"As one who has embraced the
James Goll combines his personal journey with examples from Scripture and Church history. James sets forth practical ways to sustain a real prayer life. Having known James for over forty years, I am delighted to commend to you *The Lifestyle of a Watchman.*"

Mike Bickle, International House of Prayer, Kansas City

"James Goll lives what he writes in the pages of this book. This is a life-changing book because of that fact. For anyone who is just beginning to learn to pray, it is a training manual. For others, it will satisfy that deep place in your heart that longs for a deeper relationship with God in prayer."

Cindy Jacobs, co-founder, Generals International

"Many have written concerning the importance of prayer and intercession, but few have ever addressed the character needed to maintain the lifestyle of a watchman. Across the globe, there are signs of revival. 'When the enemy comes in like a flood, the Spirit of the LORD will lift up a standard against him' (Isaiah 59:19 NKJV). The flood of God is rising. In its rising is restoration of the ancient DNA of Pentecost: watching in prayer. We give thanks to our dear friend James for adding these vital insights to strengthen the global prayer community. We have known James for more than 35 years and can testify that he lives what he teaches and always focuses on the Source of life itself—the Captain of Armies, the Lord, Jesus Christ."

Mahesh and Bonnie Chavda, senior pastors, All Nations Church, Fort Mill, South Carolina

"James Goll has been a friend and prophet to me for years. He has been a major voice in the divine moments of my personal transitions, thrusting me into new spheres of faith and breakthrough. James Goll has been that kind of man for the whole Body of Christ for years. I believe his prophetic words and prolific teaching on prayer go down in heaven as one of the great gifts ever given to the Body of Christ.

May God use this book to raise up thousands of intercessors who will frame the future of the earth. Throw yourself into this book and let the Lord light your soul on fire as you read."

Lou Engle, co-founder, TheCall

"Dr. James Goll *is* a watchman, a prophet, a teacher, a father . . . and more. He has throughly studied the mandate, activities and ministry of the watchman throughout the Scriptures and Church history, and as a result, his book *The Lifestyle of a Watchman* is filled with treasures and insights regarding this often-ignored subject. It is truly a book to acquire for your personal library, but be sure to get others to give away. Let's spread the fire!"

Patricia King, founder and CEO,
Patricia King Ministries, www.patriciaking.com

"A timely book, by one of the most important voices in the Church today. James Goll has modeled this lifestyle for decades. Only in eternity will any of us realize the full advantage we have in life because of those who paid such a price to appear before the Lord on our behalf. *The Lifestyle of a Watchman* will provide the reader with insight, inspiration and a challenge. In the wisdom forged only in trial, James takes on the monumental task of equipping us for this challenge, but he does so in doable bite-sized pieces. Brilliant!"

Bill Johnson, senior leader, Bethel Church, Redding, California;
author, *Face to Face with God* and *The Essential Guide to Healing* (with Randy Clark)

"The *Lifestyle of a Watchman* is a practical, biblical and insightful book on a lifestyle of prayer. James Goll has given the Church a gift in this book. It will help you become more acquainted with the life of prayer and the basis for greater faith in the prayers we pray."

Randy Clark, D.Min., Th.D., overseer, Apostolic Network of Global Awakening; founder, Global Awakening; author,
There Is More!, *The Healing Breakthrough* and more

The Lifestyle of a Watchman

Books by James W. and Michal Ann Goll

A Radical Faith

Angelic Encounters

The Call of the Elijah Revolution (with Lou Engle)

The Coming Israel Awakening

Deliverance from Darkness

Dream Language

Empowered Prayer

Finding Hope

God Encounters

Hearing God's Voice Today

The Lifestyle of a Prophet

The Lifestyle of a Watchman

Living a Supernatural Life

The Lost Art of Intercession

The Lost Art of Practicing His Presence

Passionate Pursuit

Prayer Storm

Praying for Israel's Destiny

The Prophetic Intercessor

Releasing Spiritual Gifts Today

The Seer

Shifting Shadows of Supernatural Experiences (with Julia Loren)

What Love Looks Like (comp.)

Women on the Frontlines (series)

Other Products

Study guides, CD and DVD class sets, audio and video messages

The Lifestyle of a Watchman

A 21-DAY JOURNEY TO BECOMING A GUARDIAN IN PRAYER

JAMES W. GOLL

FOREWORD BY BENI JOHNSON

a division of Baker Publishing Group
Minneapolis, Minnesota

Published by Chosen Books
11400 Hampshire Avenue South
Bloomington, Minnesota 55438
www.chosenbooks.com

Chosen Books is a division of
Baker Publishing Group, Grand Rapids, Michigan

Printed in the United States of America

Library of Congress Cataloging-in-Publication Data
Names: Goll, Jim W., author.
Title: The lifestyle of a watchman : a 21-day journey to becoming a guardian in prayer / foreword by Beni Johnson ; James W. Goll.
Description: Minneapolis, Minnesota : Chosen, 2017. | Includes bibliographical references.
Identifiers: LCCN 2016041241 | ISBN 9780800798093 (trade paper : alk. paper)
Subjects: LCSH: Prayer—Biblical teaching. | Abraham (Biblical patriarch) | Anna (Biblical prophetess) | Daniel (Biblical figure)
Classification: LCC BS680.P64 G65 2017 | DDC 243—dc23
LC record available at https://lccn.loc.gov/2016041241

Cover design by LOOK Design Studio

17 18 19 20 21 22 23 7 6 5 4 3 2 1

In keeping with biblical principles of creation stewardship, Baker Publishing Group advocates the responsible use of our natural resources. As a member of the Green Press Initiative, our company uses recycled paper when possible. The text paper of this book is composed in part of post-consumer waste.

With honor and gratitude in my heart, I dedicate this book to two people who are well known before the throne of God. They are both living legends of the message that history belongs to the intercessors. I would not be in the place of stature I am today without the shadows of these two diverse giants of the secret place touching my life: first, Dick Simmons of Men for Nations, based in Washington, D.C.; and second, Elizabeth (Beth) Alves of Increase International in Bulverde, Texas. Thank you for inspiring my life.

Contents

Foreword

Many years ago I had a personal encounter with the Holy Spirit. From that encounter, a deep hunger was birthed, and I fell in love with the Holy Spirit. I felt I could not get enough of Him. When my family left in the mornings, I turned on a worship CD and spent hours in His presence. I had been overtaken with the love of heaven.

In those times of worship, I began to experience prayer as I had never experienced it before. It took place in a deep place in my heart, and it felt as if my prayers were coming right from heaven, and all I did was agree with what heaven wanted to do.

It is in this intimate place with God, I learned, that we receive His heart, obtain His strategies and become His watchmen.

One of my favorite passages in the Bible is 2 Samuel 18:24–27:

> While David was sitting between the inner and outer gates, the watchman went up to the roof of the gateway by the wall. As he looked out, he saw a man running alone. The watchman called out to the king and reported it.
>
> The king said, "If he is alone, he must have good news." And the runner came closer and closer.

> Then the watchman saw another runner, and he called down to the gatekeeper, "Look, another man running alone!"
>
> The king said, "He must be bringing good news, too."
>
> The watchman said, "It seems to me that the first one runs like Ahimaaz son of Zadok."
>
> "He's a good man," the king said. "He comes with good news."

What intrigues me about this passage is that the watchman had a seeing ability, and a very good one at that. He was able to discern who a man was just by the way he was running. That is impressive!

What an honor to be able to come before the Lord in prayer and to be able to see accurately with spirit eyes what God is doing, while having Him reveal to us how to pray. As watchmen, you and I can be in partnership with the King, just as the watchman on the wall was with King David.

As you read *The Lifestyle of a Watchman*, which James has written beautifully, know that there will be keys for you to implement. I pray that this book revolutionizes and refreshes your prayer walk with the Lord.

Beni Johnson, author, *Healthy and Free*
and *The Happy Intercessor*

Acknowledgments

First, I offer my thanks to the editorial and marketing teams of Chosen Books, with whom I have had the honor of working for close to twenty years now. Jane Campbell saw potential in my lump of clay when I did not. She helped me discover my voice and taught me how to reach my audience. I will always be grateful for Jane's imprint upon my life.

Next, I thank the Lord for my excellent assistant, Kathy Deering, who has helped me develop my teachings with a smooth and timeless devotional style. Oh, I am so grateful for Kathy's coming to my aid, time and time again.

I also thank the Lord for all of the mentors who have poured into my life over the years so that I could do a better job of bringing forth equipping materials that can further God's unfolding purposes throughout the earth.

Continuing on the wall,
James W. Goll

Introduction

I am inviting you to go on a journey with me. This book is your personal invitation from my heart and life to yours.

Imagine with me for a moment that you are in a cozy cabin in the mountains, nestled on a comfy couch next to the fireplace with a steaming mug of your favorite drink next to you. You notice a book on the table and think, *I wonder what that is?* You pick it up and read the title. It is this book, *The Lifestyle of a Watchman: A 21-Day Journey to Becoming a Guardian in Prayer.*

The idea of becoming a guardian in prayer appeals to you. You have long wanted to increase your devotion to God in prayer, and this book's 21-day approach makes that desire feel within reach. But then you wonder, *What is a watchman, actually? And how does it relate to my devotional prayer life or to intercessory prayer or to what some believers call spiritual warfare?*

You are about to find out.

But wait, your mind counters further. *I am so tired of boring prayer meetings that get off course and seem to go nowhere or everywhere. I don't want any more of those. Can I stay true to my personal time of communion with God and still become a watchman?*

I assure you that you can. The emphasis of this book is less on prayer tips and more on creating a lifestyle, one in which prayer is mingled with worship and you are able to hear from the Lord and respond accordingly.

As you will see, a watchman is someone (male or female, of course) who has responded to God's invitation to intercede in prayer for particular types of needs. The lifestyle of a watchman is fairly hidden—even for a watchman who stands in plain sight on the "walls" of whatever he or she is guarding in prayer. Nobody but God sees the nights spent in watchful prayer, and only other watchmen can appreciate the joyful sacrifice of such a lifestyle.

The call to be a watchman is a call into grand adventures. It is laced with the quiet satisfaction of knowing the pleasure of the Lord, and it is underscored by the revelation that history belongs to the intercessors, the ones who watch faithfully. We are called to be co-laborers with Christ. What better way to do that than doing what Jesus does?

Intercession, you see, is Jesus' personal assignment, and we have the privilege of joining Him in it. Paul tells us, "Christ Jesus who died—more than that, who was raised to life—is at the right hand of God and is also interceding for us" (Romans 8:34). As intercessors, we get to watch with Him. There is no other way to do it.

The Format of This Book

I have divided our exploration of the watchman lifestyle into three sections: the lifestyle of *intimate intercession*, highlighting the story of Abraham; the lifestyle of *sacrifice*, focused on a widow named Anna; and the lifestyle of *consecration*, exemplified by Daniel, the prophet in exile. I have brought together these three distinct elements, as I have found them necessary for anyone who wishes to be an effective watchman in prayer.

This book contains 21 daily readings. At the end of each day's reading, you will find a closing prayer and questions for your review, which can be used personally or in a group study. Each reading develops one aspect of the watchman theme, and by the end of your three-week journey, my hope is that you will be able to see how these concepts fit together. I further hope you will find yourself confirmed in your own personal intercessory assignment.

Also, after the first chapter in each section, the remaining daily readings in the sections conclude with stories of real-life people who exemplify certain aspects of being a watchman or prayer guardian. Some of them are biblical characters. Others' stories have been entered into the history books. A good number of them are current-day watchmen. These stories give you a chance to be encouraged by the cloud of witnesses called to this work. You also will see through these stories that this lifestyle has a variety of expressions.

This book is similar in format to my book *The Lifestyle of a Prophet: A 21-Day Journey to Embracing Your Calling*, published in 2013. Each of these books stands alone, addressing different subjects, but there is some overlap.

The Intention of This Book

Let me be clear about one thing. This book is not just about the making of great watchmen or great intercessors or a great company of priestly prayer warriors. It is, first and foremost, about being a disciple of the Lord Jesus Christ. I want to be a wholehearted follower of Jesus, conformed into His image (see

Romans 8:29). If you share that desire, this book was written for you. On this 21-day journey to becoming a guardian in prayer, the Lord Himself is our goal.

I am inviting you into my personal pilgrimage as an intercessory prayer warrior with this book. On this journey, one concept has made a huge difference for me in recent years. I do not know how I missed it when I was first learning the principles of prayer. It is the truth the New Testament reveals that can be stated as follows: "We are not working *toward* victory; we are working *from* victory." Where intercessory prayer is concerned, that statement becomes "We are not praying *for* victory; we are praying *from* victory."

This perspective alters a lot of things, and I am still in the process of letting it change my approach to watching in prayer. But more and more, everything I do and pray comes from my rock-solid faith that Jesus has won, once and for all, the victory. This brings a smile to my face and a dance to my step. I want to invite you into the same lifestyle.

God's watchmen are joyful, prayerful men and women. They are not agitated. They do not moan or complain about the state of affairs. They enjoy what they do, even when it is difficult. As the psalmist says, "I was glad when they said to me, 'Let us go to the house of the LORD'" (Psalm 122:1 NASB). When you realize you have an invitation to partner with God—not just to pray *to* Him but to pray *with* Him—it changes everything for the better.

So come along with me now. Learn what the lifestyle of a watchman includes. This book may help you discover your personal calling in God. I sure hope so! I know firsthand that being one of the Lord's watchmen on the walls is a wonderful calling, and I would love to have your company.

SECTION 1

The Lifestyle of Intimate Intercession

"You are My friends if you do whatever I command you. No longer do I call you servants, for a servant does not know what his master is doing; but I have called you friends, for all things that I heard from My Father I have made known to you. You did not choose Me, but I chose you and appointed you that you should go and bear fruit, and that your fruit should remain, that whatever you ask the Father in My name He may give you."

John 15:14–16 NKJV

READING FOR DAY 1

Abraham: Confident Friendship with God

The dramatic high points of the life story of the patriarch Abraham are familiar to most people. The account of his life takes up a good portion of the book of Genesis (from 11:26 to 25:10), chronicling his movement from his native city of Ur to the land of Harran, until eventually he reached the land of Canaan. It was an epic journey in every way, and his guidance came from God's direct call:

> The LORD had said to Abram, "Go from your country, your people and your father's household to the land I will show you.
>
> "I will make you into a great nation, and I will bless you; I will make your name great, and you will be a blessing. I will bless those who bless you, and whoever curses you I will curse; and all peoples on earth will be blessed through you."
>
> So Abram went, as the LORD had told him.
>
> Genesis 12:1–4

Although God had promised to make Abraham into "a great nation," Abraham and his wife, Sarah, were unable to have children. Then one day, the Lord told Abraham in a vision that he and Sarah would, in fact, have a son (see Genesis 15:4–6), and, to make the crazy story short, they did. Sarah became pregnant in her extreme old age and bore Isaac. Amazing!

Within a few years, though, God spoke again, telling Abraham to offer Isaac as a human sacrifice. What? Kill the miracle child, the one upon whose life the future depended? But Abraham was willing because God had asked for it. At the last minute, God provided a ram for sacrifice instead, and Isaac's life was spared.

Many sermons have been preached about Abraham's phenomenal faith in the face of such desperate requirements. His faith was the key to the fulfillment of every one of God's original promises. Abraham walked more closely with God than anyone knew was possible. What a heritage to leave behind. What a lineage!

But one of the key things I want us to notice about Abraham's life, at least as it relates to our purposes in this book, is that he demonstrated an intercessor's heart before God that was rooted in extreme intimacy. In fact, he is the first person in the Old Testament who is called God's *friend* (see 2 Chronicles 20:7 and Isaiah 41:8). This kind of relationship with a deity was unheard of. How did Abraham learn to relate to God with the kind of give-and-take that only close friends share?

Scripturally, it corresponds to *righteousness*:

> And the Scripture was fulfilled which says, "Abraham believed God, and it was accounted to him for righteousness." And he was called the friend of God.
>
> James 2:23 NKJV

Abraham obeyed God, but he was never subservient like a slave. When God told him to do something, Abraham felt free to ask questions. He even suggested things as one friend to another. This unusual relational style was based in Abraham's security of being in right standing with God. Faith, righteousness and friendship are distinct ingredients that combined to create an intimate intercession.

Over the decades, Abraham learned to recognize God's voice, and he knew he could reason with God. He trusted God as a friend. Intimate friendship with God—that was Abraham's key to his extraordinary faith and his bold work of intimate intercession.

A Bold Friendship

The story about Abraham's courageous bargaining with God over the fate of the evil cities of Sodom and Gomorrah is a prime example of his intercessor's heart and shows beyond a shadow of a doubt that Abraham deserved his unique nickname, "the friend of God." Always remember, communication is a two-way street, and watchful intercession involves a relational interaction.

This is where Abraham demonstrated the quality of his relationship with God. He knew he was debating the fate of the city with his sovereign Creator, not an earthly ruler. He knew he was subject to God's will. Yet he dared to stand in God's way, holding up his hand to say, "Wait a minute!" and taking time to prevail upon God's goodness and sense of justice.

We see here their interactive relationship:

> "Should I hide my plan from Abraham?" the LORD asked. "For Abraham will certainly become a great and mighty nation, and all the nations of the earth will be blessed through him. I have singled him out so that he will direct his sons and their families to keep the way of the LORD by doing what is right and just. Then I will do for Abraham all that I have promised."

> So the LORD told Abraham, "I have heard a great outcry from Sodom and Gomorrah, because their sin is so flagrant. I am going down to see if their actions are as wicked as I have heard. If not, I want to know."
>
> The other men turned and headed toward Sodom, but the LORD remained with Abraham. Abraham approached him and said, "Will you sweep away both the righteous and the wicked? Suppose you find fifty righteous people living there in the city—will you still sweep it away and not spare it for their sakes? Surely you wouldn't do such a thing, destroying the righteous along with the wicked. Why, you would be treating the righteous and the wicked exactly the same! Surely you wouldn't do that! Should not the Judge of all the earth do what is right?"
>
> Genesis 18:17–25 NLT

The rest of the story is sordid. You can read about it in the nineteenth chapter of Genesis. As it turned out, God did not find even ten righteous people in the whole place. When angels disguised as men tried to warn Abraham's nephew, Lot, to escape Sodom with his small family before it was too late, depraved citizens tried to waylay them and commit sexual acts with them that have since become known by the name of the doomed city (sodomy).

Before the fire and brimstone fell and incinerated Sodom, imagine Abraham standing there, earnestly bargaining with his God. He did not hesitate to risk God's wrath as he appealed to God's sense of compassion and fairness. Even though it put his nephew's family in jeopardy, Abraham could have acquiesced to God's decision. He knew how wicked those people were; they deserved to be wiped off the face of the earth.

Abraham did not appeal to God because of his relatives in the city, nor on the basis of his own righteousness. Despite his wealth and status, Abraham knew his track record was spotty. I have skipped over most of the other stories that have come out of Abraham's life, some of which show his human side all too well (see, for example, Genesis 12:10–20 and chapter 20).

No, he appealed to God on the basis of *God's* perfect righteousness, and he knew this would help his petitions meet with approval. He also trusted God's mercy to cover him if his bartering seemed impertinent.

Thus Abraham, a mere mortal, dared to stand in the gap between the wrath of God and the wicked citizens of Sodom. He was willing to sacrifice himself, if necessary. He became a man like the intercessor God sought to find years later, speaking through the prophet Ezekiel: "I searched for a man among them who would build up the wall and stand in the gap before Me for the land, so that I would not destroy it; but I found no one" (Ezekiel 22:30 NASB).

Like you and me, Abraham was not born with a supernatural gift of friendship with God; he came to know God's nature and character over time. The relationship was initiated by God when the future patriarch was still known as Abram (see Genesis 12:1–3). Through all the ups and downs of the years, Abraham learned about God's faithfulness. Whenever he took matters into his own hands (as he did when he lied twice about his wife, Sarah), he suffered rebukes. His circumstances did not always seem to line up with the amazing promises. He was promised a son. He was promised influence that would impact the world. He carried a lot of responsibility, and he found it challenging to manage everything. Yet Abraham kept pressing on. He kept choosing to follow the Lord of life. Our choices matter in a similar way.

The Power of Trust

Abraham trusted God, and that was viewed by the Lord as righteousness: "And Abram believed the LORD, and the LORD counted him as righteous because of his faith" (Genesis 15:6 NLT). Abraham's trust in God made him the ideal intercessor.

We, too, can stand in the gap because of our trust in Jesus' righteousness. Our motives will never be pure enough and our words will always be inadequate, but by the cleansing power of the shed blood of Jesus, we can stand up in the teeth of the storm of God's withering judgment and plead for His mercy.

We must operate by a different kind of economy, one that is based on the currency of Jesus' righteousness. Paul connects the dots for us:

> Abraham was, humanly speaking, the founder of our Jewish nation. What did he discover about being made right with God? If his good deeds had made him acceptable to God, he would have had something to boast about. But that was not God's way. For the Scriptures tell us, "Abraham believed God, and God counted him as righteous because of his faith."
>
> When people work, their wages are not a gift, but something they have earned. But people are counted as righteous, not because of their work, but because of their faith in God who forgives sinners.
>
> Romans 4:1–5 NLT

Of course, we can misplace our trust. We can be forced to wade through setbacks and disastrous events. Our trust and faith, by themselves, do not guarantee success.

In the past number of years, my faith has been pressed to the limit as I have been through trial after trial, including the loss of my dear wife, Michal Ann, to cancer and enduring cancer myself three times over a nine-year period. But I will never stop trusting the Lord with all my heart, and I will keep choosing not to lean on my own understanding (see Proverbs 3:5). I will continue to live as a man of faith. I am tempted to put my trust in my feelings, my circumstances, the medical profession or even other people, but the only kind of faith with a guarantee attached to it is faith in the God of Abraham, Isaac and Jacob.

Our prayers count. They may be the only reason God lessens or delays His judgments. As I wrote in my book *The Prophetic Intercessor*, "We can use our intercessory capital to purchase seasons of mercy."[1] This is true even for ourselves and our families.

Others have modeled it for us. I think of good King Hezekiah. After some setbacks, he contracted a fatal illness. The prophet Isaiah paid him a visit and told him to get his house in order because God had decided that he should die. Hezekiah broke down in tears. He was too young to die; he had much more to accomplish for the sake of his people in Israel. He pleaded with God to let him live. Defying the odds, he recovered fully and lived another fifteen years. (See 2 Kings 20:1–11.) Hezekiah contended with God for his life, and God, in His mercy, acted on his behalf.

Do not get the idea that we should use this kind of prayer only in life-threatening situations, though. Look how Jesus' mother, Mary, contended with God's will over a seemingly minor matter—the wine supply at a village wedding. (See John 2:1–11.) Jesus and His disciples were there when the wine ran out. He had not yet begun His public ministry, and He was not inclined to demonstrate His supernatural power just yet. But Mary insisted He do something to help out.

"Do whatever He tells you," she instructed the servants, even though He had just told her He did not want to do anything. "Woman, why do you involve Me?" He had said to her. "My hour has not yet come."

But because His mother persisted, He followed through, changing jugs of water into fine wine and saving the celebration—and thus launching His ministry earlier than He might have wanted to.

This is the Lord we serve. Our God is someone who has all the power in the universe and upon whom we depend for every breath we take, yet He is also someone we can approach without trepidation to argue our case. He could snuff us out instantly if He wanted to, but He loves us too much to do that. His ears and His heart are open to us. He loves it when we lean toward Him in confidence. He loves when we approach Him as a friend.

A Greater Promise

God's promises to Abraham were amazing and powerful, yet Jesus has brought us *greater* blessings than those Old Testament ones. The writer of the book of Hebrews lists all of the Law-guaranteed blessings and privileges of the Old Testament priests yet goes on to say, "But in fact the ministry Jesus has received is as superior to theirs as the covenant of which he is mediator is superior to the old one, since the new covenant is established on better promises" (Hebrews 8:6).

When Abraham was a childless, elderly nomad—by no means a patriarch yet—God promised him a heritage he could hardly imagine, let alone believe. And to the endless benefit of generations of his descendants (both physical and spiritual), he suspended his natural incredulity and said yes. He had no guarantees. He simply moved forward, relating to God as he went, taking one step at a time. We can do that, too.

Abraham took hold of the words God had spoken to him without even having the benefit of having the Scriptures, and especially the words of Jesus, as we do. For instance, we know that "man shall not live by bread alone, but by every word that proceeds from the mouth of God" (Matthew 4:4 NKJV). We live by every word that proceeds from the mouth of God. God has spoken. God is speaking. God will continue to speak to His friends.

Remember, confident friendship with God is based in communication. Intimate intercession is a two-way street. God speaks, we listen and we respond. We speak, God listens and God responds.

As we start our 21-day journey together, I am pointing us toward the father of our faith and to the first man the Bible ever called the friend of God. But friendship with God is not a special gift of the Holy Spirit available only to an elite few. It is available to each and every person who follows Jesus, as He said:

> "You are My friends if you do whatever I command you. No longer do I call you servants, for a servant does not know what his master is doing; but I have called you friends, for all things that I heard from My Father I have made known to you."
>
> John 15:14–15 NKJV

Years ago, I was challenged by a penetrating statement made by a man who had walked with God. He stated, "You are just as close to God as you want to be!" That statement has marked my life. My lifestyle as a watchman starts and is maintained by my personal communion with my Master and Friend. So is yours.

PRAYER

Father God, You hold the universe in Your hands, and yet You call us Your friends. I want to understand that more deeply, and I want to love You more and more. You may never present me with as many important decisions as You did Abraham, but I want to lean in to hear Your voice so I can both obey You and sometimes ask You questions. Teach me what it means to fear You, but help me to grow in the intimacy of friendship with You at the same time. May I be ready and willing if You need somebody to stand in the gap. May my eyes and heart be wide open to You at all times. Because of Your Son, Jesus, Amen.

DAY 1

EMBRACING YOUR CALLING

1. How would you describe what it means to be God's friend? In what ways have you experienced that kind of friendship with God?
2. Have you ever bargained with God like Abraham, Hezekiah or Mary did? What were the results?
3. What promises has God given you? Can you say you believe those promises are as sure as their Promiser?
4. When you get discouraged in your faith, review how God has worked with other believers. Remember that everyone gets discouraged at times, even the ones we know as giants of the faith. How can you renew your faith? How can you acquire holy tenacity?

READING FOR DAY 2

Remind God of His Word

> On your walls, O Jerusalem, I have appointed watchmen; all day and all night they will never keep silent. You who remind the LORD, take no rest for yourselves; and give Him no rest until He establishes and makes Jerusalem a praise in the earth.
>
> Isaiah 62:6–7 NASB

The Isaiah passage above speaks of watchmen as people who "remind" the Lord. What does that mean? Does He forget things? Of course not. But watchmen pray and speak to God on the basis of what He has said—His Word.

That phrase "You who remind the Lord," in fact, has been translated various ways: "You who call on the LORD" (NIV), "You who make mention of the LORD" (NKJV; see also KJV) and "You who pray to the LORD" (NLT). These word choices point to an important, fundamental truth about prayer—namely, that prayers are futile unless they reflect the heart of God.

The surest way to "pray God's heart" is to pray according to His written Word—in other words, to remind Him of His Word. This is summed up perfectly by the apostle John: "If you abide in Me, and My words abide in you, you will ask what you desire, and it shall be done for you" (John 15:7 NKJV).

In his book *With Christ in the School of Prayer*, Andrew Murray wrote about this fundamental truth:

> The vital connection between the Word and prayer is one of the simplest and earliest lessons of the Christian life. As the newly converted heathen put it, "I pray—I speak to my Father; I read—my Father speaks to me." Before prayer, God's Word strengthens me by giving my faith its justification and petition. In prayer, God's Word prepares me by revealing what the Father wants me to ask. After prayer, God's Word brings me the answer, for in it the Spirit allows me to hear the Father's voice.
>
> It is the connection between His Word and our prayer that Jesus points to when He says, "If ye abide in me, and my words abide in you, ye shall ask what ye will, and it shall be done unto you." The deep importance of this truth becomes clear if we notice the expression which this one replaces. More than once Jesus said, "Abide in me and I in you." His abiding in us was the complement and the crown of our abiding in Him. But here, instead of "Ye in me and I in you," He says, "Ye in me and my words in you." The abiding of His words is the equivalent of Himself abiding.
>
> God is the infinite Being in whom everything is life, power, spirit, and truth, in the very deepest meaning of the words. When God reveals Himself in His words, He does indeed give *Himself*—His love and His life, His will and His power—to those who receive these words, in a reality passing our comprehension. In every promise, He gives us the power to grasp and possess *Himself*. In every command, He allows us to share His will, His holiness, and His perfection. God's Word gives us God Himself!
>
> That Word is nothing less than the Eternal Son, Christ Jesus. Therefore, all of Christ's words are God's words, full of a Divine, quickening life and power. "The words I speak unto you, they are spirit and they are life."

> . . . "If my words abide in you." The condition is simple and clear. In His words, His will is revealed. As the words abide in me, His will rules me. My will becomes the empty vessel which His will finds, and the willing instrument which His will rules.[1]

The key to effective intercession is the same as the key to all of the Christian life: abiding in Christ Jesus. We stay as close to Him as we can, learning to be sensitive to His slightest whispers. Then we can pray prayers that line up with His will—prayers that are guaranteed to be answered.

Why You Need the Word

As you abide in God and in His Word, His Word will begin to abide in you. Immersing yourself in His written Word, the Bible, is the best way to familiarize yourself with God's voice.

Do not limit yourself only to the New Testament, although that is where you will find a great concentration of easy-to-use statements of truth and actual prayers that you can make your own. Make it your life's work to read and reread the entire Bible, digesting all of the chapters and verses of its 66 books. The Holy Spirit will bring it to life for you, and you will never stop discovering new insights and applications. Even the most boring genealogy or hard-to-understand story will yield up its gems if you dig long enough, and you will be able to pray out of those riches.

Pay special attention to those places where God's voice breaks through loud and clear with actual promises. Sometimes it is obvious: "The Lord God says . . . ," "Thus saith the Lord . . . ," "I have promised . . . ," "This is my covenant with you . . ." In other places, you will find reports or predictions about the promises of God being fulfilled. Naturally, the specific details of God's promises may not apply across the board, but you can still glimpse His heart through the promises He makes.

For example, through an angel God told Abraham's wife, Sarah, "By this time next year you will have a son." (See Genesis 18:10.) Now, nobody should lift those words from the page and claim them as a personal promise! But you can pray from them just the same. You might pray, for example, *Lord, Your promises are always sure. When You told barren, elderly Sarah that she would bear a son, she laughed. But Your promise was fulfilled. Now I pray that You will be faithful to [a personal promise] and that You will grant me more faith to believe Your promises to me.*

Oftentimes you will find that you are reminding God of His Word in prayer by expressing some aspect of His character, which you will have learned through long exposure to the light of Scripture. This is what Abraham did when he was pleading with the Lord for the people of Sodom and said, "Far be it from you to do such a thing—to kill the righteous with the wicked, treating the righteous and the wicked alike. Far be it from you! Will not the Judge of all the earth do right?" (Genesis 18:25). Although those words have become part of Scripture today, making them useful to us in prayer, Abraham spoke them to God because he understood God's character to be that of a righteous judge.

Over time and with practice, you can learn to incorporate the words of Scripture into your daily prayers. Use whatever version of Scripture suits you best. In other words, praying the Word does not require you to use the stilted English of the King James Version (although if that is your favorite version and it flows well for you, by all means use it).

Why You Must Persist

Again, Abraham prayed on behalf of Sodom and Gomorrah because he knew God was a righteous judge. He stood before the Judge without an intermediary or advocate. Now that Jesus the Messiah has come, how much more can we pray persuasively because of His perpetual advocacy before the Father's throne?

The answers we seek may not come immediately, but we can persist in our holy pleading, taking the persistent widow of Luke 18 as our example:

> One day Jesus told his disciples a story to show that they should always pray and never give up. "There was a judge in a certain city," he said, "who neither feared God nor cared about people. A widow of that city came to him repeatedly, saying, 'Give me justice in this dispute with my enemy.' The judge ignored her for a while, but finally he said to himself, 'I don't fear God or care about people, but this woman is driving me crazy. I'm going to see that she gets justice, because she is wearing me out with her constant requests!'"
>
> Then the Lord said, "Learn a lesson from this unjust judge. Even he rendered a just decision in the end. So don't you think God will surely give justice to his chosen people who cry out to him day and night? Will he keep putting them off? I tell you, he will grant justice to them quickly! But when the Son of Man returns, how many will he find on the earth who have faith?"
>
> Luke 18:1–8 NLT

As we saw in the previous chapter, someone who is an intercessor or a watchman stands in the gap between God's judgment and sin. The sin is very real, and the intercessor does not try to argue it away. Surely, Abraham did not. He recognized full well that Sodom and Gomorrah deserved the severest punishment for their flagrant sins. Still, he persisted in asking for mercy, and so can we.

The prayers God hears are the ones that strike a chord in His heart because they originated there. In fact, the Hebrew word for *intercede* is *paga*, which means "to strike the mark."[2] The most effective prayers do not hint around ("Oh, please, God, if it be Thy will . . ."). Instead, they take their cues from the very Word of God, and they hit the bull's-eye every time!

But God has not only given us His Word to go by. He has also sent us His Holy Spirit to be our invaluable helper. The Holy Spirit makes it possible for us to move from natural words to supernatural prayers. He gives us the energy we need to keep on praying when everything looks bleak. Without His help, none of God's watchmen could keep watch.

The English word *intercede* comes from the Latin *intercedo*, with *inter* meaning "between" and *cedo* meaning "to go"—literally, "to go between." In other words, one who intercedes mediates between parties who differ or contend with each other, and he or she does so with a view toward their reconciliation.

This is why one of an intercessor's primary functions is to remind the Lord of promises and appointments that have yet to be fulfilled. Remember Isaiah's words:

> On your walls, O Jerusalem, I have appointed watchmen; all day and all night they will never keep silent. You who remind the LORD, take no rest for yourselves; and give Him no rest until He establishes and makes Jerusalem a praise in the earth.
>
> Isaiah 62:6–7 NASB

Intercessors take up cases of justice before God, the supreme judge, on behalf of others. But there are never enough of them. Isaiah deplored the fact that intercessors are too often in short supply:

> Now the LORD saw, and it was displeasing in His sight that there was no justice. And He saw that there was no man, and was astonished that there was no one to intercede; then His own arm brought salvation to Him, and His righteousness upheld Him.
>
> Isaiah 59:15–16 NASB

Are you an intercessor—someone who cannot help but cry out to God in the face of injustice or oppression? Are you willing to volunteer for active duty as a watchman for the Lord? No one person will be assigned to every type of watch post, so do not feel daunted by the magnitude of the task. God has a growing Church full of watchman-intercessors, and books such as this one have been written to help each one find the right assignment and to understand what this call entails.

How to Pray the Word

Many times the best way to launch into intercession is to read directly from one of the prayers you find in Scripture. You can make little adjustments to the wording as you go, plugging in your name or someone else's name and adding other things that occur to you.

The Psalms are loaded with actual prayers. Many of Paul's epistles begin or end with prayers. For example, you can pray this one, which I prayed every day for ten years and still pray at least weekly:

> I keep asking that the God of our Lord Jesus Christ, the glorious Father, may give you the Spirit of wisdom and revelation, so that you may know him better. I pray that the eyes of your heart may be enlightened in order that you may know the hope to which he has called you, the riches of his glorious inheritance in his holy people, and his incomparably great power for us who believe.
>
> Ephesians 1:17–19

There were days, weeks and years I prayed these verses at least ten times a day. Why? Because I wanted these results so badly! My reasoning went like this: *If Paul prayed for the church of Ephesus, which was the model church of the time, then how much more do we need to pray this prayer today?* I prayed from various translations, and I prayed for myself as much as I prayed for others in the Church.

You can find similar ready-made prayers throughout the Bible, from Genesis to Revelation. They cover every situation, every emotional state, every level of faith. Some are filled with exultation and hope. Others are laments. There are personal heart cries as well as formal priestly prayers. We do not want to forget the Lord's Prayer (captured in Matthew 6:9–13 and Luke 11:2–4). They are all right there, waiting for you to pray them.

Here is a sampling:

> Today when I came to the spring, I prayed this prayer: "O LORD, God of my master, Abraham, please give me success on this mission."
>
> Genesis 24:42 NLT

> Then Manoah prayed to the LORD, and said, "O my Lord, please let the Man of God whom You sent come to us again and teach us what we shall do for the child who will be born."
>
> Judges 13:8 NKJV

> "You are God, O Sovereign LORD. Your words are truth, and you have promised these good things to your servant. And now, may it please you to bless the house of your servant, so that it may continue forever before you. For you have spoken, and when you grant a blessing to your servant, O Sovereign LORD, it is an eternal blessing!"
>
> 2 Samuel 7:28–29 NLT

> O God, why have you rejected us forever? Why does your anger smolder against the sheep of your pasture? Remember the nation you purchased long ago, the people of your inheritance, whom you redeemed.
>
> Psalm 74:1–2

Have You completely rejected Judah? Or have You loathed Zion? Why have You stricken us so that we are beyond healing? We waited for peace, but nothing good came; and for a time of healing, but behold, terror! We know our wickedness, O Lord, the iniquity of our fathers, for we have sinned against You. Do not despise us, for Your own name's sake; do not disgrace the throne of Your glory; remember and do not annul Your covenant with us.

Jeremiah 14:19–21 NASB

Remember, O Lord, what has befallen us; look, and see our reproach! Our inheritance has been turned over to strangers, our houses to aliens. . . . Our pursuers are at our necks; we are worn out, there is no rest for us. . . . Because of this our heart is faint, because of these things our eyes are dim. . . . You, O Lord, rule forever; Your throne is from generation to generation. Why do You forget us forever? Why do You forsake us so long? Restore us to You, O Lord, that we may be restored; renew our days as of old.

Lamentations 5:1–2, 5, 17, 19–21 NASB

Though the fig tree may not blossom, nor fruit be on the vines; though the labor of the olive may fail, and the fields yield no food; though the flock may be cut off from the fold, and there be no herd in the stalls—yet I will rejoice in the Lord, I will joy in the God of my salvation. The Lord God is my strength; He will make my feet like deer's feet, and He will make me walk on my high hills.

Habakkuk 3:17–19 NKJV

Then He said to His disciples, "The harvest truly is plentiful, but the laborers are few. Therefore pray the Lord of the harvest to send out laborers into His harvest."

Matthew 9:37–38 NKJV

Now may the God of hope fill you with all joy and peace in believing, that you may abound in hope by the power of the Holy Spirit.

Romans 15:13 NKJV

> For this reason we also, since the day we heard it, do not cease to pray for you, and to ask that you may be filled with the knowledge of His will in all wisdom and spiritual understanding; that you may walk worthy of the Lord, fully pleasing Him, being fruitful in every good work and increasing in the knowledge of God; strengthened with all might, according to His glorious power, for all patience and longsuffering with joy; giving thanks to the Father who has qualified us to be partakers of the inheritance of the saints in the light.
>
> Colossians 1:8–12 NKJV

> "Holy, holy, holy, Lord God Almighty, who was and is and is to come!" . . . "You are worthy, O Lord, to receive glory and honor and power; for You created all things, and by Your will they exist and were created."
>
> Revelation 4:8, 11 NKJV

Finally, have you considered putting your prayers to music? This should not be an unfamiliar concept; originally, all of the prayers of the book of Psalms had musical accompaniments, and many of the hymns and worship songs you know are based directly on the Word.

For example, here is the refrain from "Have Thine Own Way, Lord," which is based on Isaiah 64:8:

> Have thine own way, Lord! Have thine own way!
> Thou art the potter, I am the clay.
> Mold me and make me after thy will,
> while I am waiting, yielded and still.

You see? You have been singing scriptural prayers all along without realizing it! Now you can start singing them intentionally as prayers with all your heart and soul.

I have found this to be beneficial. I have been a singer all my life, so I find that I naturally break into singing prayers, especially if a Scripture-based hymn comes to mind. This elevates my praying into another realm, one in which I merge worship and praise with prayer and intercession.

I could say much more. Many books have been written about praying the Word; if I tried to list all of them, I am sure I would leave out some of them. (Somehow that line sounds a little like Scripture!) You can find such resources by searching online for "praying the Word."

We have been taught that reading our Bibles and praying are separate devotional activities. But a strict division between them does not exist after all. What better way to pray than to open your Bible and pray the very Word that comes from God's heart?

Dick Simmons: A Word-Based Watchman

In this first profile, I am sharing with you a dedicated, current-day watchman few others know but whom God knows deeply. He has radically influenced who I am today, as he has been one of my mentors and friends for many years. His name is Dick Simmons, and I have co-dedicated this book to him. He is a veteran, a radical intercessor and a leader of intercessors, one who has worked all his life behind the scenes, tirelessly calling heaven to earth. I call him a Word-based watchman.

These days, when most men his age would have retired, Dick continues to pray for hours a day. In 1970, he founded Men for Nations, located in Washington, D.C., on Capitol Hill, next to the Supreme Court. Men for Nations promotes intensive daily Bible study and publishes an online weekly prayer guide.[3] Its goal is to equip men to join in early-morning Word-based prayer sessions on behalf of government leaders and the nation. The headquarters of Men for Nations is located alongside the American Center for Prayer and Revival, a ministry of Dick Eastman's Every Home for Christ.

Prior to his work with Men for Nations, Dick, who is an ordained Presbyterian minister, played a key role in establishing the ministries of David Wilkerson and Pat Robertson. He founded the M-2 (Man-to-Man, now Match 2) job-therapy program in Washington State, which matches Christian men with men who are serving time in prison. He also served on the Justice Task Force under then-president Ronald Reagan, advising the administration how to mobilize private citizens for justice-related initiatives. Dick and his late wife, Barbara, served as evangelists in many settings.

Back in 1958, Dick was a student at a Bible college in New York City. He was already an intercessor. In the middle of the night, he went to pray outside on the bank of the Hudson River, crying out to the Lord for New York City at the top of his voice, saying, "Lord, I beseech Thee to send forth laborers into Your field!" It was a prayer that echoed Matthew 9:37–38 and Luke 10:2.

I wrote about this moment in Dick's life in my book *The Lost Art of Intercession*, saying:

> His agonized prayers were so loud at 2:00 a.m. (even by New York City standards!) that he suddenly was bathed in floodlights on the riverbank. Cautious police officers shouted out, "What are you doing? You have been reported for disturbing the peace because you've been waking up people!"
>
> Dick bellowed back, "Oh, I am just praying to the Lord of the harvest that He would send forth laborers into His field."
>
> The police officers must have been shocked, or else they agreed with Brother Simmons. They let him go without any charges or warnings. That very night, the Holy Spirit of God descended on a little skinny preacher in rural Pennsylvania and gave him a divine call to take the gospel to New York City. Do you know his name? It was David Wilkerson. It is no wonder that when David Wilkerson established the first Teen Challenge Center in New York City, he chose Dick Simmons to be its first director.[4]

I first met Dick in 1986 on a mission trip to Haiti, and we have shared a number of exciting adventures as intercessors over the years, some of which I wrote about in another of my books, *God Encounters*. Every time Dick and I have prayed together, we have prayed the Word, reminding the Lord of His promises. The results have been incredible. With thanks, I honor the lifestyle of Word-based watchman Dick Simmons.

PRAYER

I ask You, dear Father, for spiritual wisdom and insight so that I might grow in my knowledge of You. I pray that my heart will be flooded with light so that I can come to understand the confident hope You have given to me and to everyone You have called to Yourself. I also pray that I will come to understand the incredible greatness of Your power toward those of us who believe, the same mighty power that raised Christ Jesus from the dead and seated Him in the place of honor at Your right hand in heaven. In the name that is above every other name, Amen.[5]

DAY 2

BECOMING A GUARDIAN IN PRAYER

1. What has been your experience of intercessory prayer? Do you consider yourself an intercessor or prayer watchman? How do you feel God may be calling you to intercede in prayer today or this week?
2. If possible, locate one of your "life verses" in the Bible—a passage that holds particular significance for your

spiritual life—and see if you can reformulate it as a prayer.

3. Have you ever seen prayers change the course of history? What connection have you witnessed between specific prayers and the trajectory of your personal life, extended family life or other developments on a larger scale?
4. How have you reminded God of His Word today?

READING FOR DAY 3

An Orchestra of Prayer

These all continued with one accord in prayer and supplication.
Acts 1:14 NKJV

I once heard a story about a study conducted by a psychologist and a graduate student who wanted to find out how members of the various instrumental sections of eleven major symphony orchestras perceived each other. They reported that the percussionists were viewed as fun-loving and insensitive yet not bright. String players were considered to be arrogant, stuffy and not athletic. Brass players were described as just plain loud. The section of the orchestra that was held in the highest regard was the woodwind section, whose members were seen by the others as quiet and meticulous, if somewhat egotistical.[1]

How can such a diversity of personality types and sounds make such beautiful music together? By submitting themselves to the musical score and to the conductor.

I am sure it is not too much of a stretch for you to see the similarity between a musical ensemble of any size and a group of people praying. In this case, the conductor is the Lord Jesus Christ, and His Holy Spirit sets the tempo. The score is the Word of God. And the instruments or musicians? Of course—those are you and me!

From time to time, each of us may have solo parts to play (or pray), but our parts only work with the whole piece of music if each musician (or pray-er) comes in at the right moment and in the right way. Most of the time, we raise our voices together, making our individual contributions to the whole.

Striking the Sounds of Prayer

In the previous chapters, I mentioned the Hebrew word *paga*, translated as *intercede* in the Old Testament. *Paga* is rich with layers of meaning. Not only does it mean "to strike the mark" in the manner of a bull's-eye, as I indicated, but it also carries the following shades of meaning:

To meet. Specifically, to meet with God for the purpose of reconciliation. (See Isaiah 64:5 NASB.)

To light upon. By God's working of grace, as in the life of Jacob, our divine Helper is always ready to aid us in our intercession, moving us from the natural to the supernatural and from finite ability to infinite ability. (See Genesis 28:10–17.)

To fall upon, attack, strike down, cut down. An intercessor is God's soldier, always ready to attack an enemy at the command of his Master. (See 2 Samuel 1:11–16.)

Laid upon. The fullest expression of intercession happened when our sins were laid upon Jesus, who had identified with us, so that He could take our sins away as the perfect scapegoat (see Isaiah 53:6, 12). As Christ's Body on earth, we can intercede in a way that helps to fill up that which is lacking in Christ's afflictions (see Colossians 1:24).

Do you know what intercessors are doing when they pray? Essentially, they are painting targets that draw the powerful arrows of God's glory to earth to strike the mark. Or, to revert to the image of a group of musicians, each one of us has a special part to play in the grand heaven-to-earth orchestration, and we do this by striking the right notes at the right time.

Playing the High Notes and Low Notes

I can think of eleven different types, or "sounds," of prayer, each of which makes an important contribution to the intercession that comes before God's throne. In brief, they are as follows: thanksgiving, praise and worship; dedication (consecration) and commitment; petition, intercession and supplication; commands and decrees; and—rumbly low note—curses. These aspects of prayer align themselves into groupings, much as various instruments in an orchestra are seated together in sections. Join me in taking a longer look at each one of them.

Thanksgiving, Praise and Worship

In this type of prayer, we enter into God's presence by means of our worshipful praise and thanksgiving: "Enter into His gates with thanksgiving, and into His courts with praise. Be thankful to Him, and bless His name" (Psalm 100:4 NKJV). We thank the Lord for His goodness and greatness and for what He has done: "Great is the LORD, and greatly to be praised" (Psalm 48:1 NKJV). Our worship expresses our gratitude and devotion to Him:

> Oh come, let us sing to the LORD! Let us shout joyfully to the Rock of our salvation. Let us come before His presence with

> thanksgiving; let us shout joyfully to Him with psalms. For the LORD is the great God, and the great King above all gods. In His hand are the deep places of the earth; the heights of the hills are His also. The sea is His, for He made it; and His hands formed the dry land.
>
> Oh come, let us worship and bow down; let us kneel before the LORD our Maker. For He is our God, and we are the people of His pasture, and the sheep of His hand.
>
> Psalm 95:1–7 NKJV

> Praise be to the God and Father of our Lord Jesus Christ, who has blessed us in the heavenly realms with every spiritual blessing in Christ. For he chose us in him before the creation of the world to be holy and blameless in his sight. In love he predestined us for adoption to sonship through Jesus Christ, in accordance with his pleasure and will—to the praise of his glorious grace, which he has freely given us in the One he loves. In him we have redemption through his blood, the forgiveness of sins, in accordance with the riches of God's grace that he lavished on us.
>
> Ephesians 1:3–8

Consecration and Commitment

Because we have been set apart for the Lord, we can enter into the high-priestly prayer of Jesus (see John 17:19). We present, or dedicate, our bodies as an act of spiritual worship (see Romans 12:1–2). Following the example of our Lord Jesus, we say, "Into your hands I commit my spirit" (Luke 23:46; see also Psalm 31:5). Our whole lives belong to Him now: "Commit your way to the LORD, trust also in Him" (Psalm 37:5 NKJV). We trust Him with every detail.

Petition, Intercession and Supplication

If we ask according to the will of God, then we can be sure that God will hear us and act on our behalf:

> Now this is the confidence that we have in Him, that if we ask anything according to His will, He hears us.
>
> 1 John 5:14 NKJV

> "Therefore I say to you, whatever things you ask when you pray, believe that you receive them, and you will have them."
>
> Mark 11:24 NKJV

We have already seen that standing in the gap (see Ezekiel 22:30–31) between God and sinful humans is one of the highest honors that can be bestowed on a believer. You stand between God's punishment for unrepented sin and those who have sinned, and you plead for mercy (see Isaiah 59:15–16). As James 2:13 tells us, "Mercy triumphs over judgment."

Ask for a spirit of grace and supplication, and remember that you cannot lift the cry without God's grace (see Zechariah 12:10). The only ones who do not receive mercy are those who, blinded by their self-righteousness, do not come to God (see Hebrews 4:16).

Draw near to God with gratitude and confidence. Listen for His heartbeat. Then just ask Him for whatever you need, for yourself or for others. Just ask!

Commands and Decrees

We have an example of commanding prayer in Joshua, who spoke to God and then released a command to the sun and moon, whereupon the sun stood still for an entire day (see Joshua 10:12–15). Similarly, Jesus commanded blind eyes to see and deaf ears to hear. His disciples commanded the lame to walk and more (see Acts 3, for example).

Even more reliably effective are decreed blessings. Here is one such example:

> "'The LORD bless you and keep you; the LORD make His face shine upon you, and be gracious to you; the LORD lift up His countenance upon you, and give you peace.'

> "So they shall put My name on the children of Israel, and I will bless them."
>
> Numbers 6:23–27 NKJV

Curses

Jesus famously cursed the fig tree that had no fruit, such that it withered and died within a day (see Matthew 21:18–21). Paul seems to have cursed a disciple named Alexander, who was dangerous to people and who stubbornly resisted correction (see 1 Timothy 1:20; 2 Timothy 4:14).

A curse is a command and a punishment. Only very rarely and with careful discernment should someone "play God" by relegating another person (or a thing, such as the fig tree) into the hands of the enemy. Usually a person's sin will incur its own punishment, anyway (see Romans 2:5).

Orchestrating Intercessory Prayer

Holy, believing, persevering prayer is the kind of prayer that will secure God's divine answer. As members of the heavenly orchestra, each one of us must undertake ongoing training and show a real dedication to practice, practice, practice.

We cannot play our assigned part casually. A life of intercession requires a person to develop a number of characteristics, such as these (pulled, in the order in which they appear, from Luke 11:5–8): urgency, protectiveness toward others, humility, confidence, patience, perseverance and acceptance of reward for a job well done.

A successful intercessor must keep some important things in mind. For example, he or she must remember the corporate purpose at hand (see 1 Thessalonians 3:10; Isaiah 62:6–7; Luke 18:7–8), as well as the needs of specific individuals (see 2 Corinthians 1:11; Ephesians 6:19; Philippians 1:19).

Any musician knows that he or she must remain open to correction and that he or she is always learning and growing. It is the same with praying. In order to pray as well as possible, we must never stop communing with God, meditating on the Word of God, praying Word-based prayers and praying for our circumstances to change.

I can think of at least ten conditions that must be met before effective intercession is assured:

1. Faith (see Mark 11:23–24; Matthew 21:21–22; 1 John 5:14–15)
2. Persistence (see Luke 18:1–8; Matthew 7:7–11; Isaiah 30:18–19; 62:6–7; Luke 11:5–13)
3. A holy life (see Psalm 66:18; Isaiah 59:1–2; 1 John 3:19–22)
4. Honoring one's spouse (see 1 Peter 3:7)
5. Following the will of God (see 1 John 5:14–15)
6. Praying in the name of Jesus (see John 14:13–14, 26; 16:23–24)
7. A pure motive (see James 4:2–3)
8. Boldness (see Hebrews 4:16)
9. Forgiveness (see Matthew 6:15)
10. Unity (see Matthew 5:23–24; 18:19–20)

Are any of these ten conditions particular sticking points for you? Let God's Spirit highlight the remedy, and then set a goal of living more fully in the light of God's love.

Growing into a Natural Rhythm

Intercession is spiritual work—the work of faith. Prayer transacts the business of heaven. As the Lord told the prophet Jeremiah, "*Work* for the peace and prosperity of the city where

I sent you. . . . *Pray* to the Lord for it, for its welfare will determine your welfare" (Jeremiah 29:7 NLT, emphasis added).

Just as children grow in stature and maturity, exchanging play-acting for their adult roles in life, so we grow into prayerful intercession as a completely natural part of our supernatural lives. Prayer should be just as ubiquitous and pervasive in our lives as other work is.

> Therefore we also pray always for you that our God would count you worthy of this calling, and fulfill all the good pleasure of His goodness and the work of faith with power, that the name of our Lord Jesus Christ may be glorified in you, and you in Him, according to the grace of our God and the Lord Jesus Christ.
>
> 2 Thessalonians 1:11–12 NKJV

As a seasoned watchman today, I can tell you that I have grown in my capacity and effectiveness as a guardian of prayer. No start is perfect. It is that way in the natural, and it is that way in all the spiritual disciplines, as well. It is true that "practice makes perfect," and the more time I practice praying the Word of God or watching with the Lord, the more proficient I become. So be patient with yourself, knowing God is at work with you.

The Apostle Paul: A Watchman of Unceasing Prayer

The best way to learn how to pray is to sit at the feet of a person who knows how to do it. Although the apostle Paul is primarily known for his apostolic teaching, including his strategic blueprint for the Church, he is also known as a man of deep prayer. He is the one who wrote these passages:

> Rejoice always, pray without ceasing, in everything give thanks; for this is the will of God in Christ Jesus for you.
>
> 1 Thessalonians 5:16–18 NKJV

> With all prayer and petition pray at all times in the Spirit, and with this in view, be on the alert with all perseverance and petition for all the saints, and pray on my behalf.
>
> Ephesians 6:18–19 NASB

Clearly, prayer was as natural to Paul as breathing.

As Paul prayed his way through his eventful life, he urged all of Jesus' followers to do the same. We know he started praying as soon as the Lord Jesus apprehended him on the road to Damascus, because of what the Holy Spirit told the disciple Ananias: "Arise and go to the street called Straight, and inquire at the house of Judas for one called Saul of Tarsus, for behold, *he is praying*" (Acts 9:11 NKJV, emphasis added).

By reading the book of Acts and the epistles of Paul with prayer in mind, we can see Paul's lifelong pattern of talking to God and listening to Him. In the accounts of his experiences, we see every facet of intercession. We read about the curse he declared on a wayward church member who did him harm (see 1 Timothy 1:20; 2 Timothy 4:14), and we see him singing the most exalted praises of God. In passage after passage, we find him on his knees or standing with arms upraised, praying without ceasing.

Let me direct your attention to the following examples, every one of which must have been duplicated dozens of times during Paul's life:

> Dear brothers and sisters, the longing of my heart and my prayer to God is for the people of Israel to be saved.
>
> Romans 10:1 NLT

> I thank my God always concerning you for the grace of God which was given to you by Christ Jesus, that you were enriched in everything by Him in all utterance and all knowledge, even as the testimony of Christ was confirmed in you, so that you

come short in no gift, eagerly waiting for the revelation of our Lord Jesus Christ, who will also confirm you to the end, that you may be blameless in the day of our Lord Jesus Christ.

1 Corinthians 1:4–8 NKJV

My little children, of whom I travail in birth again until Christ be formed in you . . .

Galatians 4:19 KJV

I have not stopped thanking God for you. I pray for you constantly.

Ephesians 1:16 NLT

Every time I think of you, I give thanks to my God. Whenever I pray, I make my requests for all of you with joy. . . . God knows how much I love you and long for you with the tender compassion of Christ Jesus.

I pray that your love will overflow more and more, and that you will keep on growing in knowledge and understanding.

Philippians 1:3–4, 8–9 NLT

We always pray for you, and we give thanks to God, the Father of our Lord Jesus Christ. . . . So we have not stopped praying for you since we first heard about you. We ask God to give you complete knowledge of his will and to give you spiritual wisdom and understanding.

Colossians 1:3, 9 NLT

I want you to know how much I have agonized for you and for the church at Laodicea, and for many other believers who have never met me personally.

Colossians 2:1 NLT

We always thank God for all of you and pray for you constantly.

1 Thessalonians 1:2 NLT

How we thank God for you! Because of you we have great joy as we enter God's presence.

1 Thessalonians 3:9 NLT

Dear brothers and sisters, we can't help but thank God for you, because your faith is flourishing and your love for one another is growing.

2 Thessalonians 1:3 NLT

I thank God, whom I serve, as my ancestors did, with a clear conscience, as night and day I constantly remember you in my prayers.

2 Timothy 1:3

I thank my God always, making mention of you in my prayers.

Philemon 1:4 NASB

Paul's whole life was a prayer. He did everything out of a sense that everything that happened was in God's hands and that he could talk with God about it all. Whether his praying was easy or difficult did not matter. To him, "prayer was neither a duty nor a burden. It was the natural turning of the heart to the only place from where it could possibly obtain what it sought for others."[2]

The apostle Paul has become one of my most important mentors, as I pray his prayers daily. As an intercessory prayer guardian, you can do the same.

PRAYER

Lord, once again I want to express my deepest gratitude to You for all You have done for me. When I die, I know You will bring me to heaven to live eternally with You.

But in the meantime, You are bringing heaven into my life here and now. How can I thank You enough? Like those who worship before Your throne in heaven, may I never stop throwing myself at Your feet. May I never cease learning about You and following You more closely, praying without ceasing. In love, because of Jesus, Amen.

DAY 3

BECOMING A GUARDIAN IN PRAYER

1. What are some of your characteristics as an "instrument" in God's orchestra of prayer? Are you loud or quiet? Do you play the high notes or the low ones, or both? Are you keeping your eyes on the conductor? Have you practiced yet today?
2. How have you grown in your prayer life as you have matured as a Christian? What aspect of prayer would you consider your "growing edge" at the current time?
3. How is it possible to "pray without ceasing"? Think of some ways your prayer could become more like breathing.
4. Take some time to skim one of Paul's epistles and notice how his life of prayer infiltrates every page.

READING FOR DAY 4

Nothing Happens without Prayer

> "Ask, and it will be given to you; seek, and you will find; knock, and it will be opened to you. For everyone who asks receives, and he who seeks finds, and to him who knocks it will be opened. Or what man is there among you who, if his son asks for bread, will give him a stone? Or if he asks for a fish, will he give him a serpent? If you then, being evil, know how to give good gifts to your children, how much more will your Father who is in heaven give good things to those who ask Him!"
>
> Matthew 7:7–11 NKJV

John Wesley, who was known to start every day with at least two hours of prayer in his room, famously said, "God does nothing except in response to believing prayer." Because I come from a strong Wesleyan influence, these words—and John Wesley himself—have had a dramatic impact on me. This line of his also makes me think of another often-used line: "Pray as though it all depends on God; work as though it all depends on you."

While it could be argued that God does plenty of things without human invitation, Wesley was establishing an important point, which is that prayer is important and that our faith in prayer matters.

He knew, too, where to find the Scriptures that supported the idea. For example, these words of Jesus Himself testify to the importance of prayer:

> "And all things, whatsoever ye shall ask in prayer, believing, ye shall receive."
>
> Matthew 21:22 KJV

> "You did not choose Me, but I chose you and appointed you that you should go and bear fruit, and that your fruit should remain, that whatever you ask the Father in My name He may give you."
>
> John 15:16 NKJV

> "Most assuredly, I say to you, whatever you ask the Father in My name He will give you."
>
> John 16:23 NKJV

Jesus' apostles stated the same truth in various ways in their letters to the young churches:

> Do not be anxious about anything, but in every situation, by prayer and petition, with thanksgiving, present your requests to God. . . . And my God will meet all your needs according to the riches of his glory in Christ Jesus.
>
> Philippians 4:6, 19

> First of all, then, I urge that entreaties and prayers, petitions and thanksgivings, be made on behalf of all men.
>
> 1 Timothy 2:1 NASB

> This is the confidence which we have before Him, that, if we ask anything according to His will, He hears us. And if we know

> that He hears us in whatever we ask, we know that we have the requests which we have asked from Him.
>
> 1 John 5:14–15 NASB

You may be thinking, *Ah, but there is a catch! We can ask anything we want, so long as it lines up with the will of God.* Yes. But why would you want anything else but the will of your all-loving Father? Do you think you know better than He does?

So, the real question is not whether or not prayer works but *what* to pray. How can you know what lines up with God's will so that you can pray with complete confidence? Does Wesley's quote above about "believing prayer" imply that some prayer is unbelieving prayer?

The best way to answer this is to soak your mind and spirit with Jesus' words. Marinate in the Word. Find a Bible that prints all of the words of Jesus in red ink, and read those words over and over. In doing this, the wind of the Spirit will find something in your heart to quicken into full faith. Then your desires will align with His and your prayers will be just right. The prayers of the Bible are like a blueprint for us to follow.

Come Like a Child

Another question is, Why does God need our prayers? Why does He seem so intent on having us pray for every single thing? Is He not sovereign and merciful and willing to take care of everything, whether or not His people ask Him each time?

Again, yes. But in His goodness, He wants you to come closer to Him. The most straightforward way to do that is through simple, confident prayer. Like trusting children, we come to Papa. He supplies what we need in exactly the right measure. When we point to someone else's need and tell Him about it, asking for His help, He is quick to respond. This is more than just a Q&A session. Prayer is our response to an invitation straight from Papa God's heart to ours to come into a greater intimacy with Him.

He likes it when we say, as His disciples did, "Lord, teach us to pray" (Luke 11:1). That happens to be a great prayer in itself, because it is a sincere request about a very real need and comes from a humble, childlike heart. I recommend that you pray it, too.

Children do not need an advanced degree in theology in order to feel confident about approaching their parents with questions or requests. Our petitions and prayers are not supposed to be part of a complex tool kit for Christian living. We should not need a detailed manual to know how to pray effectively. Our prayers are one part of our daily conversation with our Father in heaven. We ask Him for things, and we express our gratitude for what He has done in response to our honest, childlike requests.

Jesus did not make it complicated. Here is what He said:

> "But when you pray, go into your room, close the door and pray to your Father, who is unseen. Then your Father, who sees what is done in secret, will reward you."
>
> Matthew 6:6

This lack of complexity should hold just as true for our minor personal requests as for sweeping global needs we bring to Him in prayer. In both cases, we are echoing the prayer of Jesus: "Your Kingdom come on earth as it is currently being manifested in heaven" (see Matthew 6:10). We do not need to tell God how to handle everything. He is God; He knows already. We just need to present the needs to Him.

We also need to come to Him often. We need to say, *Look, Father! This burden is too great for me [or for so-and-so]. I'm bringing it to You. Please show me how to pray for it. What is*

Your heart toward this? Be my vision, and give me revelation so that I can pray according to Your will.

Recently, I was struggling with some intense physical pain due to a failed disc surgery. The sciatic nerve pain was intense, and I was getting fairly worn out by the entire ordeal. One evening, I rolled over in bed and reminded God of His Word. I prayed something like, *I have heard that Your grace is perfected in weakness. Well, right now I feel pretty weak, so I am asking You to extend great grace to me. I qualify according to Your Word.* I cast my cares upon Him and then attempted to go to sleep.

That night I slept all night, which I had not done in days, and I woke up in the morning from comforting dreams. As the morning unfolded, I noticed that I was thinking clearly and felt "bright." I declared to God and myself, *I'm back!* Now, I wish I had been totally healed, but I was strengthened, the brain fog had lifted and I made my next ministry assignment. God cares. He really does!

Present Your Needs

Do not let it be said of you, "You have not because you ask not" (see James 4:2)—or, worse, "You have not because you ask amiss, looking to your own pleasures" (see verse 3). Remember, again, that *intercession* means "hitting the mark." Asking amiss is like missing the mark. You may ask with great fervor and compose prayers that use wonderful images and religious phrases, but if you are thinking only of your enjoyment or if your prayers are motivated by your desire to eliminate a situation that is causing you anxiety, you will run out of spiritual steam before you run out of words.

Your anxieties do not make a good source for your faith. In fact, they make you miss the mark. Anxiety is fear, and fear must be vanquished by faith. "Why are you fearful, you of little faith?" Jesus asked His disciples in the midst of the storm (see Matthew 8:26). They were trying to hang on in their own strength and protect themselves. We do that all the time.

Our personal efforts fall so very short. Therefore, we ask amiss much more often than we need to. You will not ever be able to conquer your fears outside of His love (see 1 John 4:18). Let Him help you out of your fears and into faith, so that you can ask aright. Then you can present your needs—and the needs of others—to Him with full confidence that He not only hears your prayers but intends to answer them.

R. E. Miller: Revival Watchman for Argentina[1]

In the early 1950s, an American missionary named R. Edward Miller was working in a small city in Argentina. He had been laboring for years without results, and he felt he had tried everything he knew how to do—except sustained, concerted intercession.

Without telling the people in his congregation, he began to pray eight hours a day, asking God for revival in his life and in theirs, as well as in the wider community. All by himself, he prayed and prayed, eventually adding fasting to his regimen because he was so determined to get results.

After at least six months of dogged daily prayer, the Lord spoke one word to the tired missionary: *Continue!* So he kept praying for several more months. This was a one-man prayer watch.

Eventually the Lord spoke again. This time He told Miller to announce nightly prayer meetings at the church from eight in the evening until midnight, starting the following Monday evening. Miller objected, saying, *Lord, are You sure? If I hold prayer meetings, the only ones who come will be the little old ladies. And all they will do is sit and watch me pray.*

The Lord seemed to nod and say, *I know.*

Miller went ahead and announced a week of nightly prayer meetings. As he predicted, the only people from his congregation who showed up were three of the little old ladies. And, yes, all they did was sit silently and watch their pastor pray for four hours.

At midnight, he asked if any of them had received a word from God. One of the women raised her hand and reported having had a strange desire to come up and knock on the wood table in the front of the sanctuary, but that seemed too foolish to be a real word from God. They all went home for the night.

Next night, same thing. The same three ladies arrived, sat down and did nothing but watch Miller pray his heart out for four hours. At the end of the evening, the same woman reported having the same sense about knocking on the wooden table. This was crazy. They adjourned for the night once again.

The next two nights were exactly the same. The woman did not want to make a fool of herself, so she refused to knock on the table.

Miller wondered, What if obedience to this strange instruction would turn out to be the key to something big? The missionary tried to figure out a way to get the lady to at least try it out.

It was the final night of the scheduled meetings. Again, only those three little old ladies came into the sanctuary to watch him pray. This time, when he found out she had the same impulse for the fifth night in a row, he said, "Sister, we're *all* going to walk around the table and knock on it." He figured she could not refuse to follow through if the rest of them were doing it.

He went first. He walked past the table and struck it with his hand. *Thunk*. The other two women did the same. *Clunk. Thunk*. Finally, the third woman stepped up to the table and knocked her knuckles on it.

Suddenly, the Holy Spirit came. The four of them were overwhelmed with the glory of the presence of God. On the spot, the three women were baptized in the Spirit, and they began to worship God in languages they had not learned.

The news spread fast, and more people began to join them in nightly prayer times. After everyone in the congregation had been touched by God, the revival spread to the capital city of Buenos Aires, where in 1954 thousands of people gathered in an outdoor stadium. The great Argentine revival of the early 1950s had begun—all because one man watched and prayed and followed through to the best of his ability.

You see, it is true. Nothing happens without prayer!

PRAYER

Father of mercies, here I am, holding out my hands to You. Here are some of the things that weigh heavily on my heart: [name them]. Teach me to pray for each one of these with renewed energy and clarity of purpose. I invite You to convince me of the importance of my simple prayers, because I want to be a faithful watchman on the wall. Make the eyes of my heart clear and steady. Direct my attention to what You want me to see and understand. Help me pray the effective, fervent prayers of a person who is righteous in Your sight, because I want my prayers to "avail much" [see James 5:16 NKJV]. Because of Your Son, Jesus, Amen.

DAY 4

BECOMING A GUARDIAN IN PRAYER

1. How are you responding to the idea that nothing happens except through prayer? What evidence do you have that this is true? What makes you struggle with the idea? How might you respond to that struggle?
2. Have you ever prayed about a matter for a long time before you saw results? Did you pray long enough to get an answer? What was the outcome of your prayer?
3. How would it look for you to become more childlike in your prayer life? Do you find yourself resisting that idea at all?
4. How has anxiety tainted your prayers lately? What are you afraid of? Identify the threat and bring it to Jesus. Spend time reviewing the truth of His Word about that particular fear and its antidote—God's perfect love. Ask God to replace your fear and anxiety with faith and trust.
5. When the Holy Spirit seems to suggest something strange to you in prayer, how can you discern whether it is God's voice or not? How can you obtain the wisdom to know what to do?

READING FOR DAY 5

In Times of Crisis

O Lord, You are my God. . . . You have been a strength to the poor, a strength to the needy in his distress, a refuge from the storm, a shade from the heat; for the blast of the terrible ones is as a storm against the wall. . . .

He will swallow up death forever, and the Lord God will wipe away tears from all faces; the rebuke of His people He will take away from all the earth; for the Lord has spoken.

And it will be said in that day: "Behold, this is our God; we have waited for Him, and He will save us. This is the Lord; we have waited for Him; we will be glad and rejoice in His salvation."

Isaiah 25:1, 4, 8–9 NKJV

Too much news comes at us from too many sources, and most of it seems to be bad: mass shootings, natural disasters, degenerate crimes—all of human wickedness on display, day after day. Sometimes it makes us want to say, with King David, "Oh, that I had wings like a dove! I would fly away and be at rest" (Psalm 55:6 NKJV), especially when we are coping with personal hardship on top of it. We know we cannot continue to live in a state of crisis forever.

I am sure you have seen those articles with titles like "How to Stay Safe in a Crisis," "Who Can Help You in a Crisis?" and "Ten Things to Do in a Crisis." They appear on the internet after every hostage crisis, horrific hurricane or other major catastrophe. And they are well meant and helpful, up to a point. But never do they suggest the single best response to any crisis: *Pray*.

To be sure, even nonreligious people may find it instinctive to pray, *Oh God, help!* Occasionally you hear stories about how one of those emergency exclamations brought angels to the scene. But since most of the crisis-preparedness advice is not written by Christians, you never find intensive, intentional, strategic prayer mentioned as a viable option in an emergency. But I assure you it is one of the best options available to us.

Get Desperate

Did you know it is okay to be desperate? When it comes to praying effectively enough that God will come to the rescue, desperation is actually a key ingredient. In fact, I do not believe any of us would pray much at all, either on our own behalf or for the benefit of others, without being spurred on by true desperation. Desperation makes you pray bold prayers. In those moments, you know you have no other recourse except God, which means your faith in Him is absolute. As the psalmist says, "Trust in Him at all times, you people; pour out your heart before Him; God is a refuge for us" (Psalm 62:8 NKJV).

Now, desperate praying is not the same as whimpering in fear, "Oh God, oh God." True intercessors who fall to their knees in a time of crisis are anchored on the One who holds the universe in His hands. They have been here before, and they have seen God come through. Their fears make them pray until they achieve a breakthrough and His peace takes over their hearts. They know God will hear them, and they know He will act.

Think back to the reading from Day 1, where Abraham negotiated with God before the total destruction of two wicked cities, Sodom and Gomorrah. Was Abraham pacing back and forth, tearing out his hair with anxiety? Was he charging ahead to take matters into his own hands, to "play God" and try to intervene to rescue his nephew and his family? No.

On the contrary, he was calm and deliberate—but relentless in his pursuit of a solution to a crisis that might preserve the lives of his family members. He was strategic, bargaining his way down in numbers until he stopped at ten. Were there even ten righteous men in the city? No, but God showed mercy to Lot and his daughters anyway. The rescue was meant to include Lot's wife and the men his daughters were meant to marry, too. Surely the deliverance offered all of them was the direct result of Abraham's intervention.

Abraham wanted desperately to save Lot's family, even as he knew the wickedness of the citizens of Sodom and Gomorrah deserved God's fiery judgment. He did not waste his energy on panic. Like a man who is drowning, he knew it would not do any good to flail around frantically. His only hope was to relax as much as he could under the circumstances, trusting that his prayers might keep his relatives afloat.

We can do the same. Regardless of what kind of desperate situation confronts us, we can pray and thereby bring God's Kingdom to bear on it. Jesus told us to pray, "Your kingdom come. Your will be done on earth as it is in heaven" (Matthew 6:10 NKJV)—and we are to do this all of the time, even in the midst of the darkest "perfect storm" of events. Of course, we will be desperate for relief, but we become more and more desperate for the Kingdom. Nothing less will satisfy us in our quest. We will do whatever it takes to pray the Kingdom to earth; we will pray 24/7, we will fast and we will press uncompromisingly against opposition.

Witness the Lineage

You see, desperation, when coupled with faith and humility, moves the heart of God. Both the Old and New Testaments are filled with stories that prove it. And often what seems like personal desperation, such as Rachel's desolate yearning for a child, turns into something bigger in God's grand scheme of things. "Give me children, or else I die!" she cried out (Genesis 30:1 NKJV). God listened, and He acted. He gave her Joseph, who became Jacob's favorite son and went on to play a crucial role in the salvation of his extended family and, by extension, the people of Israel.

Other biblical accounts show how urgent, persistent prayer can preserve a nation. Moses is the best example:

> Moses sought the favor of the LORD his God. "LORD," he said, "why should your anger burn against your people, whom you brought out of Egypt with great power and a mighty hand? Why should the Egyptians say, 'It was with evil intent that he brought them out, to kill them in the mountains and to wipe them off the face of the earth'? Turn from your fierce anger; relent and do not bring disaster on your people. Remember your servants Abraham, Isaac and Israel, to whom you swore by your own self: 'I will make your descendants as numerous as the stars in the sky and I will give your descendants all this land I promised them, and it will be their inheritance forever.'" Then the LORD relented and did not bring on his people the disaster he had threatened.
>
> Exodus 32:11–14

> Once again I fell prostrate before the LORD for forty days and forty nights; I ate no bread and drank no water, because of all

> the sin you had committed, doing what was evil in the LORD's sight and so arousing his anger. I feared the anger and wrath of the LORD, for he was angry enough with you to destroy you. But again the LORD listened to me.
>
> Deuteronomy 9:18–19

You do not have to be named Moses to move the heart of God. Anyone can approach Him in the midst of any kind of a crisis, whether they are male or female, young or old, famous or just an everyday person.

Take Hannah as another example. Like Rachel, she was barren. On an annual pilgrimage to Shiloh, Hannah poured out her heart to the Lord God, promising that if He would only open her womb, she would dedicate the child to Him (see 1 Samuel 1). Samuel was born to her. Once again, as with Rachel, a fervent plea to God about a personal matter turned into something bigger, as Samuel grew up to become one of the best-known and best-positioned leaders in Israel's history, not to mention an excellent intercessor.

In the annals of other biblical "crisis intercessors," we should not forget Elijah, Elisha or Isaiah. First, we see Elijah sitting on Mount Carmel with his head between his knees (see 1 Kings 18:42). In obedience to God's word, he had prayed that it would not rain, and for three years a terrible drought had gripped the country. Elijah had also conquered the prophets of Baal in a dramatic spectacle. Now it was time to pray back the rain.

For this prayer, the only observer would be his servant. Elijah sat there on the mountainside like a woman in childbirth, travailing, until a small cloud began to form in the distance. He did not give up. (A woman in childbirth cannot give up, either!) At long last, the heavy rains he had predicted began to sweep down out of the sky. Elijah's tenacious intercession had won the day.

Then, before he went to heaven, Elijah anointed Elisha as his successor. Elisha asked for a double portion of Elijah's spirit, and he received it. In crisis after crisis, he not only intervened in the name of God but also performed prophetic actions to demonstrate his complete reliance on God. Elisha prayed while lying on top of the dead Shunammite boy and brought him back to life (see 2 Kings 4:32–35). He salvaged a pot of poisonous stew by obeying God's Spirit and throwing a handful of flour into it so that none of his fellow prophets were harmed (see 2 Kings 4:38–41). When an enemy army was about to prevail over the people of God, Elisha's prophetic eyes could see the heavenly forces that surrounded them, and his prophetic declaration—a form of intercessory prayer that is especially useful in a crisis—saved the day (see 2 Kings 6:15–18).

These are just a few of the many stories of how God used Elisha to intervene in crises. His God-saturated advice and prophetic actions often opened the way to the fulfillment of God's will, even though other people did not follow through very well sometimes. I am thinking of the time near the end of Elisha's life when he told King Jehoash what to do in order to help ensure his victory over Syria (see 2 Kings 13:15–19). Elisha told the king to shoot an arrow from an open window and then to strike the ground with the rest of the arrows in his quiver. King Jehoash did so, but after striking the ground only three times, he stopped. Elisha was dismayed. If only the king had kept striking again and again, his actions would have ensured a complete victory of repeated strikes. This is a good picture for intercessors to keep in mind; by "striking" in prayer persistently and repeatedly, our godly cause can surely triumph.

The prophet Isaiah was just that kind of persistent intercessor, even though he was required to live his whole life between prophetic revelation and its fulfillment, yearning and crying out the whole time:

> For Zion's sake I will not hold My peace, and for Jerusalem's sake I will not rest, until her righteousness goes forth as brightness, and her salvation as a lamp that burns.
>
> Isaiah 62:1 NKJV

> On your walls, O Jerusalem, I have appointed watchmen; all day and all night they will never keep silent. You who remind the LORD, take no rest for yourselves; and give Him no rest until He establishes and makes Jerusalem a praise in the earth.
>
> Isaiah 62:6–7 NASB

It seems as though Isaiah and the others never missed a chance to dig into prayer. They were completely sold out to God. No matter the circumstances, they trusted, prayed and spoke in faith.

Join the Effort

There will never be another Isaiah or Elisha or Elijah, but that is okay because now God's Spirit has been given to the whole Church. You and I are privileged to partner with God. And His Son, Jesus, the greatest intercessor of all, shows us the way:

> He is also able to save to the uttermost those who come to God through Him, since He always lives to make intercession for them.
>
> Hebrews 7:25 NKJV

Jesus ever lives to intercede, and His coming to earth represented the greatest act of intercession, the one upon which all other intercessions can rest. Jesus is our ultimate role model for the watchman lifestyle.

The Ruler of the universe has established some nonnegotiable future events in His eternal plan, such as the Second Coming, Satan's definitive defeat and the establishment of the new heavens and new earth. However, He has chosen to give His people a dynamic role in determining everything else. In response to the prayers of ordinary people like you and me, God closes down the enemy's oppression and pours out blessings. We cannot understand why He does things this way, but He requires our intercession.

Jesus said:

> "But when he, the Spirit of truth, comes, he will guide you into all the truth. He will not speak on his own; he will speak only what he hears, and he will tell you what is yet to come. He will glorify me because it is from me that he will receive what he will make known to you. . . . My Father will give you whatever you ask in my name. Until now you have not asked for anything in my name. Ask and you will receive, and your joy will be complete."
>
> John 16:13–14, 23–24

James echoed his brother Jesus' words when he said, "You do not have because you do not ask" (James 4:2 NASB).

You could say that our participation with God by means of our intercession is one of the Bible's primary themes. Consider these verses, for example:

> "But this kind does not go out except by prayer and fasting."
>
> Matthew 17:21 NASB

> Therefore the LORD longs to be gracious to you, and therefore He waits on high to have compassion on you. . . . He will surely be gracious to you at the sound of your cry; when He hears it, He will answer you.
>
> Isaiah 30:18, 19 NASB

> I sought for a man among them who would make a wall, and stand in the gap before Me on behalf of the land, that I should not destroy it; but I found no one.
>
> Ezekiel 22:30 NKJV

Our puny, desperate prayers have power! Our choices about what to pray about (or not pray about) and how to pray make a bigger difference than we realize. We have the power to open doors of blessing for ourselves and others, and we have the power, through our neglect, to relegate people to darkness.

Some people stress their faith in the sovereignty of God, but I am afraid their "faith" is sometimes the equivalent of a failure to act. An unbiblical faith declares—incorrectly—that God will accomplish everything without our input. Yet God has set up His Kingdom so that, animated by His Spirit, His people can be His hands and feet and voice on earth wherever they may go. We are His children, His delegated representatives, who listen to their Father's wishes and follow His instructions.

This means your humble place of prayer is really one of the governmental hubs of the Kingdom of God. Whether you are praying on a solo prayer walk or in a closet, on top of a mountain or at the bottom of a valley, your prayers traverse the globe and reach into dark prisons.

You see, together we make a great team. People who know me have heard this line many times, because it is one of my favorite things to say. It is true! Even when we do most of our praying in a private prayer spot, we are never alone. The whole Church, past and present, encompasses us. Our prayers echo the prayers of others, and others' prayers echo ours. Together, a great outcry rises to heaven, and God acts in response.

The New Testament marks the beginning of the time when every believer could have a voice before the throne, because Jesus had at last bridged the divide created by sin. When we read account after account of God's intervention in the book of Acts, we know why it can be called not only the Acts of the Apostles but also the Acts of the Holy Spirit. We can point to one example after another of crisis-type intercession in the New Testament, and after a while we see something: The entire collection of letters and books turns out to be one extended account of highly effective crisis intercession!

No wonder. The Church came under severe persecution from the beginning, and the welfare of its members was always uncertain at that time. Becoming a follower of Jesus Christ was a life-and-death matter. Yet believers continued to speak out for the name of Jesus, refusing to hide their light under a bushel. When they were persecuted, they stayed their course and prayed.

Revealingly, they prayed not so much for protection as for the grace to be good witnesses in the midst of every kind of harassment. See this example:

> "Now, Lord, consider their threats and enable your servants to speak your word with great boldness. Stretch out your hand to heal and perform signs and wonders through the name of your holy servant Jesus."
>
> After they prayed, the place where they were meeting was shaken. And they were all filled with the Holy Spirit and spoke the word of God boldly.
>
> Acts 4:29–31

Truly, the early Christians were the best examples of what we mean when today we say, "Faith is spelled R-I-S-K." The crisis of the moment spurred them to pray, and they did so with full assurance that the Spirit who had filled them once would fill them again and again. The dangers were real, but they considered them part of the cost of discipleship.

When their lives were threatened, these early believers prayed for safety only if that would best serve God's purposes. They were not passive but rather engaged in passionate conversation with God about what was happening, and they were quick to urge each other to pray even more:

> Pray in the Spirit on all occasions with all kinds of prayers and requests. With this in mind, be alert and always keep on praying

> for all the Lord's people. Pray also for me, that whenever I speak, words may be given me so that I will fearlessly make known the mystery of the gospel, for which I am an ambassador in chains. Pray that I may declare it fearlessly, as I should.
>
> Ephesians 6:18–20

Wake Up

Crises and disasters are not all bad. In fact, they can be good news—if you understand what the prophet Haggai was talking about when he said the following:

> "This is what the Lord Almighty says: 'In a little while I will once more shake the heavens and the earth, the sea and the dry land. I will shake all nations, and what is desired by all nations will come, and I will fill this house with glory,' says the Lord Almighty. 'The silver is mine and the gold is mine,' declares the Lord Almighty. 'The glory of this present house will be greater than the glory of the former house,' says the Lord Almighty."
>
> Haggai 2:6–9

When everything seems to be shaking, people get desperate—and that's when God's glory will come in greater measure than ever before. When God's intercessors summon Him, He will come. His glory will fill the Temple, as it did in Solomon's time (see 2 Chronicles 7:1). However, these days the Temple is not a structure made of blocks of stone in Jerusalem. It is the Body of Christ in every city and every land around the globe.

Next time you hear bad news about something that has happened somewhere on the earth, think of it as God's wake-up call. Every natural disaster, every military coup, every injustice is a call to prayer. These may well represent God's judgment (think of Sodom), but His judgments are always redemptive.

What will you do about it? What part does He want you to play?

Come, Lord Jesus!

Rees Howells: A Crisis-Intervention Watchman

Rees Howells was a Welshman who died in 1950 but is known to this day as a premier intercessor and organizer of intercessors in times of crisis. He was profoundly touched by the Welsh revival in the early years after 1900 and subsequently carried out Christian work, learning as he went in the "school of faith," while also holding down a secular job. After a while, he began to do Christian work exclusively, for a time serving with his wife in South Africa. In 1924, he founded the Bible College of Wales in Swansea.

It was there that I met his son, Samuel Howells, who had continued his father's work for fifty years. (Samuel died at the age of 91 in 2004.) More than anything, I wanted to know the secret behind his father's incredible track record in prayer, particularly in times of national crisis. After much gentle probing, driven by my own desperation to follow God's call into crisis intercession, this distinguished gentleman uttered ten words that have changed my life. Speaking of his father, he said, "You must understand. The Lord's servant was possessed by God." Then, by his own initiative, Samuel Howells laid hands on me as I knelt before his chair, and he pronounced over me a mantle for crisis intercession. Humbled and honored by this pronouncement, I was undone—consumed by God alone! From that moment on, I pursued God with true desperation. I still do, although I do not believe I will ever wear quite the same mantle that either of the Howells men wore.

Rees Howells, Samuel said, was "possessed by God." He was initially driven by a desire to be possessed by the Holy Spirit, but God fueled his desperation and converted it into prayer for the crisis of the moment. The holy fire of God possessed him to a degree that is seldom seen (and also possessed, to a lesser but still impressive degree, his son). You see, Rees Howells's passion for God caused him to stand before God, often alongside fellow intercessors, praying and wrestling in a way that was reminiscent of Abraham's great bartering session over Sodom and Gomorrah. In Rees Howells's case, the wrestling concerned dire national developments. His fervent prayer right before World War II is the best example.

Rees always sought to know God's will and wisdom before he led his team of intercessors to pray strategically and tirelessly. Often they would receive divine revelation about the enemy's plans and God's strategies for thwarting them, which meant they could hit the mark every time, even without the benefit of news reports or links to secret intelligence.

When Hitler's focus turned to England and war was on Britain's doorstep, Rees reassured his band of intercessors, "The Holy Spirit does not know doubt, misery or worry, these are of self."[1]

Matt Lockett further reports:

> As news of Hitler's advance came over the radio and in the newspapers each day, Rees and his company of intercessors would press into prayer for God's purposes to prevail.
>
> Royal Air Force pilots were outnumbered four to one at the beginning of the Battle of Britain. On all accounts, it should have been a losing battle. However, when the Nazi advance was mysteriously turned away right when all hope seemed lost, Winston Churchill famously said of the small group of pilots who had maintained air supremacy: "Never has so much been owed by so many to so few."
>
> Those words ought to inspire us today—those who are contending in prayer for spiritual air supremacy, standing in the victory of the cross of Christ like Rees Howells and his company.

"How thankful we are that God had this company of hidden intercessors, whose lives were on the altar day after day as they stood in the gap for the deliverance of Britain."[2]

The current director of the Bible College of Wales gives founder Rees Howells and his band of intercessors credit for changing history in other instances, as well, saying:

> Mr. Howells and the wonderful saints at the Bible College of Wales turned the course of human history. It was this band of intercessors that prayed right through World War II and prevailed in their prayers. They prayed through the 1948 mandate when the UN was voting if Israel was going to be a new nation and again, their prayers prevailed. After Rees Howells' death in 1950, under the directorship of his son Samuel Howells, they also prayed through the Cuban missile crisis as the US and USSR hurtled towards Armageddon and God turned the crisis around.[3]

Whether or not you feel you have an anointing for crisis intercession, it is important to know that a chorus of prayer from a hidden-away band of people can make a difference, and it is good to know that dedicated watchmen, possessed by God's love, have responded to such a call in every generation. Do you hear God calling you?

PRAYER

Lord, I am inspired by these true stories of people like me who were able to change history by means of prayer. I want to follow in their footsteps. However, I am afraid I will lapse into my ordinary thinking about prayer, which sometimes means not thinking about prayer at all. So I pray that You will reach into my heart and change it.

Make my desires match Yours. Remind me that You are in charge of everything that happens to me and that I can entrust myself to You, confiding in You and conversing with You. Train me to turn to You first when a crisis hits. Show me how to consult You for direction. Set my feet on the path You have laid out for me. I can pray this way because Your Son intercedes for me. Amen.

DAY 5

BECOMING A GUARDIAN IN PRAYER

1. When a crisis hits, have you noticed you tend to rise to the challenge with prayer? Does this happen more with certain kinds of crises than with others? If so, you could have a specific call to crisis intercession. Pay attention to the patterns of your prayers, and pay attention to the voice of the Holy Spirit.
2. Besides the biblical accounts I described in this chapter, what other stories illustrate crisis intervention through prayer? They are everywhere. (If you cannot think of one offhand, simply page through the Bible until you find one, and then read it thoughtfully to gain new insights.)
3. Why can you rejoice in times of upheaval, threat and uncertainty? How could you have responded to a recent time like this with more faith and prayer? Make your response to this question personal.
4. What most captures your heart about this chapter? Can you tell why?

READING FOR DAY 6

Live to Intercede

> Jesus . . . because He continues forever, holds His priesthood permanently. Therefore He is able also to save forever those who draw near to God through Him, since He always lives to make intercession for them.
>
> Hebrews 7:24–25 NASB

Jesus told His disciples, and therefore He is telling us, to pray all the time (see Luke 18:1), which is what He did when He was on earth. You are no doubt familiar with the wristbands that ask the rhetorical question "What would Jesus do?" Well, here is part of the answer: Jesus would pray.

The fact is that Jesus prayed constantly, lifting up His heart to His Father wherever He went. Just think of the many snapshots from the gospels that show Jesus in prayer: when He was being baptized in the Jordan River by John; when He prayed for the little children; the many times He went out to pray alone in the wee hours; the night He spent in prayer before selecting His twelve disciples; the time He took Peter, John and James up to the Mount of Transfiguration; the night He prayed with desperation in the Garden of Gethsemane; and when He hung from the cross.

Prayer was like breathing to Jesus. He did not do anything without praying first. No other man had ever prayed as He did, and nobody ever has since. Not only did Jesus seek guidance and solutions to problems in prayer, but He also beseeched His Father to spread the Kingdom and to work His will on earth. And He expressed His thanks and praise, over and over. As E. M. Bounds put it, "Prayer was the secret of His power, the law of His life, the inspiration of His toil and the source of His wealth, His joy, His communion and His strength."[1]

The Model Prayer

The disciples watched all this. I wonder if they were baffled as they observed Jesus' lifestyle firsthand. They had never witnessed anybody praying so much. How did He do it? He was urging them to pray, too, but how could they possibly do it the way He did?

That is when they asked Him to teach them to pray, and He responded with what we now call the Lord's Prayer:

> Our Father in heaven, hallowed be Your name. Your kingdom come. Your will be done on earth as it is in heaven. Give us this day our daily bread. And forgive us our debts, as we forgive our debtors. And do not lead us into temptation, but deliver us from the evil one. For Yours is the kingdom and the power and the glory forever. Amen.
>
> Matthew 6:9–13 NKJV

This is Jesus' model prayer—not that He expected us to limit ourselves to these precise words, but He wanted us to learn from it how to pray prayers that strike the mark. Most of us have memorized it, so it is not difficult to recite it to ourselves when we are casting about for just the right angle from which to pray. Is it time for praising God's glory? Would it be best to pray for some kind of provision ("daily bread")? Should I repent and ask for forgiveness? Have I kept up to date in forgiving other people? Today, how can I pray to avoid the temptation to sin and to be kept safe from the harm Satan would like to inflict?

At the outset, we pray, "Your kingdom come. Your will be done on earth as it is in heaven." We can cover a lot of ground with that prayer, as praying it aligns us perfectly with God's will. It opens the way for heaven to penetrate the earthly realm. This is the best way to pray for anything. Far from being a cop-out or a cover-all kind of prayer, it gets right to the heart of the matter. Whatever wrong you may be praying to be put right, having more of the Kingdom of God always means that more of the will of God is going to be expressed here on earth.

A person who prays for God's Kingdom to come puts himself or herself in alignment with heaven, praying that heavenly solutions will be released on earth to alleviate human agony. This person is eager for God's amazing love to right the wrongs. Such a person is a true intercessor-watchman, someone who pours his or her heart into the effort.

When you pray from the Lord's model prayer, you grow in character year by year, and that makes you more likely to keep on watching and praying until the very end of your life on earth.

Often one of the very first prayers taught to children, the Lord's Prayer can never be outgrown by adults. It helps us express our spiritual oneness with God, as well as our desire to live every part of our lives within that unity. It is both a personal prayer and a universal prayer. It reminds us that our relationship with God is a father/child one, characterized by loving dependence, hope and trust. The prayer also verifies that the perfect relationship is one where we do the asking and receiving and God does the answering and giving.

For years, I have taught on the model prayer of Jesus, and often these questions come up: Was Jesus exhorting His disciples to pray only in a personal devotional style, or was this an example of a watchman at work, identifying with the needs of others and thus asking, confessing and even repenting as an ambassador on their behalf? Is that why Jesus used terms such as *our* and *us* in the prayer? It seems to me that Jesus was presenting an unselfish way of praying to our Father.

This prayer is an intercessor's model prayer because it is the prayer taught by the Chief Intercessor, Jesus Himself. It presupposes there is no lack whatsoever in heaven. So when we call heaven to earth, we are calling down heaven's abundant provision—heaven's joy, heaven's peace and more.

We often ask the question, "What would Jesus do?" But perhaps the better question is, "What are we to do?"

The Great Intercessor

We know Jesus is the Great Intercessor because of Scripture passages like the one offered at the beginning of the chapter, which says, "He always lives to make intercession for them" (Hebrews 7:25 NASB; see also Romans 8:34 and 1 John 2:1). Just as intercessory prayer was a major part of Jesus' ministry on earth (see, for example, John 17 and Luke 22:32), so it remains a part of His heaven-enthroned life. This is known as His high-priestly ministry.

Like the priests of the Old Testament, Jesus has won our redemption and salvation by means of blood—His own. His ongoing intercession takes place in the shadow of the cross, which means He does not need to repeat the blood sacrifice, as the earthly priests did. Charles Wesley captured this reality in his hymn "Arise, My Soul, Arise":

Arise, my soul, arise; shake off thy guilty fears;
The bleeding sacrifice in my behalf appears:
Before the throne my surety stands,
Before the throne my surety stands,
My name is written on His hands.

He ever lives above, for me to intercede;
His all redeeming love, His precious blood, to plead:
His blood atoned for all our race,
His blood atoned for all our race,
And sprinkles now the throne of grace.

Five bleeding wounds He bears; received on Calvary;
They pour effectual prayers; they strongly plead for me:
"Forgive him, O forgive," they cry,
"Forgive him, O forgive," they cry,
"Nor let that ransomed sinner die!"

The Father hears Him pray, His dear anointed One;
He cannot turn away, the presence of His Son;
His Spirit answers to the blood,
His Spirit answers to the blood,
And tells me I am born of God.

My God is reconciled; His pardoning voice I hear;
He owns me for His child; I can no longer fear:
With confidence I now draw nigh,
With confidence I now draw nigh,
And "Father, Abba, Father," cry.

We should not fall into the unconscious assumption that the Father is the wrathful judge and Jesus is the "nice one" who pleads our case. Our three-in-one God operates in complete love and unity. Remember that it is the Father who sent His beloved Son to be sacrificed. Because He loves us so much, the Father made it possible for those He had given to His Son (see John 17 again) to emerge from their earthbound rags and be clothed in righteousness. Jesus taught us that our Father God is accessible and approachable to each one of His followers.

Jesus, the Great Intercessor, taught His twelve disciples—and, again, therefore us—to pray as He does now. As we have seen already, that method of prayer is intercession.

Remember that the word translated *intercession* in the New Testament, *paga*, has several nuanced meanings. One is "to strike the mark." Another is "laid upon," translated as "made intercession" (NIV) or "interceded" (NASB) in Isaiah 53:12. Intercession reached its fullest and most profound expression when our sins were "laid upon" Jesus. He was able to identify fully with us, so that when our sins were laid upon Him as the scapegoat, He could carry them away.

Even those of us who are earthbound intercessors can enter into an aspect of this. Colossians 1:24 calls us to share on behalf of His Body, which is the Church, in filling up that which is lacking in Christ's afflictions as we intercede when sin is laid upon us. This does not sound easy. How on earth can we do it? Only with the powerful assistance of the Holy Spirit.

The Groaning Prayer

The Holy Spirit lives within us and is always ready to bid us to pray—and to help us pray according to God's will. The prayers that He inspires will always be answered because they line up with God's will:

> The Spirit also helps our weakness; for we do not know how to pray as we should, but the Spirit Himself intercedes for us with groanings too deep for words; and He who searches the hearts knows what the mind of the Spirit is, because He intercedes for the saints according to the will of God.
>
> Romans 8:26–27 NASB

I have often paraphrased this passage as follows:

> Often we do not know what or how to pray effectively. But as we admit our limited abilities and yield to the direction of our Helper, the Holy Spirit, God will give Him the language of perfect prayer through us that is too deep for natural articulation.

Of course, the Spirit helps us pray with understanding as well as with "groanings too deep for words." But our ability to understand a situation is never going to be comprehensive enough to pray fully; only God Himself can know everything.

Seasoned prayer teacher Wesley Duewel explains this further:

> God the Father understands the Spirit's meaning as He groans within us (Romans 8:27). Our weakness (v. 26) is that our human words cannot adequately and fully articulate the depth of divine longing, just as our personality cannot experience the fullness and depth of the Spirit's longing. We can express it truly but not totally. We are finite; He is infinite.
>
> . . . Our knowledge is limited, so we do not know what is best to pray for in each situation. The Spirit's very definite and infinitely deep desire must be expressed in groanings rather than in our words, since our words are inadequate. Spirit-born groaning is always in accord with God's will. The Spirit could desire nothing other. But God can translate these groanings into His fullest understanding and do "immeasurably more than all we ask or imagine, according to His power that is at work within us" (Ephesians 3:20).[2]

This kind of praying is often called *travail* because of its resemblance to labor and childbirth. Not only do the prayers strike the mark more accurately with the Spirit's help, but prayer that is strongly Spirit-led changes *us* as we pray, too. We abandon ourselves to God more completely, and we become more open to whatever He may wish us to do.

Every one of us has hidden pockets of resistance to God, and prayer in the Spirit can flush those out. Praying in the Spirit molds our spirits and pushes us through tight and painful places toward the broad, unrestricted places of heaven. This kind of praying is humbling in a liberating way. Self-satisfied intercessors will turn away from it, but people who know they are weak and who are desperate for more of God will have difficulty *not* praying with "groanings too deep for words," under the direct influence of His Holy Spirit.

Often you will be able to tell what kind of praying the Holy Spirit is stirring in you, even when it does not come with recognizable words. Sometimes it will express love. Other times verbalizations will become urgent as the Spirit rises up with righteous indignation to fight against a foe. He will use human vessels to pronounce the judgment and the will of God on opposing forces, whether or not the human intercessor knows much about the situation.

Praying by the power of the Spirit takes different forms to suit both the intercessor and the occasion. The Holy Spirit, who dwells within us, does not have to teach us "praying lessons" and then leave us on our own. He is always with us, always helping us practice what He has taught us, always expanding on what we need to know. He kindles in our hearts the desire to pray, and He fans the sparks into flame—that is, audible utterances. As E. M. Bounds wrote, "He prays for us, through us and in us. We pray by Him, through Him and in Him."[3]

Jude, our fellow disciple, wrote:

> But you, dear friends, must build each other up in your most holy faith, pray in the power of the Holy Spirit, and await the mercy of our Lord Jesus Christ, who will bring you eternal life. In this way, you will keep yourselves safe in God's love.
>
> Jude 1:20–21 NLT

The apostle Paul added:

> And pray in the Spirit on all occasions with all kinds of prayers and requests. With this in mind, be alert and always keep on praying for all the Lord's people. Pray also for me, that whenever I speak, words may be given me so that I will fearlessly make known the mystery of the gospel, for which I am an ambassador in chains. Pray that I may declare it fearlessly, as I should.
>
> Ephesians 6:18–20

> Be anxious for nothing, but in everything by prayer and supplication with thanksgiving let your requests be made known to God.
>
> Philippians 4:6 NASB

By praying in the power of His Holy Spirit, we can be ambassadors of Jesus Christ on earth, representing His desires and decisions as much as we reflect His character and His heart to the world around us. As He prays, so we pray—and by *we*, I mean the entire Body of Christ, with each of us picking up part of the praying.

Jesus: Our Watchman-Savior

Jesus is both the Savior who has rescued us from death and our premier Watchman, ever standing guard against the work of the evil one in the lives of those He loves. From the beginning of His ministry on earth, He preached the same message as His forerunners: "Repent and believe" (see Matthew 4:17). He is our Watchman-Savior because He not only warns us to repent and believe but also is the One who has made it possible to repent and be forgiven, to be saved from death and punishment.

Jesus Himself prayed in the Spirit with "groanings too deep for words." When His friend Lazarus died, He arrived on the scene to see His friend's sisters, Martha and Mary, distressed and weeping:

> Then, when Mary came where Jesus was, and saw Him, she fell down at His feet, saying to Him, "Lord, if You had been here, my brother would not have died."
>
> Therefore, when Jesus saw her weeping, and the Jews who came with her weeping, *He groaned in the spirit and was troubled*. And He said, "Where have you laid him?"
>
> They said to Him, "Lord, come and see."
>
> *Jesus wept*. Then the Jews said, "See how He loved him!"
>
> . . . Then Jesus, *again groaning in Himself*, came to the tomb.
>
> John 11:32–36, 38 NKJV, emphasis added

Jesus told the other mourners to remove the stone that blocked the tomb entrance, and John reports that Jesus lifted up His eyes and prayed, "Father, I thank You that You have heard Me" (verse 41). What did the Father hear? Groaning and weeping. Those were Jesus' only prayers. Because those prayers were heard, they were answered with the glorious resurrection of Lazarus, who had been dead four days already.

Jesus' prayers were too deep for words because His heart was torn open with loving compassion. Death had inflicted unspeakable distress on His dear friends. He had to resort to prayers that went beyond what His native Aramaic or any other earthly language could articulate.

What does this mean for us as intercessory guardians? As I put it in my book *The Prophetic Intercessor*:

> Simply that we have an invitation to enter into the intercessory ministry of Christ that extends beyond our limited knowledge. In no way does our experience compare with the depth of Christ's propitiatory, intercessory act of the cross. That has already been accomplished! Nonetheless, we are invited to enter the depths of the heart of Jesus, and release sighs and groans

too deep for man's natural vocabulary. Whatever the distinctive purpose of these ancient forms of intercession, just yield. Let Him do it.[4]

For three years, Jesus walked the earth, praying and working miracles. But now, for all eternity, He lives to make intercession. In a word, Jesus lives for prayer. May we follow Him watchfully all the way.

PRAYER

O my Lord, who am I that You should invite me to share Your power of intercession? And why am I so slow of heart to understand, believe and exercise this wonderful privilege to which You have redeemed Your people?

Give me Your grace, that my life's work may become praying without ceasing, to draw down the blessing of heaven on all my surroundings on earth.

I come now to accept my calling, for which I will give up everything and follow You. Into Your hands I will willingly yield my whole being. Form, train and inspire me to be one of Your prayer forces, those who watch and strive in prayer, who have power and victory. Take possession of my heart, and fill it with the desire to glorify God in the gathering, sanctification and union of those whom the Father has given You. Take my mind and give me wisdom to know when prayer can bring a blessing. Take me wholly, and prepare me as You would a priest, to stand always before God and to bless His name.

Now and through all my spiritual life, let me want everything for You and nothing for myself. Let it be my experience that the person who has and asks nothing for himself receives everything, including the wonderful grace of sharing Your everlasting ministry of intercession. Amen.[5]

DAY 6

BECOMING A GUARDIAN IN PRAYER

1. Skim through at least one of the gospels and make note of all the times Jesus prayed. (Remember, prayer is simply communicating with the Father. The word *prayer* itself may not always appear in the passages.)
2. See if you can articulate how you have personally benefited from Jesus' perpetual heavenly intercession. What has His intercession made possible in your life? Can any of us come to faith without it?
3. Have you ever experienced prayerful "groanings too deep for words"? What were the circumstances? How were your inarticulate prayers answered?
4. If Jesus is always praying and interceding, why do we need to pray at all? How do you know? Join your prayers with His right now.

READING FOR DAY 7

Don't Give Up

> And pray in the Spirit on all occasions with all kinds of prayers and requests. With this in mind, be alert and always keep on praying for all the Lord's people.
>
> Ephesians 6:18

Do not lose heart. Keep up the good work. Keep on praying. Remember, all prayer counts!

In the last chapter, we saw Jesus teach His disciples what we now call the Lord's Prayer. Having told them *what* to pray, He then began to explain *how* to pray: "Now He was telling them a parable to show that at all times they ought to pray and not to lose heart" (Luke 18:1 NASB). He then told them the story of the persistent widow, which is quoted in full in the reading for Day 2.

Many of us think of that story of the widow and the judge when the subject of *importunate* (persistent) praying comes up. Yet we can easily get distracted by the gruff personality of the judge or the aggressive approach of the widow and lose track of the main point, which is that persistence in prayer is a virtue that will not go unrewarded. The better you know God, the more passionately you will pray. God wants it that way. He wants you to cling to Him. He wants you to know that a casual, offhand approach to Him will not succeed.

The Word of God is filled with stories that illustrate this. For starters, we opened this section of the book, in the reading for Day 1, with the story of Abraham pleading for the salvation of Sodom and Gomorrah, keeping up the pressure through several rounds of negotiation with God. That story makes me think of Jacob wrestling all night with the angel of the Lord (see Genesis 32:24–31) and Moses praying straight through forty days and nights so that he could hear God on behalf of the people of Israel (see Exodus 34:28; Deuteronomy 9:9–11; 10:10). The sometimes mixed motives of these men of God did not weaken their absolute conviction that God would listen to them and answer their prayers eventually.

Time after time, in both the Old and New Testaments, we see that important matters deserve importunate prayer. Here is another one of Jesus' parables about it:

> Then He said to them, "Suppose one of you has a friend, and goes to him at midnight and says to him, 'Friend, lend me three loaves; for a friend of mine has come to me from a journey, and I have nothing to set before him'; and from inside he answers and says, 'Do not bother me; the door has already been shut and my children and I are in bed; I cannot get up and give you anything.' I tell you, even though he will not get up and give him anything because he is his friend, yet *because of his persistence* he will get up and give him as much as he needs.
>
> "So I say to you, ask, and it will be given to you; seek, and you will find; knock, and it will be opened to you. For everyone who asks, receives; and he who seeks, finds; and to him who knocks, it will be opened."
>
> Luke 11:5–10 NASB, emphasis added

Notice that phrase: "because of his persistence" (translated as "shameless audacity" in the New International Version and "importunity" in the King James Version). It seems kind of brash, doesn't it? Does God really want us to pester Him that way? If He truly loves us, why does He seem to withhold blessing until we have asked and asked? Perhaps He is giving us a test to see how much we want a breakthrough and if we really believe He wants to release it.

Quitters Never Win

Evidently, the Lord is not irritated in the least by our often-repeated requests. I wonder if sometimes He postpones His answers purely to motivate us to pray longer and harder, and furthermore to force us to ask Him for everything we need instead of operating by our own strength and limited wisdom. It appears that importunity, or persistence, in prayer is made up of equal parts intensity (like wrestling) and patience. We need to come to a full revelation that He is a good, good God.

This kind of praying may be loud and even somewhat physical in its expression. Or not. It can just as easily be calm and quiet—but relentlessly so. As E. M. Bounds put it in his powerful little book *The Necessity of Prayer*:

> Importunate prayer is a mighty movement of the soul toward God. It is a stirring of the deepest forces of the soul, toward the throne of heavenly grace. It is the ability to hold on, press on, and wait. Restless desire, restful patience, and strength of grasp are all embraced in it. It is not an incident, or a performance, but a passion of soul. It is not a want, half-needed, but a sheer necessity.[1]

Instead of settling for halfhearted prayers that will be quickly abandoned when they seem to go nowhere, God wants us to put our whole heart and soul into our praying. Requests that are easily forgotten represent hardly more than fleeting impulses, whereas petitions that cause us to latch on to the hem of Jesus' garment reflect both the degree of our desperation and the depth of our faith.

Look how often the Lord Jesus praised this kind of relentless faith. Remember the Syrophoenician woman? She was not a Jew; she had no real claim on His time. But she had a big need, and she was convinced He alone could help her:

> Jesus got up and went away from there to the region of Tyre. And when He had entered a house, He wanted no one to know of it; yet He could not escape notice. But after hearing of Him, a woman whose little daughter had an unclean spirit immediately came and fell at His feet. Now the woman was a Gentile, of the Syrophoenician race. And she kept asking Him to cast the demon out of her daughter. And He was saying to her, "Let the children be satisfied first, for it is not good to take the children's bread and throw it to the dogs." But she answered and said to Him, "Yes, Lord, but even the dogs under the table feed on the children's crumbs." And He said to her, "Because of this answer go; the demon has gone out of your daughter." And going back to her home, she found the child lying on the bed, the demon having left.
>
> Mark 7:24–30 NASB

This woman was insistent and persistent, but she was not disrespectful or impertinent. Her fervency matched the magnitude of her need. To her unending grief and distress, her beloved little daughter had become demon-possessed. When the mother was offered a clear opportunity to receive a miracle from God, she was not going to give up easily and go home. No, like the persistent widow in the other story, she was going to press her case to a successful conclusion, even if she got thrown out of the house. She refused to worry about fine points of religion.

Jesus put her off for a while, but she persisted. Her undaunted faith impressed Him more than anything. In Matthew's telling of the story, Jesus said, "O woman, your faith is great; it shall be done for you as you wish" (Matthew 15:28 NASB). Because of the woman's faith in Him, she had a bold hope, and that made her hang on. She shows us that without a doubt, quitters never win.

Hope and Hard Work

When Jesus told His disciples they ought always to pray and not lose heart, He was saying that they should hope in Him. When you have hope, you have the wind under your wings:

> Those who hope in the LORD will renew their strength. They will soar on wings like eagles; they will run and not grow weary, they will walk and not be faint.
>
> Isaiah 40:31

Paul reiterated this truth when he wrote to the church in Corinth, "Therefore we do not lose heart, but though our outer man is decaying, yet our inner man is being renewed day by day" (2 Corinthians 4:16 NASB).

Generations of believers can testify to the importance of hope. Because of hope, they were able to keep on serving, both in physical ways and in spiritual ways (i.e., by praying without ceasing). Paul told the Galatian Christians, "Let us not lose heart in doing good, for in due time we will reap if we do not grow weary" (Galatians 6:9 NASB). I believe that the "doing good" he mentioned includes praying for others and entrusting them to God's care.

Effective prayer cannot be an activity that is undertaken merely for self-fulfillment. Prayer can look like hard work. It might appear to take something out of you. Every time you "pray through" something difficult, you must remind yourself what an honor and privilege it is to be a guardian of prayer. We need God's help, and He is ready and willing to give it.

After all, you are not applying your prayer energy against human fiascos or generalized malevolence. For the most part, your enemies are unseen. In prayer, you wrestle with those enemies of the name that is above all other names: "For we do not wrestle against flesh and blood, but against principalities, against powers, against the rulers of the darkness of this age, against spiritual hosts of wickedness in the heavenly places" (Ephesians 6:12 NKJV).

When your prayer wrestling goes so long that you really do not know if you can take much more, should you blow the whistle, give up and go home? Not if you are convinced of the ultimate victory of the Mighty One. Replacing your feeble spirit with one that never, ever gives up, you must gather strength and courage at each delay and postponement of your hope, redoubling your efforts in prayer until you reach V-day at last.

Take blind Bartimaeus as your example. Do not let the Lord pass you by. Do not worry about offending the Lord with your urgent pleas. Disregard what other people think, too. Look at his example:

> When Bartimaeus heard that Jesus of Nazareth was nearby, he began to shout, "Jesus, Son of David, have mercy on me!"
>
> "Be quiet!" many of the people yelled at him.
>
> But he only shouted louder, "Son of David, have mercy on me!"
>
> When Jesus heard him, he stopped and said, "Tell him to come here."
>
> So they called the blind man. "Cheer up," they said. "Come on, he's calling you!" Bartimaeus threw aside his coat, jumped up, and came to Jesus.
>
> "What do you want me to do for you?" Jesus asked.

> "My Rabbi," the blind man said, "I want to see!"
>
> And Jesus said to him, "Go, for your faith has healed you." Instantly the man could see, and he followed Jesus down the road.
>
> Mark 10:47–52 NLT

Dropping everything, Bartimaeus ran blindly in the direction of Jesus' voice. Then, healed and able to see, he followed Jesus down the road. We do not know how things worked out for him down the road, but he was going in the right direction as long as he was following Jesus. This will happen for us, too. Our persistent pleas for mercy and relief will always make us into better Jesus-followers.

Be prepared for setbacks, delays, betrayals, apparent dead ends and more. They are part of the package. Does a soldier on the front line give up right in the thick of the battle? I hope not. Calling on all of his courage and training, he intensifies his fighting, disregarding his personal comfort. He knows the only way through the mess he is in is straight through the middle, and retreat is not a good option.

May we be commended by our God as good soldiers of Jesus Christ. Even in the midst of the fight, may we share His joy. May each of us "be joyful in hope, patient in affliction, faithful in prayer" (Romans 12:12).

E. M. Bounds: A Prolific Prayer Writer

Edward McKendree Bounds (1835–1913) was a Methodist preacher during the Civil War. I have a strong affinity for him for a number of reasons. First, he was born in northern Missouri, as I was. Second, his heritage was Methodist, as is mine. Third, he had a spirit of prayer on his life, as people say that I do. And fourth, interestingly, he ended up right in Franklin, Tennessee, where I currently live. He came here as a chaplain for the Fifth Missouri regiment of the Confederate Army, and he marched with the troops right down Henpeck Lane, where my ministry headquarters used to be located. Bounds led in prayer during a time of war, and I, too, have been called to lead in prayer during tumultuous times.

Bounds led a prayer revival that lasted. To this day, worship and prayer meetings are held in that same downtown Franklin, Tennessee, church. True prayer can have that kind of a lasting impact.

During his long and eventful ministry, Bounds wrote a number of books about prayer. Most of these are still in print today. The titles include *The Necessity of Prayer*, *The Essentials of Prayer*, *Power through Prayer*, *Purpose in Prayer*, *The Reality of Prayer* and *The Weapon of Prayer*. The insights and exhortations contained in his books have a timeless appeal for intercessors who keep watch. Here is one about wrestling in prayer:

> The wrestling quality in importunate prayers does not spring from physical vehemence or fleshly energy. It is not an impulse of energy, not a mere earnestness of soul; it is an inwrought force, a faculty implanted and aroused by the Holy Spirit. Virtually, it is the intercession of the Spirit of God, in us; it is, moreover, "the effectual, fervent prayer, which availeth much." The Divine Spirit informing every element within us, with the energy of His own striving, is the essence of the importunity which urges our praying at the mercy-seat, to continue until the fire falls and the blessing descends. This wrestling in prayer may not be boisterous nor vehement, but quiet, tenacious and urgent.[2]

These words echo the words of an old Methodist hymn, "A Charge to Keep I Have," that Bounds must surely have sung:

> A charge to keep I have,
> a God to glorify. . . .

Help me to watch and pray,
and on thyself rely.

In the original foreword of the book *The Necessity of Prayer*, a fellow pastor named Claude Chilton Jr. wrote:

> Edward McKendree Bounds did not merely pray well that he might write well about prayer. He prayed because the needs of the world were upon him. He prayed, for long years, upon subjects which the easy-going Christian rarely gives a thought, and for objects which men of less thought and faith are always ready to call impossible. From his solitary prayer-vigils, year by year, there arose teaching equaled by few men in modern Christian history. He wrote transcendently about prayer, because he was himself, transcendent in its practice.
>
> As breathing is a physical reality to us so prayer was a reality for Bounds. He took the command, "Pray without ceasing" almost as literally as animate nature takes the law of the reflex nervous system, which controls our breathing.[3]

What a wonderful prayer watchman E. M. Bounds was! If you do not have any of his books already, look for them. Let their words grow roots in your soul as you build your personal library of books written by effective, persistent prayer warriors. Let this man's words light a fire in your heart for unrelenting, watchful prayer.

PRAYER

Lord, have I weakened in my zeal for praying? I pray for a new wave of Your grace so that I can recover my passion and eagerness to see You act in response to my requests. Position me and equip me to pray over the long haul, and reignite the Spirit's fire within me whenever it grows dim. Help me identify the specific needs You want me to pray for, and show me new ways to approach You in prayer. Reveal to me the strategies of my unseen enemies so that I can elude traps and go on to watch and pray for another day. I rely on You for every breath. Amen.

DAY 7

BECOMING A GUARDIAN IN PRAYER

1. What obstacles to your exercise of persistent prayer have you encountered? How have you overcome those obstacles in the past, and how can you overcome them now?
2. What has been your experience of prayer as work? Does thinking about the work of prayer energize you or dishearten you? Why?
3. What watchman-mentors might you have in your life who can model for you practical ways of exercising importunate, persistent, faith-filled prayer? (Remember to consider potential mentors who have graduated to heaven already, leaving you their books.)
4. Which of your regular prayer petitions has occupied your attention the longest? Are you still zealous for it? How can you become more persistent and dedicated in praying for it?

SECTION 2

The Lifestyle of Sacrifice

The LORD is my light and my salvation; whom shall I fear? The LORD is the strength of my life; of whom shall I be afraid? . . . One thing I have desired of the LORD, that will I seek: that I may dwell in the house of the LORD all the days of my life, to behold the beauty of the LORD, and to inquire in His temple. . . . Therefore I will offer sacrifices of joy in His tabernacle. . . . When You said, "Seek My face," my heart said to You, "Your face, LORD, I will seek." . . . I would have lost heart, unless I had believed that I would see the goodness of the LORD in the land of the living. Wait on the LORD; be of good courage, and He shall strengthen your heart; wait, I say, on the LORD!

Psalm 27:1, 4, 6, 8, 13–14 NKJV

READING FOR DAY 8

Anna: Praying the Promises

We do not know very much about the widow Anna. She is mentioned only once in the Bible, in the narrative about Mary and Joseph bringing their newborn son, Jesus, into the Temple to perform the post-childbirth purification offering required by Jewish law. She and a man named Simeon crossed paths with the holy family in important ways that day. Here is what the narrative tells us:

> Eight days later, when the baby was circumcised, he was named Jesus, the name given him by the angel even before he was conceived.
>
> Then it was time for their purification offering, as required by the law of Moses after the birth of a child; so his parents took him to Jerusalem to present him to the Lord. . . .
>
> At that time there was a man in Jerusalem named Simeon. He was righteous and devout and was eagerly waiting for the Messiah to come and rescue Israel. The Holy Spirit was upon him and had revealed to him that he would not die until he had seen the Lord's Messiah. That day the Spirit led him to the Temple. So when Mary and Joseph came to present the baby

Jesus to the Lord as the law required, Simeon was there. He took the child in his arms and praised God, saying, "Sovereign Lord, now let your servant die in peace, as you have promised. I have seen your salvation, which you have prepared for all people. He is a light to reveal God to the nations, and he is the glory of your people Israel!"

Jesus' parents were amazed at what was being said about him. Then Simeon blessed them, and he said to Mary, the baby's mother, "This child is destined to cause many in Israel to fall, and many others to rise. He has been sent as a sign from God, but many will oppose him. As a result, the deepest thoughts of many hearts will be revealed. And a sword will pierce your very soul."

Anna, a prophet, was also there in the Temple. She was the daughter of Phanuel from the tribe of Asher, and she was very old. Her husband died when they had been married only seven years. Then she lived as a widow to the age of eighty-four. She never left the Temple but stayed there day and night, worshiping God with fasting and prayer. She came along just as Simeon was talking with Mary and Joseph, and she began praising God. She talked about the child to everyone who had been waiting expectantly for God to rescue Jerusalem.

Luke 2:21–22, 25–38 NLT

Anna had waited decades for that day, and because she never gave up, she was ready when it came. She does not seem to have had any assurance, as Simeon did, that she might actually see the Savior with her own eyes. However, she maintained her watch, day after day, month after month, year after year, praying fervently that the Messiah would come to rescue the Jewish people.

The name *Anna* is the Greek form of the Hebrew name *Hannah*, and it means "grace." This woman was dedicated! Anna may have been elderly, but she was active, worshiping and praying in the Temple around the clock and also fasting from food on a regular basis. Apparently, she had no family who could look after her; even after she became an octogenarian, she saw no reason to retire from what she had started to do decades earlier.

How could Anna have lived right within the Temple, as the passage says? Even the priests were restricted from setting up permanent housekeeping there, and Anna was a widowed woman. Probably she had a chamber in some of the living quarters that existed around the Temple precincts, although nobody knows for sure. When Luke wrote that "she stayed there day and night," he must have meant, at the least, that she was inside the Temple whenever the doors were open. Every single day. No vacations. The Temple was God's house, and Anna wanted to live with Him.

Although we have not been told many details about Anna's life, we know all we need to know. We know she was consumed with a burning passion: waiting for and interceding for the coming of the Messiah. We know her passion was both inspired and sustained by the Holy Spirit; otherwise she would never have continued faithfully for so long. We know she had been living this life upward of sixty years—assuming she had gotten married in her early teens, according to the custom of the day, only to be widowed before she reached her mid-twenties. Apparently, their marriage brought forth no children, or she would not have been able to live this lifestyle. (Moms with young children reading this book right now—breathe. A lifestyle of sacrifice looks different for each one of our lives!)

Anna's was not a meaningless existence. In the Temple, surrounded by God's presence, her quiet demeanor was devoid of self-interest, her mind and heart filled with divinely inspired insights and vitality. She was waiting for her long-expected Messiah. I have often said Anna was the first Jesus fanatic!

Luke does not record what Anna said when she saw Jesus, but he does say she "talked about the child to everyone," and it is not hard to imagine she did this because she was overjoyed.

I can see the scene. The day started out like all the others, with its well-worn rhythm of sacrificial worship and its hum of human voices. Then Anna overheard something—just a few words, but they were momentous ones. There was a stirring in the Temple that bright sunshiny day. Something was up. I imagine Anna's heart started racing as she recognized the manifest presence of God.

A man named Simeon, a gifted seer, had taken a woman's eight-day-old baby boy into his arms. His aging voice thick with emotion, he uttered God-inspired words. Could it be true? Yes! The hope of Israel had arrived at last!

Simeon's prophecy came from one whose faith had matured through faithful waiting and watching. He, like many good Jews, was longing for the deliverance of the nation of Israel. Evidently, God had revealed to Simeon that he would not die until he had laid his own eyes on this Messiah.

When he saw that infant bundled in his mother's arms, Simeon's heart must have leaped. His joyful prophetic proclamation contained a statement of great import: "I have seen Your salvation."

This baby—Simeon did not even know His name, and he did not need to. He had seen the child with spiritual eyes for many long years, and now he beheld the Promised One with natural eyes, as well—God's gift of salvation. The Word had become flesh!

In other words, to see this baby was to see God's salvation.

And by the way, Simeon added, this salvation would also bring pain. Not everyone would welcome Him with open arms. Many would reject Him. Kill Him. To put your hope in Jesus, to identify fully with Him, is an invitation to die to yourself—but out of the pain comes an unexpected gift of joy.

Everyone in that cluster of people—Simeon, Anna, Joseph and Mary—was acquainted with a lifestyle of sacrifice. They were committed to waiting for the fulfillment of God's promises. They were used to accepting the cost of sacrifice and faithfulness. They were ready for the next level. And they beheld His glory.

As they took their leave of each other, Simeon and Anna had completed their lifelong assignments. They showed us how it is done—what some of us today call *prophetic intercession.*

Prophetic Intercession

It takes a powerful prophetic vision to sustain such a ministry of prayer for so long. Anna had been praying for more than sixty years straight. Most of us cannot imagine doing that. We may grasp a general vision for being a watchman, and we may shoulder a few prayer burdens when urgent needs flare up, but we falter easily. Only the rare prayer ministry has staying power.

Why do we not see Anna's secret? Her focus was not on "doing ministry" or on God's promises as much as it was on the Lord Himself. Everything else had been stripped away—husband, family, home. She had discovered her watchman calling as she turned her heart, day and night, to the Author and Sustainer of life. *He* was her goal, the prize she was reaching out to touch.

Anna spoke of her hope to those who would listen, but hers was not a public ministry. She was a woman of the secret place, interceding in accord with God's purposes.

Anna's worshipful intercession was fueled by her prophetic senses. When she turned her heart to God, what did she see? What was on His heart? What were His promises? Well, those were what she would wait for, expectantly and actively. As I put it in my book *Prophetic Intercession*:

> Anna was looking for a Deliverer, the Messiah, the hope of Israel. She was one of a special task force of prophetic intercessors whom God had ordained for that generation. They were the ones who were listening and watching for the Lord's appearing. Like Joshua they were waiting at the doorway of the tent of meeting in hopes that they would be the first to see the shining forth of the Lord's great presence. Anna was doubtless praying through those beloved prophetic promises of a coming Messiah.[1]

So, what is prophetic intercession, and how does it work?

Prophetic intercession is the desire to pray, given by the Holy Spirit, for a person or situation about which the intercessor may have little information. Such prophetic prayers express God's heart. The Holy Spirit nudges the intercessor to pray so that God can intervene in the situation. This matches the prayer Jesus taught His disciples: "Your kingdom come. Your will be done on earth as it is in heaven" (Matthew 6:10 NKJV).

Far from being meaningless, rote repetition, prayer requests engendered in the heart of God are sure things. John tells us, "This is the confidence we have in approaching God: that if we ask anything according to his will, he hears us. And if we know that he hears us—whatever we ask—we know that we have what we asked of him" (1 John 5:14–16).

In the power of the Holy Spirit, a prophetic intercessor takes every unfulfilled promise God has made to His people and pleads it before God's throne. It takes an army of intercessors to cover everything, so each one carries a specific assignment.

Prophetic intercessors combine the ministries of the priests and the prophets. Priests supplicate on behalf of the people before the Lord, and prophets bring God's word down from heaven to the people. Prophetic intercession does both. Prophetic intercessors do not simply pronounce the word of the

Lord; they pray His words of promise back to Him. Their efforts give birth to the fulfillment of the words, bringing them into being.

This kind of praying combines a number of spiritual disciplines—listening, watching and waiting, and believing God will open our spiritual eyes (see Ephesians 1:17–19). We are in eager anticipation that He is already at work and inviting us to labor with Him. These spiritual disciplines are combined with the gifts of the Holy Spirit, such as the discerning of spirits, the gift of prophecy and possibly even the gift of faith. This revelatory realm of intimate intercession now becomes interactive.

The first step of prophetic intercession is waiting. We must wait in order to hear God's voice and get some idea of the burden that He wants us to take up in prayer. He may share with us a word of warning, a hindrance in the way, a condition that needs to be met, a vision or a revelatory promise. Then—and only then—can we take that word and pray it back to Him, relying on His Spirit to inspire us.

Intercessory Sacrifice

This kind of prayer does not come without significant effort—even sacrifice—on the part of the one who prays. In a real way, prophetic intercessors conspire with God for the release of His glory on the earth.

The word *conspire* means "to breathe together," and that is what such intercessors do with God. This is no light thing. It is more like the violent panting of childbirth or like God's infusion of life into Adam's nostrils after He had created him from the dust of the earth (see Genesis 2:7). It suggests intensity and costly effort. It is like the sound of the violent wind filling the Upper Room when God breathed His Spirit into the first members of the Church.

Such prayer must come forth from a heart that is wholly engaged; there can be nothing tentative or halfway about it. Just as Anna had to remain at her post for sixty-plus years, so we may need to endure for the long haul, clinging to God's promises without wavering. What if Anna had yielded to the temptation to give up? For sure, such temptation would have been part of the burden of those long years. No tangible reward presented itself. The experience of God's glory, when it came, would have helped, but that can be forgotten in the dry seasons.

When you look at Anna's life from the outside, it appears to be placid and protected. *Not bad*, you think. *I could get used to just hanging out in the Temple all the time. Looks like a hassle-free existence.* We forget about her continuous deprivations of all kinds. Anna's lifestyle was sacrificial to the uttermost.

When you are overworked and tired, have you ever found yourself envying someone who has recently retired? *It just looks so restful*, you think. *Just imagine how well I could read Scripture and pray if I had that much downtime.* You may look at someone like Anna in a similar way, thinking, *Wow. For most of her life, she did nothing but worship and wait. I could handle that.*

Maybe.

Now, I love contemplation and turning aside to be with the Lord. But let me tell you from personal experience that being forced into solitary confinement, spending weeks on end alone due to major physical problems, or being widowed and trying to fulfill a lonely, long-term assignment is not all sweetness and rose-scented breezes. Sure, it looks nice from the outside—all that time to yourself. But you fail to realize how difficult it can be and what a sacrifice it represents. I now understand Anna's lifestyle in a way I never dreamed I would. Yet I know all things still work together for good (see Romans 8:28).

When you are confined like that, you not only cannot move about freely but also cannot even think or pray in a straight line sometimes. You hurt. Your time is divided between not sleeping and wishing you could sleep. Often you lie awake at night, wishing God would send a word or set you to praying for something specific, and with the exciting results that others report. But so often, nothing happens. You just wait, hoping your waiting is not in vain.

If, like Anna or me, you have lost your spouse and your "nest" is empty, you are on your own. A good day for you is one in which you keep your focus and hope and joy. Most days, you feel as if you inhabit a waiting room. Naturally, you might want a break, a reward, even a shred of encouragement. Is it worth it? How can you know? Only by keeping your eyes on the prize of the One you know is faithful and true.

Like Anna, you can stay the course that has been set before you. Just keep your eyes on the Lord. Anna was waiting for her Messiah. You will be looking for something specific, too. Even though some of the time it may feel like you are waiting in the fog for a ship to come in, where else would you rather be? You have a divine assignment to pray through the promises of God for your generation.

Accept the conditions. God has set them up, and He will help you daily (and nightly). With the apostle Paul—who had his share of hardship—learn to be content with your circumstances:

> Not that I speak in regard to need, for I have learned in whatever state I am, to be content: I know how to be abased, and I know how to abound. Everywhere and in all things I have learned both to be full and to be hungry, both to abound and to suffer need. I can do all things through Christ who strengthens me.
>
> Philippians 4:11–13 NKJV

I appreciate Paul's choice of words. He did not say, "I was always perfectly content," or, "I am comfortable," or even, "I am content." He said, "I have *learned* to be content in every circumstance."

Paul had it hard much of the time. People wanted to argue with him, put him in prison, kill him. He was beaten, stoned and shipwrecked. By nature, he was the kind of man who fought back, so I imagine that learning contentment was far from easy for him. But he accepted the hardships, even the extreme ones, as part of doing God's business.

If Paul, Simeon, Anna and so many others could learn to be content in a sacrificial lifestyle, so can I. So can you. It is, indeed, an honor to be a forerunner and call forth God's prophetic purposes in your generation.

The examples make it clear: The life of God's watchmen can include sacrifice and times of solitude. Watchmen will be exposed to the elements. They may feel alone and even in the dark at times. That comes with the territory. The privilege of entering into the intercession of Christ is worth every sacrifice.

You and I can be co-laborers with Christ! Thank you, Anna, for showing us how it is done. And thank You, God, for inviting us to partner with You in the birthing of Your dream in the earth by praying Your Word into being. What a joy has been set before us!

PRAYER

Dearest Lord, increase my faith and my trust in Your ability to take care of me even when You assign me to watchman duty and I must accost enemies in the dark or—sometimes this is harder—find that I have nothing to do but watch and wait. Enable me to rejoice in the hardest things, and keep me steady. As I listen for Your words of direction and encouragement, keep me from mistaking other voices for Yours. I rededicate my life to You, Lord. I give You permission to do whatever You want with me. My only plea: Keep me close to You, right at the foot of Your cross. For the joy set before me, and for Jesus' sake, Amen.

DAY 8

BECOMING A GUARDIAN IN PRAYER

1. Do you know any Annas? If you do, what can you learn from them? What is their central prayer passion? How long have they been praying for that concern? What sacrifices have they made along the way?
2. Anna did not often receive encouragement from anyone, but Simeon encouraged her (albeit unknowingly) when he burst forth with a prophetic word before the baby Jesus. Do you know any Simeons—not necessarily a prophet, but someone who brings a word in due season? (See Proverbs 15:23, Galatians 6:9, and Isaiah 50:4.) How has that person encouraged you to press toward God's goal?
3. Jesus ever lives to intercede (see Hebrews 7:25), and we represent Him wherever we go. Can you think of a time when you interceded for someone or something and knew your requests were "spot on" before the throne?
4. Practically speaking, how can someone find joy in the midst of deprivation and difficulties? How have you experienced this?

READING FOR DAY 9

The Watchman Fast

> Anna, a prophet, was also there in the Temple. She was the daughter of Phanuel from the tribe of Asher, and she was very old. . . . She never left the Temple but stayed there day and night, worshiping God with fasting and prayer.
>
> Luke 2:36, 37 NLT

Anna's daily life in the Temple was devoted not only to prayer but also to fasting. Even in her extreme abstinence from food for years and decades on end, she was only following a strong Jewish tradition. Fasting from food was a common practice among the Jews from earliest times, and later, too, among the early Christians who came from Jewish backgrounds. It was a way for them to underline the importance of their prayers, a specific personal sacrifice made by people who yearned to see God's intervention in human affairs.

As a spiritual discipline, fasting can never be undertaken lightly, even when it becomes a routine part of the devotional fabric of a person's life. It is not pleasant to be hungry. Without the fuel of food, our bodies feel tired and weak. Instinctively, we want to look for something to eat in order to escape our lassitude, but someone who is fasting can only resort to more prayer.

Why on earth would you want to put yourself into such a difficult position? Because fasting works. It gets your willful self out of the way, at least partially, so you can perceive how puny you are in comparison to God Almighty. It humbles you. Every time your stomach growls, it reminds you to pray and seek His face. With normal comforts stripped away, you can more readily hear His voice. You become more sympathetic toward other people, less judgmental and harsh. Honed to the bone, your prayers become more "on point," especially when they are joined with the prayers of others.

In short, fasting brings you closer to God. It helps to release His presence in and through your life. And once fasting has helped you get in touch with God's heart and mind, it also makes you more able to reach out to others in the power of God's love.

A Long History

Tsum, the Hebrew word for *fasting*, means "to abstain from food."[1] This is the word used throughout the Old Testament to describe not a time of famine but a time of going without nourishment for some reason, even when food is not scarce.

Fasting has always been considered a natural expression of human grief, and the Bible gives us two early examples in Hannah (see 1 Samuel 1:7) and David (see 2 Samuel 3:31–37). Over time, fasting evolved into a way of making a prayerful petition more effective before God. Many times, the entire nation of Israel fasted in order to seek divine favor and protection or to circumvent God's judgment. The people combined sorrow and grief, confession of sin and intercessory prayer with their fasting—an example that groups of believers follow to this day.

The prophet Isaiah gives important reasons for fasting:

> "Is this not the fast which I choose, to loosen the bonds of wickedness, to undo the bands of the yoke, and to let the oppressed go free and break every yoke? Is it not to divide your bread with the hungry and bring the homeless poor into the house; when you see the naked, to cover him; and not to hide yourself from your own flesh? Then your light will break out like the dawn, and your recovery will speedily spring forth; and your righteousness will go before you; the glory of the LORD will be your rear guard."
>
> Isaiah 58:6–8 NASB

The benefits of this form of self-denial or sacrifice are many. This passage in Isaiah shows that, through fasting, our light will break out, our recovery will spring forth and the glory of the Lord will increase. The long-term benefits far outweigh the short-term costs.

Fasting has been a common spiritual discipline throughout Church history. The fourth-century Cyprian bishop Epiphanius wrote that it was a well-established practice in the Church to fast two days a week, specifically Wednesdays and Fridays[2] (which differentiated the Christians from devotees of other religions, such as the Pharisees, who fasted on Tuesdays and Thursdays).

Yet the Church, particularly in the West, has neglected fasting in recent times. We prefer our "microwave" approach to life—instant gratification—which makes fasting seem like a quaint and archaic relic of the past or the peculiar specialty of hermits and religious fanatics.

I believe, with many others, that the modern Church is poorer and weaker for neglecting the practice of fasting. So many believers suffer from spiritual anemia, or loss of strength and stamina, because they have never learned to fast, and so many of their prayers have failed to break through enemy ramparts.

But times are changing, and God is once again raising up those who understand the power of the watchman's fast.

More Than Growling Stomachs

It seems counterintuitive to go without food voluntarily in order to make ourselves weak and low, does it not? Yet simply because we are so fond of eating, our abstaining from food makes a strong statement about our faith and desire. When we fast, we are purposefully changing our priorities.

I should add that although going without food is the primary kind of fast we can do, fasting does not need to be limited to that. Sometimes for reasons of health or age, a believer should not fast totally from nutrition. Sometimes, like Daniel (whom we will profile in section 3), you can fast from certain kinds of food, as he and his companions adopted a plain vegetarian diet. You can also fast from certain meals, limit your caloric intake or eliminate caffeine. In our electronically overloaded world, you can fast from social media or from entertainment, like movies, videos, TV, radio and video games. You can fast from the news media or even Christian fiction, if you tend to spend a lot of time reading it. You can fast from sleep, too, replacing the hours you would normally spend in bed with active intercession, either alone or with others. (In the reading for Day 17, you can discover more about staying up all night for "the watch of the Lord.")

In other words, you can fast from just about anything that plays a prominent role in your life. Of course, you would not fast from things like attending worship services, going to work or school, or taking care of your family, but I am sure you understand what I mean.

The point is, God's watchmen will fast. They will take hold of fasting as a vital part of their equipment as guardian intercessors, and they will learn to use it on a regular basis, year after year. They do not have to enjoy it; they will just do it.

You can read whole books about fasting, and I can recommend many of them. But reading or talking about fasting is only the beginning. If you are serious about entering into a watchman lifestyle of sustained intercession, you will need to incorporate some form of fasting into your regular routine.

Do not wait to fast until you get a lightning bolt from heaven. That will not happen. The decision to fast or not belongs to you, as does the decision about what kind of fast to undertake. If you are asked to participate in a corporate fast, the timing and nature of the fast may be predetermined by a group leader, but you are the only one who can declare yes or no to the idea. Remember how Jesus put it: He said *when* you fast, not *if* (see Matthew 6:16; see also Matthew 9:14–15). He did not say, "Wait for a sign from God, and then fast," or, "Wait until you have a break from your normal responsibilities." Just do it.

A Suggested Approach

Now, with your fast being voluntary, who will police your adherence to the "rules" of each fast? Nobody. Obeying your self-imposed restrictions is just as much up to you as deciding to fast in the first place is—not that it depends entirely on sheer grit and willpower.

Here are some strategies that will help you succeed in your fast.

1. Start small.

Do not be too ambitious or you will set yourself up for failure. Perhaps you could fast one meal a couple of times before undertaking a longer fast.

2. Commit to a specific kind and length of fast.

Will you skip one meal, three meals plus snacks, three days of meals? Are you ready for a fast of more than a week—even forty days? Will you drink some nutritive juices or only water? (It is not usually advisable to deprive yourself of water.) If you will allow yourself juices or other beverages, what types of beverages will you drink? How will prayer figure into your time of fasting? Some people calculate how much money they would have spent on food during their fast so they can donate it to a charitable cause. Do you want to do that?

3. Set a firm objective and write it down.

Remembering why you are fasting will enable you to have an easier time sticking with your plan. Are you fasting as part of a group initiative for, say, revival or governmental issues? Are you praying for healing for yourself or someone else? Are you seeking guidance about a big decision? Are you concerned about resolving a conflict or solving a problem? Do you just need more of God's grace? While the decision to fast is yours to carry out, the inspiration for the objective of the fast will come from the Holy Spirit if you ask Him.

4. Ease into it.

Before a long fast, common sense would indicate starting to cut back on your food consumption. You could eat lighter meals with plenty of vegetables and dishes that are not heavy with rich sauces or fats. You could eliminate desserts and sweets or coffee, tea and colas.

5. Ease out of it.

Do not gorge yourself afterward. Trust me. You will not die if you do not take in your normal number of calories over the span of a few days. Ease back into eating normally.

6. Pay attention to spiritual preparation.

You will be subjecting your body to fasting for spiritual reasons, so it only makes sense to examine your spiritual state before and during the fast. Take an inventory of your sins, and confess them humbly to God, repenting and asking for His forgiveness. (For a personal application, see 1 John 1:9. For corporate relevance, see 2 Chronicles 7:14.) Make restitution to other people, if necessary, and be sure to forgive their offenses, as well (see Mark 11:25; Luke 11:4; 17:3–4). Pray to be filled anew with God's Holy Spirit (see Ephesians 5:18; 1 John 5:14–15). Tell your body that you will be refusing to obey its demands during this time (see Romans 12:1–2). Go into your fast expectantly (see Hebrews 11:6), reminding yourself of God's goodness and love (see Psalm 48:9; 103:8, 11–13; Romans 5:5; Galatians 4:6).

Remember what happened to Jesus during His forty-day fast at the beginning of His earthly ministry: Satan showed up. When Jesus was at His weakest, temptations flooded in (see Matthew 4:1–11; Luke 4:1–13; Mark 1:12–13). By undertaking a fast, you will be engaging in the ageless battle between the body and the spirit—so take to heart Peter's words: "Stay alert! Watch out for your great enemy, the devil. He prowls around like a roaring lion, looking for someone to devour" (1 Peter 5:8 NLT; see also Galatians 5:16–17; Ephesians 6:13).

7. Keep it secret.

As part of your prayer life, fasting should be invisible; you do not want to advertise your noble intentions. Naturally, the people you live with will need to know why you are drinking a glass of water instead of eating spaghetti with them, but for the most part, you should be able to carry out your daily activities without mentioning that you are not eating.

Jesus told His disciples how to fast, and it included this discipline of secrecy:

> "And when you fast, don't make it obvious, as the hypocrites do, for they try to look miserable and disheveled so people will admire them for their fasting. I tell you the truth, that is the only reward they will ever get. But when you fast, comb your hair and wash your face. Then no one will notice that you are fasting, except your Father, who knows what you do in private. And your Father, who sees everything, will reward you."
>
> Matthew 6:16–18 NLT

Just as there is no one way to pray, so there is no one way to fast. As thorough as prayerful communication with the Father can be, our prayers sometimes need extra reinforcement, and fasting can provide that. We need to get ourselves out of the way so that the Spirit within us can freely cry out with sighs and groans too deep for words (see Romans 8:26).

Lou Engle: The Watchman's Call to Fasting

> "Even now," declares the LORD, "return to Me with all your heart, and with fasting, weeping and mourning; and rend your heart and not your garments." Now return to the LORD your God, for He is gracious and compassionate, slow to anger, abounding in lovingkindness and relenting of evil. Who knows whether He will not turn and relent and leave a blessing behind Him, even a grain offering and a drink offering for the LORD your God? Blow a trumpet in Zion, consecrate a fast, proclaim a solemn assembly, gather the people, sanctify the congregation.
>
> Joel 2:12–16 NASB

My friend Lou Engle raises a radical voice for fasting and prayer. For decades, he has spearheaded solemn assemblies in the spirit of Joel 2, gathering thousands of fervent believers—young adults, in particular—for prolonged sessions of corporate repentance and prayerful worship, and these have always included fasting. The initiative is named TheCall, and it has become both a rallying cry and a heartfelt prayer. Lou knows that the combined prayers and fasts of many faith-filled believers can change history.[3]

Who would think stadiums could be filled with people who have purposely abstained from food and stimulants and yet celebrate in worship and prayer for hours on end?[4] Consider TheCall Azusa Now, held in the greater Los Angeles area, that formed as a way of redigging the wells of the famous Azusa Street revival of 1906. It is but one of more than 25 such rallies my friend Lou Engle has led.

Extended fasting has become so much a part of Lou Engle's life message because it has always been an integral part of the Christian message. Here is what early Church father St. Basil the Great (AD 330–379), archbishop of Caesarea, said in a sermon about fasting:

> Fasting gives birth to prophets, she strengthens the powerful. Fasting makes lawmakers wise. She is a safeguard of a soul, a stabilizing companion to the body, a weapon for the brave, a discipline for champions. Fasting knocks over temptations, anoints for godliness. She is a companion of sobriety, the crafter of a sound mind. In wars she fights bravely, in peace she teaches tranquility. She sanctifies the Nazirite, and she perfects the priest.[5]

Lou Engle and other prayer leaders have simplified and modernized the wording of this quote from Basil to read as follows: "Fasting begets prophets and strengthens strong men. Fasting makes lawgivers wise; it is the soul's safeguard, the body's trusted comrade, the armor of the champion, the training of the athlete."

Without the component of consecration and voluntary fasting, TheCall would be just another stadium event with limited impact for the Kingdom of God. But when fasting is combined with sustained and focused prayer, heaven comes to earth. I thank God for the Lou Engles around the globe today who are modeling the watchman's call to fasting.

PRAYER

Lord, I love You and am willing to lay down my life for Your Kingdom. I believe one way for me to do that is by fasting from food or something else I love and enjoy. Since fasting is part of Your call to me as a follower of Jesus and as an intercessory prayer warrior, I embrace it, difficult as it may be for me to do it. I ask You to help me. With food and other supports taken away, I will need to lean more than usual on You. Help me keep You in the forefront of my mind, and plant Your desires into my hungry heart. In the middle of my weakest moments, make me stronger than ever in effective prayer. You are asking for volunteers, and I am standing up to say, "Here I am, Lord. Send me!" [See Isaiah 6:8.] Amen.

DAY 9

BECOMING A GUARDIAN IN PRAYER

1. Have you ever fasted voluntarily? (Being too sick to eat does not count!) What was your experience like? Did it leave you discouraged from trying again, or did it draw you toward making it part of your walk with Christ?
2. What did you learn from this chapter that will help you fast to good effect?

3. Do you know anybody who fasts on a regular basis? Consider talking with them about fasting to gain insights and motivation.
4. Are you aware of carrying particular prayer burdens? How might fasting improve your prayers for a specific issue?

READING FOR DAY 10

Removing Obstacles

> Go through, go through the gates! Prepare the way for the people; build up, build up the highway! Take out the stones, lift up a banner for the peoples!
>
> Isaiah 62:10 NKJV

Isaiah's prophetic proclamation above can be read both figuratively and literally. Figuratively, intercessory watchmen understand its application to their task of helping to clear out obstacles ("stones") that lie in the path of the victorious people of God. Literally, commentators say that the "gates" and the "highway" mentioned in the passage have to do with the end of the Jews' exile to Babylon.

As you may remember from the book of Daniel, the people of Judah were conquered by Babylon, and much of the population was exiled to Babylon. (Section 3 of this book shares more about this.) Then, at the end of seventy years of captivity, Babylon was conquered by Persia, and Cyrus the Great gave permission to the Jews to return home to Jerusalem. At that point, they were free to follow leaders like Ezra and Nehemiah "through the gates" of Babylon and, after the long trek home, to rebuild the gates of Jerusalem.

Ezra's Strategic Intercession

Ezra returned first. His task was to re-teach God's laws to the people whose lives had been disrupted by the exile and who had begun rebuilding the Temple under Zerubbabel.

Ezra was a priest as well as a scribe. He returned from Babylon with a large number of other exiles—whole families together. After they had been there awhile, some of the leaders came to Ezra with an alarming report about how the people, including some of the other priests and Levites, had transgressed God's Law by intermarrying with the pagans who were in the land (see Ezra 9:1–2).

Ezra was horrified. He knew these actions defiled the entire population, and he expressed his shock and humiliation by tearing his robe and pulling out some of his hair. Others joined him, and their grief included a period of fasting (see verses 3–5).

In due time, Ezra fell onto his knees with his hands spread out and began to confess, numbering himself with the guilty. He not only confessed their grave sins; he also confessed the truth about the graciousness of God:

> "I am too ashamed and disgraced, my God, to lift up my face to you, because our sins are higher than our heads and our guilt has reached to the heavens. From the days of our ancestors until now, our guilt has been great. Because of our sins, we and our kings and our priests have been subjected to the sword and captivity, to pillage and humiliation at the hand of foreign kings, as it is today.
>
> "But now, for a brief moment, the LORD our God has been gracious in leaving us a remnant and giving us a firm place in

> his sanctuary, and so our God gives light to our eyes and a little relief in our bondage. Though we are slaves, our God has not forsaken us in our bondage. He has shown us kindness in the sight of the kings of Persia: He has granted us new life to rebuild the house of our God and repair its ruins, and he has given us a wall of protection in Judah and Jerusalem.
>
> "But now, our God, what can we say after this? For we have forsaken the commands you gave through your servants the prophets."
>
> Ezra 9:6–11

After reminding the Lord about the importance of preserving a remnant of His people (see verses 14–15), Ezra—joined by many of the guilty parties—repented publicly with bitter weeping (see Ezra 10:1–5). Vowing to reform their ways, the people were released to make right their wrongdoing (see verses 9–17).

In this way, by personally investing himself in the situation, Ezra removed the great obstacle of sin that was blocking the resettlement progress and ensured (for the time being, anyway) that the people would continue to enjoy God's favor in the land He had given them. Ezra had been commissioned to restore God-ordained worship in the land, and he cleared the way for it to be reestablished. He was a forerunner who helped ensure the establishment of the prophetic promise.

Nehemiah Clears the Way Again

The exiles returned in waves and kept trying to rebuild their cities, especially Jerusalem. One of the prominent exiles, Nehemiah, was still in Babylon, where he served as cupbearer to King Artaxerxes.

About thirteen years after Ezra's prayer initiative, a report was brought to Nehemiah that distressed him:

> They said to me, "Those who survived the exile and are back in the province are in great trouble and disgrace. The wall of Jerusalem is broken down, and its gates have been burned with fire."
>
> When I heard these things, I sat down and wept. For some days I mourned and fasted and prayed before the God of heaven.
>
> Nehemiah 1:3–4

Eventually, Nehemiah pulled himself together and prayed this magnificent prayer:

> "LORD, the God of heaven, the great and awesome God, who keeps his covenant of love with those who love him and keep his commandments, let your ear be attentive and your eyes open to hear the prayer your servant is praying before you day and night for your servants, the people of Israel. I confess the sins we Israelites, including myself and my father's family, have committed against you. We have acted very wickedly toward you. We have not obeyed the commands, decrees and laws you gave your servant Moses.
>
> "Remember the instruction you gave your servant Moses, saying, 'If you are unfaithful, I will scatter you among the nations, but if you return to me and obey my commands, then even if your exiled people are at the farthest horizon, I will gather them from there and bring them to the place I have chosen as a dwelling for my Name.'
>
> "They are your servants and your people, whom you redeemed by your great strength and your mighty hand. Lord, let your ear be attentive to the prayer of this your servant and to the prayer of your servants who delight in revering your name. Give your servant success today by granting him favor in the presence of this man."
>
> Nehemiah 1:5–11

Nehemiah's prayer captures every important element necessary for changing the situation: worship and adoration, confession of sin on behalf of his people, a reminder to God of

His prophetic promise to Moses and an appeal to God on the basis of His previous redemptive work. Only at the end of the prayer did Nehemiah make an actual request: favor with King Artaxerxes when he would ask to take a long leave of absence to return to Jerusalem to personally supervise the rebuilding process.

That prayer was answered. Nehemiah was allowed to return, and the rest of the story, which shows the same humble courage and tenacity, is told in the book known by his name: Nehemiah.

We learn from this that when there are immovable obstacles in the way, only God's strength can do the job. God was able and willing, in the case of Nehemiah's plea, to supply the hope, the strategies, the courage, the perseverance and the wisdom necessary for the situation—and our Father will supply everything for us as watchmen on our assignments today, as well.

We Face Two Obstacles

We are beginning to see a pattern here. In addition to the physical obstacles of broken buildings, fallen walls and impassable rubble, human hearts are strewn with the hindrances of sin—all kinds of sin and ungodliness. Both kinds of obstacles must be removed in order for restoration to proceed on either the physical or heart level, and God wants to accomplish both. After all, our God is a God of reconciliation, restoration, reformation and transformation.

Rebuilding the city walls, gates, Temple and houses required a large workforce of strong men under the watchful eyes of overseers and sometimes armed guards. By their combined strength and effort, they could do it if they kept at it. Rebuilding the "walls of salvation," though, requires a different kind of workforce—watchman-intercessors whose spiritual strength can pull down strongholds of evil and clear the way for the victorious Lord to enter hearts and lives.

Again, Isaiah captures the picture prophetically:

> "Nations will come to your light, and kings to the brightness of your rising. . . .
>
> "For in My wrath I struck you, and in My favor I have had compassion on you. Your gates will be open continually; they will not be closed day or night, so that men may bring to you the wealth of the nations. . . .
>
> "I will make peace your administrators and righteousness your overseers. Violence will not be heard again in your land, nor devastation or destruction within your borders; but you will call your walls salvation, and your gates praise."
>
> Isaiah 60:3, 10–11, 17–18 NASB

Isaiah's words insist that every obstacle be removed out of the way of God's people so they can return to their original places of habitation and peace: "Build up, build up, prepare the road! Remove the obstacles out of the way of my people" (Isaiah 57:14). The obstacles must be removed before anybody can repair the breach, restore the streets (see Isaiah 58:12) or do the work of building up (see Isaiah 57:14; 62:10).

But what do these "obstacles" consist of? What kinds of blockages must be removed from hearts before prayers can be heard and answered? Sin, wickedness, broken commandments—these loom like boulders between us and the targets of our prayers. And you cannot shoot arrows through boulders!

Scripture is filled with descriptions of the effects of these obstacles. For example:

> If I had not confessed the sin in my heart, the Lord would not have listened.
>
> Psalm 66:18 NLT

> The Lord is far from the wicked, but he hears the prayer of the righteous.
>
> Proverbs 15:29

> But your iniquities have separated you from your God; your sins have hidden his face from you, so that he will not hear.
>
> Isaiah 59:2

> "We know that God does not listen to sinners. He listens to the godly person who does his will."
>
> John 9:31

What tools can we use to remove these sin obstacles so that our prayers reach their target? Confession, repentance and forgiveness—in that order, and with the all-important help of the Holy Spirit. Sometimes we need a good Holy Ghost bulldozer to push the debris out of the way.

First, *confession*. We must call a spade a spade and a sin a sin. Even when it is not our own sin, we can shoulder the responsibility of sin in prayer, as Daniel did when he confessed the sins of his people, none of which he personally had committed. (See Daniel 9:9–10.) There is no use pretending we are sin-free:

> If we say that we have no sin, we are deceiving ourselves and the truth is not in us. If we confess our sins, He is faithful and righteous to forgive us our sins and to cleanse us from all unrighteousness.
>
> 1 John 1:8–9 NASB

Confession of sin is an open declaration of guilt. It is saying, "Yes, I did it. I am still doing it. I am responsible for it."

Of course, we can also confess the truth about God's great love, and that may go hand in hand with our confession of sin. We can confess we are not perfect but that God is and that God's redemptive love can pull us out of the mire of sin. We can confess—testify to—the glory of God to the people around us, which Jesus mentioned as one way to clear the way to heaven. He said, "Therefore everyone who confesses Me before men, I will also confess him before My Father who is in heaven" (Matthew 10:32 NASB).

This works both ways. Again, straight from Jesus' mouth:

> "Everyone who confesses Me before men, the Son of Man will confess him also before the angels of God; but he who denies Me before men will be denied before the angels of God."
>
> Luke 12:8–9 NASB

The facts remain the same, whether you are consulting the Old or the New Testaments:

> Let those who love the LORD hate evil, for he guards the lives of his faithful ones and delivers them from the hand of the wicked.
>
> Psalm 97:10

> "If wicked people turn from their wickedness, obey the law, and do what is just and right, they will save their lives."
>
> Ezekiel 18:27 NLT

> Seek good, not evil, that you may live. Then the LORD God Almighty will be with you, just as you say he is. Hate evil, love good; maintain justice in the courts. Perhaps the LORD God Almighty will have mercy on the remnant of Joseph.
>
> Amos 5:14–15

> Therefore, confess your sins to one another, and pray for one another so that you may be healed. The effective prayer of a righteous man can accomplish much.
>
> James 5:16 NASB

After confession comes *repentance*—a follow-up declaration of the intention to change your ways:

> "And rend your heart and not your garments." Now return to the LORD your God, for He is gracious and compassionate, slow to anger, abounding in lovingkindness and relenting of evil.
>
> Joel 2:13 NASB

> The sacrifice you desire is a broken spirit. You will not reject a broken and repentant heart, O God.
>
> Psalm 51:17 NLT

> "Repent of your sins and turn to God, for the Kingdom of Heaven is near."
>
> Matthew 3:2 NLT

Lastly, confession and repentance are followed by God's *forgiveness*, which is a huge topic we cannot cover adequately in this short reading. Rest assured that our God *will* forgive; He will not withhold His forgiveness out of meanness or spite or because we deserve punishment. Jesus came to take the punishment for our sin, and we ask for forgiveness in His name. Here are some examples of this truth:

> While they were eating, Jesus took some bread, and after a blessing, He broke it and gave it to the disciples, and said, "Take, eat; this is My body." And when He had taken a cup and given thanks, He gave it to them, saying, "Drink from it, all of you; for this is My blood of the covenant, which is poured out for many for forgiveness of sins."
>
> Matthew 26:26–28 NASB

> Then He opened their minds to understand the Scriptures, and He said to them, "Thus it is written, that the Christ would suffer and rise again from the dead the third day, and that repentance for forgiveness of sins would be proclaimed in His name to all the nations, beginning from Jerusalem."
>
> Luke 24:45–47 NASB

> Hide Your face from my sins, and blot out all my iniquities.
>
> Psalm 51:9 NKJV

> "To the Lord our God belong mercy and forgiveness, though we have rebelled against Him."
>
> Daniel 9:9 NKJV

Heartfelt confession, true repentance, total forgiveness—these three make up the spiritual "earth-moving equipment" that can clear out the wreckage of sin from human hearts, freeing up prayers that will strike the mark. It is a promise.

Our Father Hears Us

As I mentioned in the reading for Day 6, the model prayer of Jesus—the Lord's Prayer—is a corporate prayer. It says, "Our Father," "Give us our daily bread" and "Forgive us our sins." It uses the language of *us* and *ours*. Of course, we can pray it individually, and we often do. But even when we are alone when we pray it, we are uniting ourselves to our fellow sinners, near and far. We are expressing a corporate cry for mercy. We are praying to *our* Father for *our* needs.

We not only confess our individual sins, but we step into the gap on behalf of the failures and sins of others. We admit that our personal shortcomings fall within a larger framework. We ask for blessings not only for our own immediate circumstances, but also for the wider Body and community around us.

In other words, by removing the blockages and obstacles of sin, we take the limits off our prayers. Now, in the opposite spirit, we can proclaim the righteousness of God everywhere we go, calling for the release of hope, provision and promise. After all, the purpose is not only to cleanse us from sin, but also to be called up into the higher heavenly reality, where all things are possible. As Jesus taught us, "With men this is impossible;

but with God all things are possible" (Matthew 19:26 KJV; see also Jeremiah 29:11–14).

When we pray first for cleansing from sin, whether for ourselves or for others, the light of God can shine on the path before us. Then, free to pray according to the will of God, we will know the joy of abundantly answered prayer. Just look at the way Paul describes it:

> Now to Him who is able to do far more abundantly beyond all that we ask or think, according to the power that works within us, to Him be the glory in the church and in Christ Jesus to all generations forever and ever.
>
> Ephesians 3:20–21 NASB

Chastened by his severe trials, Job was given this counsel, and we can prove the truth of it in our own lives as watchmen on the wall, guardians in prayer:

> "If you return to the Almighty, you will be restored; if you remove unrighteousness far from your tent, and place your gold in the dust, and the gold of Ophir among the stones of the brooks, then the Almighty will be your gold and choice silver to you. For then you will delight in the Almighty and lift up your face to God. You will pray to Him, and He will hear you; and you will pay your vows. You will also decree a thing, and it will be established for you; and light will shine on your ways."
>
> Job 22:23–28 NASB

John Hyde: Watchman on His Knees

John Nelson Hyde—much better known as "Praying Hyde"—was born in Illinois in 1865, but he spent most of his adult life as a missionary in the Punjab region of northern India. He began to pray in earnest in order to open the way for spiritual awakening, which was conspicuously lacking in that region. In part because of his deafness, which made language-learning difficult, his mission gained very few converts, sometimes none at all, in a given year.

Hyde travailed in prayer, out of sight, while his fellow missionaries preached and taught and, eventually, reaped a great harvest. Today, his prayers are credited for a mighty revival in Sialkot (located in what is now Pakistan), which began in 1904 and continued even after Hyde's death in 1912.

In his book *No Easy Road*, Dick Eastman writes about a time when Praying Hyde had to clear his heart of obstacles before his prayers could have their good effect:

> Praying Hyde, missionary to India, reports learning an important lesson concerning fault-finding. Never in public did critical words of a piercing nature flow from his lips. In his prayer life, however, this was not the case. Once he felt a keen burden on his heart for a native Indian pastor. Upon entering his favorite place of prayer, he developed a bitter spirit toward this pastor's lukewarm walk with Jesus. In his mind he criticized that pastor and began praying a negative prayer: "Oh, Father, thou knowest how cold . . ." but something stopped him in the midst of his prayer.
>
> A finger seemed to touch Hyde's lips, sealing them shut. He heard the voice of God softly say, "He that toucheth him, toucheth the apple of mine eye."
>
> Praying Hyde at once cried out, "Forgive me, Father, in that I have been an accuser of the brethren before thee." In the anguish of this prayer, Hyde begged God to show him positive things in this pastor's life and as moments passed good points saturated Hyde's mind. As each good quality came to mind Hyde stopped and praised God for this dear pastor.
>
> Soon after Hyde's prayer, revival hit that Indian church. Clearly this was the impact of a loving spirit. Let it never be forgotten, forgiving hearts give birth to revival.[1]

Forgiveness both leads to and flows from revival. This is a perfect example of prayer evangelism, in which the obstacles are first removed through persistent, private prayer. It is important to talk to God about our neighbor before we talk to our neighbor about God.

Hyde's incessant prayers and stringent fasting may have shortened his life. He died at age 47, after reportedly exclaiming, "Shout the victory of Jesus Christ!" What a way to go out!

PRAYER

Almighty and most merciful Father, we have erred and strayed from Your ways like lost sheep. We have followed too much the devices and desires of our own hearts. We have offended against Your holy laws.

We have left undone what we ought to have done, and we have done what we ought not to have done, and there is no health in us.

Yet, good Lord, have mercy on us. Restore those who are penitent, according to Your promises declared to us in Jesus Christ our Lord. And grant, merciful Father, for His sake, that we may live a godly, righteous and obedient life, to the glory of Your holy name. Amen.[2]

DAY 10

BECOMING A GUARDIAN IN PRAYER

1. When you are in prayer, do you bump into roadblocks or obstacles in your heart? What are they? (Giving them names, such as jealousy or judgment, can help

you overturn them.) Resolve to do something about them soon.

2. Have you ever rebuilt something that was demolished in an accident or a storm? See if you can draw some parallels between the often-arduous task of physical rebuilding and the hard-to-define task of rebuilding the spiritual life on any scale. On both a physical and a spiritual level, what can impede progress? What kinds of help are needed? Imagine the discouraging words of naysayers, and see if you can defend your hope of completing your task successfully.
3. Pause and examine your heart for unrepented sin and unforgiveness. Remember what Jesus said: "If you refuse to forgive others, your Father will not forgive your sins" (Matthew 6:15 NLT).
4. For whom or for what are you willing to pray at great personal expense?

READING FOR DAY 11

Waiting in Quietness

I love the LORD, because He has heard my voice and my supplications. Because He has inclined His ear to me, therefore I will call upon Him as long as I live.

The pains of death surrounded me, and the pangs of Sheol laid hold of me; I found trouble and sorrow. Then I called upon the name of the LORD: "O LORD, I implore You, deliver my soul!"

Gracious is the LORD, and righteous; yes, our God is merciful. The LORD preserves the simple; I was brought low, and He saved me. Return to your rest, O my soul, for the LORD has dealt bountifully with you.

Psalm 116:1–7 NKJV

Times of quiet, meditative prayer may appear to be boring and unproductive, even a waste of time. Some of us have a hard time appreciating even moments of rest, seeing them as a type of filling station to get us ready for the "real" business of life—the meaningful work, the achievements that make good additions to our portfolios and so forth. I used to feel that way myself—until practice turned the discipline into a delight.

Take another look at the significant verses from Psalm 116 above. The psalmist's prayers have been answered by God, and abundantly. He had been in trouble, even in danger of death, and possibly he was depressed. God came through for him, delivering him completely from his trials.

Your average American Christian might take that prayer answer and run with it: *Now that I have been saved from my desperate situation, it is high time for me get back in the saddle!* Right?

But verse 7 puts on the brakes: "Return to your rest, O my soul, for the LORD has dealt bountifully with you." Return to your rest, it says. Slow down. Sit awhile longer. Make an additional sacrifice of your time. Rejoice quietly. See what God might want to lay on your heart. Take more time to "build [yourself] up in your most holy faith, pray in the power of the Holy Spirit, and await the mercy of our Lord Jesus Christ, who will bring you eternal life" (Jude 1:20–21 NLT). God has "dealt bountifully with you" not so that you will run away, but so that you will linger in His presence.

You will only be able to make a difference in your world by remaining firmly rooted in the secret place with God. I have found this to be true in my life experience. What I used to run from, I now run toward. After all, time spent with God is never time wasted. Truly, it is time well spent—and even gained.

The Watchman's Well

Anna had put herself in the perfect spot by situating herself in the Temple to watch and wait for the Messiah. As she worshiped and prayed without interruption, she was drawing nearer and nearer to God. By immersing herself in the glory of His presence for so long, she was given the strength to watch steadfastly for six decades. Additionally, when Jesus' parents entered the Temple, she knew that little bundle in Mary's arms was the One she had been watching and waiting her whole adult life to encounter.

In other words, separating herself from normal life and dedicating all of her time to God had filled Anna's spirit with His glory—which, of course, is what enabled her to last long enough to welcome her Savior. If she had not pressed through to the end, she would have perished from spiritual thirst before reaching the happy outcome of her long wait. It was as though Anna's lifestyle had produced a well in the depths of her soul, a well of refreshing, living water that she could draw from when she needed it, similar to the way the Lord told Isaiah that God's people "with joy . . . will draw water from the wells of salvation" (Isaiah 12:3 NKJV). Jesus prophesied along the same lines, saying that rivers of living water would flow from the hearts of those who believe in Him (see John 7:38).

Such a wellspring does not develop on its own, nor does it burst into existence overnight. Like any river, it starts small. It can be dammed up or blocked. It can get polluted. But when it is encouraged to flow and grow, it will do so.

We watchmen must be able to tap into their inner wells of God's presence in order to keep watching and praying without wearying. It is crucial for us to understand the importance of replenishing our inner wellsprings.

The Key to Peace

The prophet Isaiah spoke often of this wonderful truth:

> This is what the Sovereign LORD, the Holy One of Israel, says:
> "Only in returning to me and resting in me will you be saved.
> In quietness and confidence is your strength."
>
> Isaiah 30:15 NLT

> "You will keep him in perfect peace, whose mind is stayed on You, because he trusts in You."
>
> Isaiah 26:3 NKJV

> Have you never heard? Have you never understood? The LORD is the everlasting God, the Creator of all the earth. He never grows weak or weary. No one can measure the depths of his understanding. He gives power to the weak and strength to the powerless. Even youths will become weak and tired, and young men will fall in exhaustion. But those who trust in the LORD will find new strength. They will soar high on wings like eagles. They will run and not grow weary. They will walk and not faint.
>
> Isaiah 40:28–31 NLT

This is almost too good to believe. Too many of us miss the treasures that can be found only in long stretches of silent or almost-silent contemplation at the feet of the Lord. As watchmen, we must learn to tap into this inner source of peace and fortitude. We must learn to "practice the presence of God," as the seventeenth-century monk Brother Lawrence put it.

Remember how Jesus commended Mary of Bethany for sitting attentively at His feet instead of getting all worked up and fretful, as her sister did? (The story is told at the end of Luke 10.) That incident came from real life; it is not a fictitious parable. It has been preserved in the New Testament because Jesus wanted all of the generations of His followers to know what matters the most: sitting at His feet and listening to Him.

But is that practical? Can real people in today's frantic world find ways to sit quietly with the Lord? Speaking for myself, as a man who has maintained a high activity level, traveling from place to place and coping with numerous disruptions, I know it can be done. I wrote the following back when my four children were still living at home and I was much busier than I am today:

> One of my favorite prayer postures is sitting with a blanket over my head as a tool of helping me remove as many external distractions as possible, quiet my spirit, and commune silently with the God who lives within me. There is a time and place for aggressive postures in intercession and spiritual warfare, but I have discovered that my effectiveness in going *outward* is directly proportional to how deeply I am maintaining my *inward* devotional Mary position.[1]

I have had to make a way to spend time alone with God. Without that time, I grow agitated, anxious, on edge. With quiet, purposeful time alone in God's presence, I find peace. Echoing Saint Augustine, I have learned to exclaim, "Thou hast formed us for Thyself, and our hearts are restless till they find rest in Thee."[2]

The Gift of Still Waters

Everybody seems to know the Twenty-third Psalm, even people who are not believers. We love its promise of peace and protection under the personal care of the great Shepherd:

> The LORD is my shepherd; I shall not want. He makes me to lie down in green pastures; He leads me beside the still waters. He restores my soul; He leads me in the paths of righteousness for His name's sake.
>
> Yea, though I walk through the valley of the shadow of death, I will fear no evil; for You are with me; your rod and Your staff, they comfort me.
>
> You prepare a table before me in the presence of my enemies; You anoint my head with oil; my cup runs over. Surely goodness and mercy shall follow me all the days of my life; and I will dwell in the house of the LORD forever.
>
> Psalm 23:1–6 NKJV

When we recite that psalm, how often do we notice that the Shepherd must *lead the way* to the green pastures and still waters? On our own, we cannot find the best refreshing places. And have you noticed this, too? Once He leads us there, He stays there with us. By the still waters with Him is the best place for us to be. We never want to leave.

The psalmist-king David knew all about shepherding, because he had started out as a shepherd. He knew the secret—rediscovered by old Anna in the Temple—of attaining true peace and strength wherever God can be found. In another psalm, he says:

> How lovely is your dwelling place, LORD Almighty! My soul yearns, even faints, for the courts of the LORD; my heart and my flesh cry out for the living God. Even the sparrow has found a home, and the swallow a nest for herself, where she may have her young—a place near your altar, LORD Almighty, my King and my God. Blessed are those who dwell in your house; they are ever praising you.
>
> Blessed are those whose strength is in you, whose hearts are set on pilgrimage. As they pass through the Valley of Baka, they make it a place of springs; the autumn rains also cover it with pools. They go from strength to strength, till each appears before God in Zion.
>
> Hear my prayer, LORD God Almighty; listen to me, God of Jacob. Look on our shield, O God; look with favor on your anointed one.
>
> Better is one day in your courts than a thousand elsewhere; I would rather be a doorkeeper in the house of my God than dwell in the tents of the wicked. For the LORD God is a sun and shield; the LORD bestows favor and honor; no good thing does he withhold from those whose walk is blameless.
>
> LORD Almighty, blessed is the one who trusts in you.
>
> Psalm 84:1–12

(This psalm is appropriately inscribed on my late wife's tombstone in a quaint cemetery in Dover, Missouri. She lived this psalm. It was her life.)

The Quiet Watch

When they are on duty, watchmen are quiet, never boisterous or loud. In fact, the ability to remain silently watchful is one of the requirements of the job. Watchmen who surround themselves with too much noise cannot hear anything, and they distract themselves from what they are supposed to be doing.

At times, a watchman may need to sound an alarm or address a situation. But most of the time, a watchman remains quietly at his post, assessing the environment around him with his practiced eyes and ears for the duration of his watch, equipped for action but calm. He does not jump every time the wind rattles the window; he can discern true threats from false alarms.

A watchman waits unobtrusively until something happens. In the case of a spiritual watchman, she can discern the still, small voice of the Lord any time of the day or night. The Holy Spirit drove this point home to me one day when I heard His sweet inner voice say, *The incubation bed of the spirit of revelation is quietness.* I had been asking for an increase of the spirit of revelation, and He was showing me one of the ancient keys that would unlock hidden treasures of wisdom and revelation.

Once, I asked my dear friend Mahesh Chavda how he could manage to hear the Lord's voice so well, even when he was in the middle of chaotic, stressful ministry situations. I wanted to know what God's voice sounded like to his spiritual ears. As it turns out, Mahesh had sharpened his spiritual hearing through long watches. He chuckled and responded to me, "You must understand, the closer I get to Him, the gentler His voice becomes."

Now I have found this to be true. The more I spend time immersed in God's presence, where often nothing seems to be happening for hours and hours, the more easily I can tap into that great reservoir of His presence. It is not difficult to heed His voice. Those long resting times are not wasted, as long as I am resting in Him.

Although I like to think of myself as a man of passionate action and I am not by nature a calm or quiet person, I have learned to mature as a watchman. Even before I entered into the long season of health struggles that have often confined me to my home for weeks at a stretch in recent years, I was learning to appreciate a lifestyle of quiet, Spirit-guided contemplation. I began to read and write about people like Teresa of Ávila, Brother Lawrence and Madame Jeanne Guyon, whose lasting influence came almost entirely out of their quiet watches before the Lord.

To be honest, I have not been able to get enough of it. That is why, until the day I graduate to heaven, I want to re-create a little heaven on earth every day, watching humbly and thankfully, waiting before God and praying as if my life depends on it—because it does.

Teresa of Ávila: Watching in the Secret Place

When I was growing up in the Methodist Church, I would never have thought that a sixteenth-century Spanish nun would end up having such a profound influence on my life. But somewhere along the line, the spiritual legacy of Teresa of Ávila captured my heart.

Teresa was an adventuresome, lively, even mischievous child. As a teenager, she was torn between enjoying the attractions of the social life of a young person of her status in the city of Ávila and withdrawing into Christian piety, which for her meant committing herself to live in a convent. The convent won out.

Much to Teresa's distress, the convent failed to be the perfect place to find union with God. Still, despite many worldly distractions in the place, she had an increasing number of supernatural experiences. Eventually, she was allowed by her superiors to lead a reform movement within the Carmelite order.

Endowed with great personal charm, tact, practicality and good humor, Teresa proved to be a skilled manager. She joined her efforts with a Carmelite friar named John of the Cross, and together they established not only a reformed religious order but also a body of writing that remains unparalleled in terms of its rarefied spirituality.

Teresa's books include her autobiography and *El Castillo Interior* (*The Interior Castle*), which traces the path of a contemplative Christian through seven "mansions," or steps for growing closer to God. Starting with basic humility, she guides readers into the practice of prayer, a holy life, the "Prayer of Quiet" and on into higher spiritual states of transformative intimacy with God. Even in translation, the intensity of Teresa's language makes the material hard to grasp, but generations of God-seekers have been nourished and guided by it.

The following translation of a prayer poem written by Teresa near the end of her life portrays her confident trust in God:

> Let nothing trouble you,
> Let nothing scare you,
> All is fleeting,
> God alone is unchanging,
> Patience
> Everything obtains.
> Who possesses God
> Nothing wants.
> God alone suffices.[3]

For Teresa of Ávila, love was everything. Her entire life of prayer was the story of her intimate friendship with God Himself. Empowered by her inner journey with God, her outer works live on to this day.

Teresa of Ávila reminds me of Anna, stationed in the Temple for sixty years, because for both women, the secret place with God became their dwelling place. Poor health and old age did not deter them. They sacrificed ordinary comforts for the sake of their pursuit of intimate communion with the Lord, and they give us a shining example of what years of dedicated watching can accomplish.

As a watchman on the walls today, I plan to follow in their footsteps.

PRAYER

Christ Jesus, You have no body on earth now but mine; no hands or feet on earth but mine. Mine are the eyes through which You look with compassion on this world. Therefore, may I be well-equipped to serve You. Out of my emptiness, may I be filled with Your Spirit. Confident in Your love, may nothing trouble me or scare me. May I understand how fleeting all troubles are and how absolutely unchanging You are. Grant me patience for the journey. Because I have You, I have everything; You are utterly sufficient for every possible need. I pray in trust and joy as the beloved of Jesus, Amen.[4]

DAY 11

BECOMING A GUARDIAN IN PRAYER

1. What does the word *rest* connote to you? Do your initial associations with the word have anything to do with prayer? Why or why not?

2. When you go to your prayer closet to pray, how do you handle distractions? What practical strategies have you learned to help you keep your focus? What is your primary focus?
3. How do you hear (or not hear) the voice of God? What can you do to help His voice become clearer to you?
4. Are you a Mary or a Martha? Might it be possible for you to sit at the Lord's feet more? How would this look in your life? Take some time right now to sit quietly in the Lord's presence. Let His living water bubble up inside you. Read and meditate on Psalm 21:6, John 7:38, and Psalm 103:11.

READING FOR DAY 12

Prayers of Heaven

> And I saw between the throne (with the four living creatures) and the elders a Lamb standing, as if slain, having seven horns and seven eyes, which are the seven Spirits of God, sent out into all the earth. And He came and took the book out of the right hand of Him who sat on the throne. When He had taken the book, the four living creatures and the twenty-four elders fell down before the Lamb, each one holding a harp and golden bowls full of incense, which are the prayers of the saints.
>
> Revelation 5:6–8 NASB

John, who referred to himself in his gospel as the disciple whom Jesus loved (see John 13:23; 19:26; 20:2; 21:7, 20), had a much longer earthly life than any of the other disciples. He suffered persecution, even in his old age, and yet that never stopped him from loving Jesus back, and passionately. In fact, everything John suffered made him love Jesus more.

This made John the perfect candidate to experience—while he was still an earthbound saint—the glories of heaven. The verses above give us a glimpse of the revelation he saw and heard when God's Spirit swept him up into heaven.

We are shown a scene of overwhelming praise being given to Jesus, the Lamb who was slain. Angels and elders prostrate themselves before Him while holding musical instruments, harps and "golden bowls full of incense, which are the prayers of the saints." These prayers undoubtedly include all of the unanswered supplications of the faithful people of God who suffered many injustices, the prayers of which can be summarized by this line in Jesus' model prayer: "Your kingdom come. Your will be done on earth as it is in heaven" (Matthew 6:10 NKJV).

The Lamb is the One whose blood has opened the way to purifying judgment. Hallelujah! Wrongs *will* be righted. Righteousness *will* be established, once and for all.

John continued to write about what he saw:

> And they sang a new song, saying: "You are worthy to take the scroll, and to open its seals; for You were slain, and have redeemed us to God by Your blood out of every tribe and tongue and people and nation, and have made us kings and priests to our God; and we shall reign on the earth."
>
> Revelation 5:9–10 NKJV

This "new song" praises the Lamb for allowing Himself to be slain, so that by His death all people who assent to Him can be redeemed for an eternity of blessedness. They praise Him for opening heaven and for making them "kings and priests," with the host of related privileges and joyful responsibilities that come with such an elevated position.

John blinked and looked again and could hardly believe his eyes and ears, as countless myriads of angels joined in the heavenly worship:

> Then I looked and heard the voice of many angels, numbering thousands upon thousands, and ten thousand times ten thousand. They encircled the throne and the living creatures and the

> elders. In a loud voice they were saying: "Worthy is the Lamb, who was slain, to receive power and wealth and wisdom and strength and honor and glory and praise!"
>
> Revelation 5:11–12

What can I add to that? It is overwhelming, isn't it? No wonder the people of God keep trying, for millennia now, to worship God adequately. No wonder saintly intercessors like Anna can spend a lifetime in what some call "harp and bowl" worship, and still it seems like a drop in the bucket. In fact, it is but an appetizer for what is coming.

With the loss of my wife and other close friends and relatives in recent years, I now connect with the reality of eternity and the anticipation of heaven in a way I never did previously. Heaven has become real to me. I long and yearn for heaven. I find it easier than before to imagine the heavenly worship of generations of believers who make up a community of constant adoration.

And we, the watchmen in waiting, have the opportunity to join them in harp-and-bowl expressions of worship—praise mingled with intercession—in the here and now. It blows me away.

A Necessary Praise

As watchmen, we must not miss the fact that worship and praise are intimately wedded to intercession. These cannot be separated in the seamless garment of the ministering priest.

Praise sanctifies the atmosphere around God's throne. As a matter of fact, we learn that He is enthroned on those praises: "Yet You are holy, O You who are enthroned upon the praises of Israel" (Psalm 22:3 NASB). Because of the praise and worship of the people of God, He is lifted up and exalted on a throne of authority and blessing, from which He reigns supreme.

Praise paves the way into God's presence: "Enter his gates with thanksgiving; go into his courts with praise. Give thanks to him and praise his name" (Psalm 100:4 NLT). As we glorify God, He turns the river of blessing back upon us. Clothed with what Isaiah calls the "garment of praise" (Isaiah 61:3), we can walk out of our sin-stained rags and dance with joy before His throne. We do not seem like the same people who used to be weighed down with troubles. He has come to save us. He has come to

> give [us] beauty for ashes, the oil of joy for mourning, the garment of praise for the spirit of heaviness; that [we] may be called trees of righteousness, the planting of the LORD, that He may be glorified.
>
> Isaiah 61:3 NKJV

Thanksgiving to God even delivers us from strongholds of darkness: "Giving thanks is a sacrifice that truly honors me. If you keep to my path, I will reveal to you the salvation of God" (Psalm 50:23 NLT). This means that praise is a weapon of honor—and a very effective one. Satan cannot tolerate the praises of the One who defeated him on the cross. Often we can worship our way out of a dead-end alley of defeat and get our feet back on the highway of holiness, as Isaiah describes:

> And a great road will go through that once deserted land. It will be named the Highway of Holiness. Evil-minded people will never travel on it. It will be only for those who walk in God's ways; fools will never walk there.
>
> Isaiah 35:8 NLT

Everywhere in the Bible, we can find examples of the effectiveness of prayers of praise. Here is a sampling:

- Not until Jonah offered up a sacrifice of praise when he was at his lowest point did God deliver him. (See Jonah 2:1–10.)

- Paul and Silas were set free from their prison cell supernaturally as they declared their praises to the Lord. (See Acts 16:25–26.)
- Even the praises of children (or adults who become childlike) will silence Satan's lies and shut down his evil activities: "Through the praise of children and infants you have established a stronghold against your enemies, to silence the foe and the avenger" (Psalm 8:2).

I do not intend to make it sound like praising God is always one big, happy-clappy party. Often enough it is not as easy as it seems. It is not called a "sacrifice of praise" (Hebrews 13:15) for nothing. Like any sacrifice, it will cost you something.

Jack Hayford explains it this way:

> Why is praising God a sacrifice? The word "sacrifice" (Greek, thusia) comes from the root thuo, a verb meaning "to kill or slaughter for a purpose." Praise often requires that we "kill" our pride, fear, or sloth—anything that threatens to diminish or interfere with our worship of the Lord.
>
> We also discover here the basis of all our praise: the sacrifice of our Lord Jesus Christ. It is by Him, in Him, with Him, to Him, and for Him that we offer our sacrifice of praise to God. Praise will never be hindered when we keep its focus on Him, the Founder and Completer of our salvation.

A Proclamation of Victory

Watchmen have a distinctive assignment: proclamation. Like the prophets of old, they stand watch over the people and places God has designated. When they see something, they say something.

Like representatives of royalty or holy priests, watchmen declare the appropriate words at the right point in time. Proclamations are announcements, pronouncements, invitations and declarations. Those made in the name of the Lord express the power of heaven. You can see how praise and proclamation flow together seamlessly:

> I will proclaim the name of the Lord. Oh, praise the greatness of our God! He is the Rock, his works are perfect, and all his ways are just. A faithful God who does no wrong, upright and just is he.
>
> Deuteronomy 32:3–4

Jesus made seven statements when He was dying on the cross. The most important one was His proclamation, "It is finished!" (John 19:30 NKJV). He had completed the unthinkable: God had become sinless man and had voluntarily sacrificed Himself so that, henceforth, anyone who believed in Him would not have to pay for his or her own sins with death but could live eternally.

From this perspective of victory, we must learn to pray by proclaiming the worth of our God. Because of the One we praise, we are not the losers. He has already won the battle for all time. As His children on earth and as pray-ers, we have been called to enforce the victory of Calvary. Praising Him all the way, we declare and proclaim what He has accomplished—and our prayers strike the mark.

Our prayers proclaim His victory everywhere and under all circumstances. Just look at how many ways our proclamations effect change:

- Proclamations of the cleansing power of Jesus' blood take away the stain of sin from our eyes, ears, lips, tongues, hearts and minds, cleansing us from the corruption of the world that otherwise contaminates our ability to apply His victory. (See Revelation 12:11.)

- Proclamations of blessing from leaders to the people under them bring protection and peace. (See Numbers 6:24–26.)
- Proclamations of protection are effective—for ourselves, for our families and for others. (See Joshua 24:15; Psalm 17; 24:1–2; Isaiah 25:1–3.)
- Proclamations about the fulfillment of God's will help to bring it to pass. (See Jeremiah 29:14; 30:3.)

Our proclamations of Christ's victory will always hit the bull's-eye of prayer. As we proclaim the abundance of heaven and the righteous love of our heavenly Father, we are able to call forth heaven to earth. The Kingdom comes and God's will is done, just as it is in heaven.

An Ousting of Opposition

We overcome Satan when we testify personally to what the blood of Christ has done for us, according to the Word of God: "Let the redeemed of the LORD say so, whom He has redeemed from the hand of the enemy" (Psalm 107:2 NKJV).

We enforce the victory of the cross as we continue to proclaim its benefits. The most powerful plea we can bring before the throne of God is the shed blood of His Son. The counterclaims of the enemy, our flesh and the world around us evaporate when we plead the blood of Christ. No amount of prayer know-how matches the effectiveness of this one declaration.

Charles Spurgeon once said:

> Do not reckon you have prayed unless you have pleaded, for pleading is the very marrow of prayer. He who pleads well knows the secret of prevailing with God, especially if he pleads the blood of Jesus, for that unlocks the treasury of heaven. Many keys fit many locks, but the master key is the blood and the name of Him that died and rose again, and ever lives in heaven to save unto the uttermost.[1]

Why is the blood of Christ so persuasive? In the Old Testament, on the Day of Atonement, the priest would go from the altar of incense to the most holy place, beyond the veil. There, he would take blood from the bull or goat and sprinkle it with his finger on the mercy seat and on the horns of the altar, seven times each. Only the high priest could enter the holy of holies, and only on that particular day of the year. Moreover, he could not have access to the holy presence of God without the shedding of sacrificial blood.

Since Jesus' death and resurrection, we live under the New Covenant, and the blood that atones for sin is His own:

> You have come to Mount Zion and to the city of the living God, the heavenly Jerusalem, and to myriads of angels, to the general assembly and church of the firstborn who are enrolled in heaven, and to God, the Judge of all, and to the spirits of the righteous made perfect, and to Jesus, the mediator of a new covenant, and to the sprinkled blood, which speaks better than the blood of Abel.
>
> Hebrews 12:22–24 NASB

Did you see that? Jesus' blood "speaks better than the blood of Abel." That is because Jesus was more innocent of sin than Abel was. Abel, you will remember, was murdered by his brother, Cain. When the Lord accosted Cain about his brother's death, asking him where Abel was, Cain retorted, "Am I my brother's keeper?" The Lord said, "What have you done? The voice of your brother's blood is crying to Me from the ground" (Genesis 4:9–10 NASB). The innocent blood of Abel had made itself heard in God's ears, and God had responded. How much more clearly does the pure blood of the crucified Son of God speak into the Father's ears?

Yes, Jesus' blood, too, cries out from the ground. I can think of at least seven ways His blood was shed:

1. In Gethsemane, when His sweat became like drops of blood (see Luke 22:44).
2. When He was struck and beaten before the high priest (see Matthew 26:63–67).
3. When some of His beard was pulled out (see Isaiah 50:5–6).
4. When His back was scourged (see Matthew 27:26).
5. When the soldiers mocked Him and pressed the crown of thorns into His scalp (see Matthew 27:29).
6. When He was nailed to the cross (see Matthew 27:35).
7. When the soldier pierced His side with a spear (see John 19:34).

By testifying to what the blood of Jesus has accomplished, we enforce His triumph over the powers of darkness. His blood cries out and intercedes for us—and the more we declare its benefits, the more clearly that cry arises. In John's revelation, we see that "they [the believers] overcame him [the accuser of the brethren, Satan] because of the blood of the Lamb and because of the word of their testimony, and they did not love their life even when faced with death" (Revelation 12:11 NASB).

In order to better proclaim the saving benefits of Jesus' sacrifice, take a look at these passages from Scripture and what they allow you to proclaim:

Forgiveness. "All things are cleansed with blood, and without shedding of blood there is no forgiveness" (Hebrews 9:22 NASB). You can proclaim, "I have been forgiven through the blood of Jesus."

Cleansing. "If we walk in the Light as He Himself is in the Light, we have fellowship with one another, and the blood of Jesus His Son cleanses us from all sin" (1 John 1:7 NASB).

You can proclaim, "The blood of Jesus has cleansed me from all sin."

Redemption. "In Him we have redemption through His blood, the forgiveness of our trespasses, according to the riches of His grace" (Ephesians 1:7 NASB). You can proclaim, "The blood of the Lamb has redeemed me."

Justification. "Much more then, having now been justified by His blood, we shall be saved from the wrath of God through Him" (Romans 5:9 NASB). You can proclaim, "By the blood of Jesus I am justified, just as if I never sinned."

Sanctification. "Therefore Jesus also, that He might sanctify the people with His own blood, suffered outside the gate" (Hebrews 13:12 NKJV). You can proclaim, "I have been sanctified through Jesus' blood for a holy calling. I have been brought out of Satan's territory by the blood of Jesus."

Peace. "For it was the Father's good pleasure for all the fullness to dwell in Him, and through Him to reconcile all things to Himself, having made peace through the blood of His cross" (Colossians 1:19–20 NASB). You can proclaim, "Peace has been established for me through the blood of the cross."

Access to the throne. "Since we have confidence to enter the holy place by the blood of Jesus . . . let us draw near with a sincere heart in full assurance of faith, having our hearts sprinkled clean from an evil conscience and our bodies washed with pure water" (Hebrews 10:19, 22 NASB). You can proclaim, "I have confidence to enter the most holy place by the blood of Jesus."

When we praise God and proclaim all He has done, we join the vast company of heaven that worships continuously before His heavenly throne. Our prayers rise before Him with unmistakable clarity, like incense from golden bowls, every one of them capturing His generous attention.

Mike Bickle: Harp-and-Bowl Watchman

Mike Bickle is a forerunner and a watchman who has made it his life's work to hasten Jesus' coming again. He is best known as the founder of the International House of Prayer (IHOP) in Kansas City, Missouri, but his far-reaching ministry includes evangelistic outreaches, along with social and justice initiatives. IHOP was officially launched in 1999, and by now, hundreds of other 24/7 houses of prayer have been created across the nation and world.

The IHOP style of prayer has come to be known as "harp and bowl," after the passage in Revelation 5:8 that describes the prayer happening before God's throne: "[They] fell down before the Lamb, each one holding a harp and golden bowls full of incense, which are the prayers of the saints." In a mirrored way, teams of singers, musicians and intercessors at IHOP have kept worship and prayer going around the clock since 1999, combining several forms of intercession with Spirit-led, Word-based devotional worship in ever-new variety. People who are not part of the teams join in, as well. In round numbers, the ministry has about a thousand staff members and another thousand interns, who are mostly young people who raise their own support.

As large as the ministry is, Mike believes each person's contribution is significant. Considering the fact that one of the fundamental longings of the human heart is to make a deep and lasting impact, he sees a bigger picture happening here of worshipful watchman-intercessors on earth blending their voices with those in heaven.

He writes:

> We play a small but significant role in a very large drama, in a great conflict with eternal consequences. We are not some footnote to the script. God did not create the world because He was bored. He is not peering down on us as if we were a collection of highly-functional gerbils in a cage, wondering what we're going to do next. He is looking for people who will partner with Him to bring about His purposes on Earth. . . .
>
> God has big plans for people, real people like you and me. . . . God is looking for people who want to make a deep and lasting impact, people who will partner with Him on a level far exceeding just working a job or pursuing personal happiness. . . .
>
> The goal of impacting lives is excellent, but incomplete. While many people find legitimate fulfillment in serving others, we want our lives to count in eternity as well. Fortunately, that is where we have the greatest potential for impact: not impact on another person for a few decades, or even on our culture for a century, but impact on the entire world as well as our own lives for eternity. . . .
>
> We must consider the ultimate meaning of the work to which we are putting our hands. If we're leading a small band of intercessors, the intercession we are making is preparing the ground for a Kingdom that will last a thousand years.[2]

I have had the honor of knowing this zealous man for more than forty years. He has always been a man of the Word, a man of prayer, a defender of truth—and he has one of the most gregarious personalities I have ever known. Mike fills every room with his overflowing passion for Jesus. He makes you feel valued and significant.

I was on Mike's staff in Kansas City for about a decade. I know his character, his wife, his sons and his legacy. Someday I would like to dedicate a book to this dear, godly man of prayer. I am not much like Mike Bickle, but I admire him greatly, and I know his infectious desire for the "one thing" has had a profound impact on my life and ministry.

Whether or not you live in Kansas City, where IHOP is keeping the fires of prayer and worship continuously burning, you, too, can join in with the heavenly throng right now, right where you are. Proclaim His glorious worth. Pray as much as you can, and bring many others with you into the throne room.

PRAYER

In the name of Jesus, who sits on the highest heavenly throne and whose shed blood has cleansed me from all unrighteousness, I joyfully proclaim that I am redeemed, justified and sanctified. Jesus is my Lord, and I trust Him with everything. I hold up my two hands to represent the harp and bowl that are held by my fellow worshipers in heaven, and I make melody in my heart before the Lord, acclaiming Him and asking confidently for the blessings of heaven to surround me and spill into the lives of the people around me. Bowing before the King, Amen.

DAY 12

BECOMING A GUARDIAN IN PRAYER

1. In Revelation 5:8, what do the harps and golden bowls stand for? What are the implications of these objects in your prayer life? Do you feel one of them is more significant in your prayer life than the other? Why?
2. Reflect on this statement: "Praise paves the way to His presence." How have you found this to be true?
3. Review this paragraph from the reading: "Watchmen have a distinctive assignment: proclamation. Like the

prophets of old, they stand watch over the people and places God has designated. When they see something, they say something." How has proclamation played a role in your prayer life as a watchman (if it has)? What forms can the proclamations of a watchman take?

4. Write out a personal proclamation of faith, incorporating a variety of aspects. Then turn it into a prayer of thanksgiving.

READING FOR DAY 13

Absolute Trust

> Trust in the LORD and do good; dwell in the land and cultivate faithfulness. Delight yourself in the LORD; and He will give you the desires of your heart. Commit your way to the LORD, trust also in Him, and He will do it. . . . Those who wait for the LORD, they will inherit the land. . . . I have been young and now I am old, yet I have not seen the righteous forsaken or his descendants begging bread. All day long he is gracious and lends, and his descendants are a blessing. . . . Wait for the LORD and keep His way, and He will exalt you to inherit the land.
>
> Psalm 37:3–5, 9, 25–26, 34 NASB

Throughout the 21 days of this study, I am holding up for you important traits that watchmen must know and cultivate. Therefore, within this section on a lifestyle of sacrifice, it is time to take a look at what it means to sacrifice our protective self-interest in favor of absolute trust in God.

Consider these questions: Who is in charge of your life? Who gives you guidance? As a disciple of Christ Jesus, I learned early about dying to myself on a daily basis, but I sometimes dig in my heels when I am faced with a situation that seems overwhelmingly difficult. It can take a while to learn how to trust that God will always, always take care of me and that even when He tells me to do something that does not seem to make sense, my obedience to His directive will bring more grace. Who would think that trusting absolutely in God could be such an adventure? As it turns out, it is hardly a burden at all, because it brings me so close to my loving Father.

Missionaries often learn this level of trust on the field, especially when they carry a responsibility for many others. That is why so many missionary veterans say, "God is slow, but He is always on time." I am sure that dear, Temple-praying Anna would endorse that outlook.

In Anna, we see an example of someone who trusted God with her whole being. She was a model of faithfulness in both senses of the word: Not only was she faithful and steadfast, praying for sixty years straight, but she was also faith-*filled* and totally trustful. As a watchman, she had absolute faith that her long wait would be worth it because she knew the One upon whom she waited was completely and utterly trustworthy. He *would* come; she just did not know when or how. She believed God's promise would come to pass, but she left the details to the One who had promised.

Only Believe

Anna knew God would be faithful to fulfill the promising words of His prophets. Somehow she knew she was supposed to wait and pray and watch in the Temple. She did not know exactly what she was looking for, but her eyes of faith enabled her to recognize the infant Messiah when He was carried into the Temple in His mother's arms.

In the Temple that day, God engineered a complex, seemingly impossible intersection. Just think about it: Anna happened to walk past the seer Simeon, who was speaking to Mary and Joseph and their newborn son. Thus, the elderly woman met the new baby she had been waiting for all her life. That meeting represented another intersection, one that was invisible except to the eyes of faith: the meeting of heaven and earth. Anna's job description? She was to wait—sixty years!—for the moment of intersection, exercising her faith in watchful prayer.

Anna is such a model for us as watchman-intercessors, showing us how to invest our time and energy as we fulfill the assignments God has given us. Anna demonstrates how to link our desires to His, how to ask Him to act and, of course, how to wait in absolute trust for Him to do so.

I relate to Anna. Like her, I have been widowed. In my case, I was suddenly a single dad with four children, and I was still fighting cancer myself. I felt I had to learn how to trust God all over again. Some things I will understand later, but for now I will trust the Lord with all my heart.

We watchmen have the great privilege of praying for heaven to intersect with earth, and often we are able to see the sparks when the connection is made. I like to quote this easy-to-remember principle that is rooted in Jesus' teaching from Mark 11:22–24: "Pray until the promise; praise until the provision." We could also add the words "Testify to what God has done," because that is how faithful Anna followed up on that hallowed moment.

Here is how it will look for you. You will faithfully and faith-fully pray until a promise from God—a promise that comes from His Word—becomes a "now word" (a *rhema* word) planted in your spirit by the Holy Spirit. Then, even as you keep seeking Him in prayer and He fine-tunes your requests, you will begin to thank Him. You will thank Him that He has heard your prayers and that He is already sending the answer. As He adjusts your thinking and raises your expectations, you will thank Him all the more. You will begin to "breathe" faith, in and out, in a naturally supernatural way.

God's part is to execute the impossible. Your part is quite simple: Believe. As Jesus said, "Only believe" (Luke 8:50 NKJV).

Jesus also said, "All things are possible to him who believes" (Mark 9:23 NASB; see also Matthew 19:26). That does not mean all things are a good idea or all things are in God's will, but it does mean He is bigger than everything, everywhere, visible and invisible, and He can do anything. He will show you the way. You can trust Him.

Live by Faith

You and I are able to live by faith because we are *kept* by faith:

> For by grace you have been saved through faith; and that not of yourselves, it is the gift of God.
>
> Ephesians 2:8 NASB

> [You] are kept by the power of God through faith for salvation.
>
> 1 Peter 1:5 NKJV

Enabled by your faith, you are able to bring the Kingdom to bear on your little corner of the earth. You are able to defeat the devil and all of his works, just as John says: "For every child of God defeats this evil world, and we achieve this victory through our faith" (1 John 5:4 NLT). Throughout your life journey, your faith makes the connection between you and God. In fact, the Bible says, "Without faith is it impossible to please Him, for he who comes to God must believe that He is, and that He is a rewarder of those who diligently seek Him" (Hebrews 11:6 NKJV).

Faith is active, not passive. I do not want you to get the idea that the job of a watchman is mind-numbingly tedious.

Even in her long, long wait, Anna was active. She was walking, talking, praying. She was fasting, focusing, rejoicing. She did not weary of it; she was in touch with God. She and all of the other faith-filled men and women of the Bible were people of obedient action. When God told them to do (or not to do) something, they acted on whatever He said, even if it seemed crazy. Give up normal life and go live in the Temple? *Well, all right. I trust You.* Go take your only son, the one whose birth was a miracle, and sacrifice him on an altar? *Yes, God. My life is in Your hands.* Fast for forty days? Pray all night? *If that is what faith looks like, I will do it gladly. I trust You, Lord.*

Faith and trust are not physical objects you can touch. They are learned responses. They form our perspective on life. They inform our conduct. They connect us to the Source of all life. Faith and trust come from Him in the first place, and we give them back to Him—faithfully: "Through Christ you have come to *trust* in God. And you have placed your *faith* and hope in God because he raised Christ from the dead and gave him great glory" (1 Peter 1:21 NLT, emphasis added).

Faith and trust are not physical objects, but faith is something solid. As the King James Version defines it in Hebrews 11:1, faith is "the *substance* of things hoped for" (emphasis added). The New Living Translation uses the modern word *reality* to talk about faith: "Faith shows the reality of what we hope for; it is the evidence of things we cannot see."

How can you cultivate and strengthen your faith and trust in God? Here are some practical ideas:

- **Faith arises by the preaching of the Gospel.** Word-based preaching is one of the most effective "faith fertilizers" around. (See Romans 10:8, 14; John 1:1; 1 Thessalonians 2:13; Titus 1:3.)
- **Faith arises through reading the written Word or hearing it read.** Exposure to the Word is key to faith growth.

(See Romans 10:17; Psalm 119:105; Luke 24:13–32; Acts 17:13.)

- **Faith arises in times of prayer.** Every time you receive something from God, your faith grows. (See Jeremiah 33:3.)
- **Faith arises by means of a word of testimony or an exhortation.** This is another example of faith coming by hearing. We can testify personally to encourage each other to trust God more. (See Hebrews 10:23–25; Colossians 3:16; John 4:29.)
- **Faith arises because of dreams and visions.** When Paul had his extraordinary experience on the road to Damascus, his heart was changed completely and faith was born. Faith-building is the only reason I can think of for God to communicate with us through dreams, visions and other supernatural experiences. (See also Acts 27:22–25.)
- **Faith arises because of the audible voice of God.** In the Damascus event, both Paul and then the disciple named Ananias heard the audible voice of God, without which their faith would not have been adequate. (See also Matthew 3:16–17; Revelation 1:8.)

You can cultivate and encourage great faith and trust. In fact, the Bible urges us to do so:

> But you, beloved, building yourselves up on your most holy faith, praying in the Holy Spirit, keep yourselves in the love of God, looking for the mercy of our Lord Jesus Christ unto eternal life.
>
> Jude 1:20–21 NKJV

Trust in the Word

As a faithful watchman, you cannot harbor doubts about something God has said in His Word. You may not understand everything you read there (who does?), but doubts are like invasive weeds when you are trying to cultivate a garden of faith and trust. Thanks to the Holy Spirit, who reminds you of God's truth—and thanks to our easy access to the written Word—you no longer have to resort to wearing a tasseled garment to remind yourself of the details of your faith (see Numbers 15:38–41). You can lean hard on the Word, and you know it will not fail you.

The Word is as strong as the Lord God Himself. Jesus is known as "the Word" (see John 1:1), and King David wrote, "Forever, O LORD, Your word is settled in heaven" (Psalm 119:89 NKJV). The Word of God was not produced within a finite time frame; it is the product of eternity, both timeless and permanent. Jesus said, "Heaven and earth will pass away, but My words will by no means pass away" (Matthew 24:35 NKJV). The Word is unshakable, indestructible and wholly true. There is no firmer foundation upon which to establish your faith. Trust it absolutely.

The invincible authority of the Lord of the universe stands behind the Word of God. I count that precious Book as my dearest friend, like Jesus Himself. Together, the Word of God (the Bible) and its Author are the source of life. I want to put my entire faith in the truth and not in what I can figure out on my own. How about you?

I like to put it this way: This Spirit-inspired Book will take the warp out of your life. It will set your feet on the straight and narrow way, and it will keep you from veering off it. When you expose yourself to its light, you can see heaven. When you turn away, you cannot.

If you grow weary as a watchman on the wall and you are looking for a mentor to help you, look in the Word. You will find more potential mentors there than I will ever be able to profile in a book like this one. The Bible itself has been my best mentor all my life. Whenever I hit a serious pothole in my life journey, I always go back to the Word. When cancer came, I went to the Word. When my wife died, I went to the Word. When I did not know how to move forward, I went to the Word. When I struggle in any way, I reach for absolute trust by going back to the Word.

The Word helps me interpret and verify my experiences and to understand the guidance that the Spirit gives me. In other words, it shows me how to walk trustfully and obediently, which is a way of pure joy. I think of the words of the old hymn "Trust and Obey":

> Trust and obey,
> For there's no other way
> To be happy in Jesus,
> But to trust and obey.

God's watchmen do not have grim faces and victim mindsets, even when they must stand and face the darkness. Their eyes are clear and bright because their hearts are fixed on God. Their spirits may be groaning in prayer, but their groaning is born of hopeful yearning. Along with all of creation and on behalf of others, they intercede in the power of the Holy Spirit:

> We ourselves, who have the firstfruits of the Spirit, groan inwardly as we wait eagerly for our adoption to sonship, the redemption of our bodies. For in this hope we were saved. . . . In the same way, the Spirit helps us in our weakness. We do not know what we ought to pray for, but the Spirit himself intercedes for us through wordless groans. And he who searches our hearts knows the mind of the Spirit, because the Spirit intercedes for God's people in accordance with the will of God.
>
> Romans 8:23–24, 26–27

Naturally, even those whose faith and trust are rock solid can experience jarring earthquakes from time to time. (Over the past decade or so, my personal life has felt like an endless series of volcanic eruptions.) But once you are a man or a woman of faith, shake-ups can only make you stronger. Your trust in God grows stronger with every adversity. You put your trust in the Lord with intentionality. You choose not to lean on your own understanding anymore (see Proverbs 3:5). You trust with your heart, not with your head. You do not have to go to graduate school or a bunch of conferences to learn how to walk in faith. You trust the God of heaven and earth, with whom you can speak anytime you wish. You have taken the sound advice of the seasoned psalmist who wrote:

> Do not put your trust in princes, in human beings, who cannot save. When their spirit departs, they return to the ground; on that very day their plans come to nothing. Blessed are those whose help is the God of Jacob, whose hope is in the LORD their God.
>
> Psalm 146:3–5

Absolute trust—it is within your reach.

George Müller: Unshakable Watchman

George Müller was born in Prussia (Germany) in 1805 and lived most of his very long life in Bristol, England, where he is best known for the orphanages he founded and operated completely by faith. He cared for as many as two thousand orphans at a time, but he never made an appeal for funds or goods. Instead, taking to heart the words "Give us this day our daily bread," he "prayed in" every morsel of food, every stick of furniture, every staff member and every scrap of clothing his orphans needed.

Müller recorded his prayers and their answers in his journals. He claimed that over the course of his ministry, thirty thousand prayers were answered almost immediately. Many times he would get up from his knees, only to be summoned to the door to receive a donation.

Müller also ran Bible schools for children and adults, distributed Bibles and other materials, and ran a sizable missionary support organization. For the last 68 years of his ministry, he did not draw a salary, take out a loan or go into debt, even for a day. He trusted God for everything. He wrote:

> In looking back upon the Thirty One years, during which this Institution had been in operation, I had, as will be seen, by the Grace of God, kept to the original principles, on which, for His honour, it was established on March 5, 1834. For 1, during the whole of this time I had avoided going in debt; and never had a period been brought to a close, but I had some money in hand. Great as my trials of faith might have been, I never contracted debt; for I judged, that, if God's time was come for any enlargement, He would also give the means, and that, until He supplied them, I had quietly to wait His time, and not to act before His time was fully come.[1]

Lest we think Müller found it easy to pray so trustingly, he explained how he used to struggle to feel like doing it. Eventually he learned to start by reading the Word of God and then to move into conversing with God about it. Here is how he described it:

> The difference, then, between my former practice and my present one is this: Formerly, when I rose, I began to pray as soon as possible, and generally spent all my time till breakfast in prayer, or almost all the time. At all events I almost invariably began with prayer, except when I felt my soul to be more than usually barren, in which case I read the word of God for food, or for refreshment, or for revival and renewal of my inner man, before I gave myself to prayer. But what was the result? I often spent a quarter of an hour, or half an hour, or even an hour, on my knees, before being conscious to myself of having derived

> comfort, encouragement, humbling of soul, etc.; and often, after having suffered much from wandering of mind for the first ten minutes, or quarter of an hour, or even half an hour, I only then began *really to pray*. I scarcely ever suffer now in this way. For my heart being nourished by the truth, being brought into *experimental* [experiential, relational] fellowship with God, I speak to my Father and to my Friend (vile though I am, and unworthy of it) about the things that he has brought before me in his precious word. It often now astonishes me that I did not sooner see this point.[2]

Any of us could profit from this idea, it seems to me. Prayer is a conversation, an extension of a flourishing relationship between a believer and the Lord Himself. Why not let Him have the first word (Word) and then reflect with Him about it, moving naturally into other topics of concern? That is true prayer. Into the bargain, our faith and trust and confidence in the Lord will grow daily as we see the results of our prayers. Our trust in God will continue to grow until it becomes complete on that glorious day when each of us sees Him face to face.

PRAYER

Father God, I want to learn to come to You as my Papa, someone who loves me dearly and whom I can trust with my whole heart, like a child. You hold the answer to every question I can ever think of, and You hush my fears about the future. As I sit at Your feet and listen to You, You remind me again of Your Good News, and You say, "For in the gospel the righteousness of God is revealed—a righteousness that is by faith from first to last" (Romans 1:17).

I need more faith. I can see mountains ahead, and they are steep. Holy Spirit, be my Helper every step of the way as I navigate my journey. I trust You more right now than I did at the beginning of this prayer. I can feel faith arising in my heart, and I know it is new. Thank You! I love You, because of Jesus, Amen.

DAY 13

BECOMING A GUARDIAN IN PRAYER

1. Think about this line from the chapter: "We watchmen have the great privilege of praying for heaven to intersect with earth, and often we are able to see the sparks when the connection is made." Testify to a time when you saw the "sparks." What did God do in response to your prayers? As far as you know, did it make a permanent difference? Do you feel you should pray further about some aspect of the situation?
2. How do times of difficulty and shaking make your faith stronger? What does it mean to say that Jesus is the "pioneer and perfecter" (Hebrews 12:2; some translations read "author and finisher") of your faith?
3. Read and reflect on this verse from the Word: "If some did not believe, their unbelief will not nullify the faithfulness of God, will it?" (Romans 3:3 NASB). How can this statement of truth help sustain your prayers for wayward people?
4. In your next time of prayer, give George Müller's idea a try. Open your Bible anywhere, and read for a while. When the Word makes you think of something you can talk to God about, go ahead and do it. You do not need to use big words or complete sentences. You could say, *Papa, I never did understand this story. Why is it in*

the Bible? What do You want me to learn from it? Or, *Lord, this makes me think of so-and-so, who used to recite this passage.* Or, *Ouch, I am just like that sinner. Please walk me through to freedom.* Notice when your faith begins to bubble up. Then you will be underway, really praying!

READING FOR DAY 14

Called to Battle

> Prepare the table, set a watchman in the tower, eat and drink. Arise, you princes, anoint the shield!
>
> For thus has the Lord said to me: "Go, set a watchman, let him declare what he sees." . . . And he listened earnestly with great care. Then he cried, "A lion, my Lord! I stand continually on the watchtower in the daytime; I have sat at my post every night."
>
> Isaiah 21:5–8 NKJV

The word *watchman* brings to my mind an image of a vigorous person with sharp eyes and a straight, military bearing, someone like a soldier on guard duty or a uniformed security guard. This watchman stays alert so he can sound an alarm if a threat materializes. If necessary, this watchman will use force to protect the premises. He spends his time casing out the potential for damage from interlopers and menacing intruders.

Such an image can be useful when explaining the duties of a spiritual watchman—an intercessor who is on prayer guard duty. The lifestyle of a spiritual watchman involves staying alert, awake and ready for action when nothing much is happening, interspersed with times of action. An intercessory watchman is called to play a particular role in the great battle between the forces of good and evil. A watchman—a prayer guardian—is called to spiritual warfare.

Army of the Lord

The Lord God is the Commander in Chief of the heavenly army, and His watchmen are warriors assigned to guard duty in the gates. We know this military title is true because the Scriptures tell us it is: "The LORD is a warrior; the LORD is His name" (Exodus 15:3 NASB). This Commander of ours is in charge of the whole earth and everything in it, and He has gone to war to reclaim what the enemy has stolen:

> The earth is the LORD's, and the fulness thereof; the world, and they that dwell therein. For he hath founded it upon the seas, and established it upon the floods. . . . Lift up your heads, O ye gates; and be ye lift up, ye everlasting doors; and the King of glory shall come in. Who is this King of glory? The LORD strong and mighty, the LORD mighty in battle. Lift up your heads, O ye gates; even and be ye lift up, ye everlasting doors; and the King of glory shall come in. Who is this King of glory? The LORD of hosts, he is the King of glory.
>
> Psalm 24:1–2, 7–10 KJV

> And I saw heaven opened, and behold, a white horse, and He who sat on it is called Faithful and True, and in righteousness He judges and wages war.
>
> Revelation 19:11 NASB

This battle has been raging for a long time. Since the angel Lucifer contended for glory with God and was exiled from the heavenly courts, there has always been enmity between the children of light and those who willfully remain in darkness:

> "How you are fallen from heaven, O Lucifer, son of the morning! How you are cut down to the ground, you who weakened the nations! For you have said in your heart: 'I will ascend into heaven, I will exalt my throne above the stars of God.'"
>
> Isaiah 14:12–13 NKJV

> "Do not think that I came to bring peace on earth. I did not come to bring peace but a sword. . . . He who loves father or mother more than Me is not worthy of Me. And he who loves son or daughter more than Me is not worthy of Me. And he who does not take his cross and follow after Me is not worthy of Me."
>
> Matthew 10:34, 37–38 NKJV

No one can remain neutral in the conflict; everyone fights on one side or the other. Since you are reading this book, you must have chosen the Lord's side already! His is the winning side; ever since Jesus came as Messiah, His ultimate victory is guaranteed. But those of us who have chosen His side have work to do, assignments to fulfill. A good number of us have been tapped for guard duty.

Being a watchman for the Lord means that we serve the King of glory in an active combat situation:

> I have commanded My consecrated ones, I have even called My mighty warriors, My proudly exulting ones, to execute My anger. A sound of tumult on the mountains, like that of many people! A sound of the uproar of kingdoms, of nations gathered together! The LORD of hosts is mustering the army for battle.
>
> Isaiah 13:3–4 NASB

This kind of combat happens largely behind the scenes. Only rarely do we see troops in full battle array. The enemy troops, often under the watchful eyes of the Lord's sentinels, are invisible: "For we do not wrestle against flesh and blood, but against principalities, against powers, against the rulers of the darkness of this age, against spiritual hosts of wickedness in the heavenly places" (Ephesians 6:12 NKJV).

For the Lord's warriors, it is not a question of whether or not to wrestle, but rather how to wrestle. We are part of God's army, which means that He will train us and tell us what to do. For our part, we cannot relax into a passive role, assuming the rest of the army will take care of the fighting, nor should we undertake every campaign as if we had to do all of the wrestling on our own.

The Lord wants soldiers who will be quick to respond—just as quick to jump into active battle as to pull back and regroup. He wants to keep us from overconfident presumptuousness on the one hand and casualties on the other.

You see, most of our combat takes place hand to hand, one on one; that is the nature of wrestling. Our enemies, however, will resort to anything, including fiery guided missiles or spiritual "smart bombs" (see Ephesians 6:16). In other words, our battlefield conduct, our weapons and our techniques are different from the opposition's. The enemy forces are ruthless and desperately wicked. They will resort to anything. Sometimes they seem to be winning. We need to keep up our courage and keep our spiritual wits about us at all times.

Unsurprisingly, much of the battle occurs inside our heads and hearts. Before we can effectively reach out to help other people, we must firm up our own fidelity to the King. In order to be joyful warriors and not frazzled or worried soldiers of the Lord, we must learn how to work *from* victory instead of *toward* it. Jesus said on the cross, "It is finished!" He won the victory over evil once and for all. Our job is to enforce the victory of Calvary through our lifestyle of prayer.

A Mental Sentry

Ochuroma, the Greek word for *stronghold*,[1] refers to a fortress and is derived from a word meaning "to fortify, through the idea of holding safely." Strongholds keep out invaders. Not only do strongholds of righteousness repel the kingdom of darkness, they also launch the volleys that demolish invincible-seeming enemy strongholds:

> We are human, but we don't wage war as humans do. We use God's mighty weapons, not worldly weapons, to knock down the strongholds of human reasoning and to destroy false arguments. We destroy every proud obstacle that keeps people from knowing God. We capture their rebellious thoughts and teach them to obey Christ.
>
> 2 Corinthians 10:3–5 NLT

It takes a series of battles, each waged successfully, to bring every one of our thoughts and our willfulness into obedience to our Lord. Author and speaker Dean Sherman explains:

> I have heard people use the term *strongholds* to refer to humanism, Islam, communism, and other religions and institutions. However, in II Corinthians, *strongholds* does not refer to massive, complex systems, human or demonic. Here it refers to the strongholds of the mind. These strongholds are castles in the air built up in our minds through wrong thinking—through unbelieving, depressed, fearful, and negative thinking. . . .
>
> Every military post has guards. They stand quietly at their posts until they hear a rustling in the bushes. Then they immediately ask: "Who goes there?" and are prepared to evict any intruder. We too need to post a guard at the gate of our minds to check the credentials of every thought and every imagination, ready to cast down that which is not true, not righteous, or not of God. If it doesn't belong, out it goes. This is spiritual warfare: being alert to every thought.

> The Bible says, "As he thinks within himself, so he is" (Proverbs 23:7). One of the devil's greatest schemes is to nullify the effectiveness of Christians who are genuinely saved. Even if they go to heaven when they die, Satan will be happy to blunt their lives while on earth. He disables them, stealing their days, months, and years by influencing them to think wrongly. Unfortunately Satan has successfully neutralized thousands of potential victors this way.[2]

So we see how each of us must win on the crucial battlefield of the mind before seeing through other battles. We must make every effort to build up our stronghold of righteousness. We see the importance of this in another part of Psalm 24, which I quoted earlier in this reading:

> Who shall ascend into the hill of the LORD? or who shall stand in his holy place? He that hath clean hands, and a pure heart; who hath not lifted up his soul unto vanity, nor sworn deceitfully. He shall receive the blessing from the LORD, and righteousness from the God of his salvation. This is the generation of them that seek him, that seek thy face, O Jacob.
>
> Psalm 24:3–6 KJV

The bottom line is this: Righteousness is essential. So is humility. Even the mightiest warriors, like Joshua, need it:

> And it came to pass, when Joshua was by Jericho, that he lifted his eyes and looked, and behold, a Man stood opposite him with His sword drawn in His hand. And Joshua went to Him and said to Him, "Are You for us or for our adversaries?"
>
> So He said, "No, but as Commander of the army of the LORD I have now come."
>
> And Joshua fell on his face to the earth and worshiped, and said to Him, "What does my Lord say to His servant?"
>
> Then the Commander of the Lord's army said to Joshua, "Take your sandal off your foot, for the place where you stand is holy." And Joshua did so.
>
> Joshua 5:13–15 NKJV

Even Joshua needed humility. Have you discovered this yet in your life as a believer in Christ Jesus and as a watchman for the Lord? Humility is an appropriate garment to wear at any age!

Find Your Post

Too many intercessors never discover their distinct calling because they are too busy thinking someone else's calling would be more rewarding. Yet we will only find fulfillment in pursuing the particular calling that God has chosen for us. The only intercessor who has been called to pray for everything (and equally well) is Jesus Himself. The rest of us must "specialize," as He leads. Take a look at some of these diverse options:[3]

General "list" intercessors. These prayer warriors love to use prayer lists and never seem to get bored with them. They tend to be more disciplined than others and do not depend on receiving a special unction or burden before they engage in intercession.

Personal intercessors. These watchman-intercessors will bring a single person to the Lord for a period of months or even years. They are not campaign-oriented prayer warriors as much as they are "shield-bearers" for specific people, in particular for Christian leaders.

Financial intercessors. Financial intercessors have been given a gift of faith for finances from the individual level to the ministry, city, regional or even national level. They love to intercede for financial provision to be released for the work of a ministry or for the prosperity of a city or nation. These special forces are equipped to believe for the great transfer of wealth for the work of the Lord.

Crisis intercessors. Crisis intercessors pray more for urgent emergency situations than for long-term matters. When a crisis occurs, these individuals spring into action, alert and fully engaged—even in the middle of the night. I am one of these, often called to attention to intercede for God's intervention in world events.

Spiritual warfare intercessors. These strategic intercessors confront demonic strongholds like spiritual commandos. Often they will pray on-site, and they may possess the spiritual gift of discerning of spirits. (See my book *Releasing Spiritual Gifts Today* for teaching on this subject.)

Worship intercessors. In an environment of praise and worship, inspired prayers pour forth from these priestly intercessors. We are in the midst of one of the greatest global worship movements in history. The Holy Spirit is raising up a glorious combination of worshiping intercessors and interceding worshipers.

Government and reform intercessors. These people often pray for state, national and international leaders by name. They may also seize on specific moral and legislative issues that they will carry regularly before the throne of grace.

People-group and missions intercessors. Mission endeavors motivate these people to pray for the Gospel of the Kingdom to penetrate every tribe and nation. These are the intercessors who continue to pray through the 10/40 and/or the 40/70 prayer window and who will pray to the Lord of the harvest for Muslims, Hindus, Hispanics or other specific people groups.

Salvation and revival intercessors. These valuable prayer warriors know all of the Scriptures about the lost and laborers for the harvest. They make great backup people for outreach ministries.

Israel intercessors. These watchmen pray for the peace of Jerusalem, the Middle East and the Jewish people worldwide.

They weep over Jerusalem as Jesus did, and they pray for the Isaiah 19 "highway of reconciliation" to be established.

Church and leadership intercessors. These men and women are modern-day Aarons and Hurs who will lift and hold up the arms of the Moseses of their generation. They pray for the unity of the Church, for revival and for protection for leaders and their initiatives.

Prophetic intercessors. Those who pray out of the burdens they hear, see, feel and receive from the Spirit of God are prophetic intercessors. Their grace combines the Old Testament offices of prophet and priest and is empowered by the New Testament provision of grace. Their prayers are more spontaneous than agenda-driven. (This is where the waters of God run the deepest in my own life. See my book *The Prophetic Intercessor* for a defining work on this subject.)

As a prayer watchman-warrior, you will sit some battles out. You will be meant to participate only in certain ones. Some will be for today, others for tomorrow or another time. Some battles are never to be fought at all. Only the Holy Spirit can and should direct the action—and you can be sure that He always leads into triumph: "Thanks be to God, who always leads us in triumph in Christ, and manifests through us the sweet aroma of the knowledge of Him in every place" (2 Corinthians 2:14 NASB).

Elizabeth Alves: Prayer-Shield Watchman

My wife used to call Elizabeth (Beth) Alves a "grandmother of the prayer shield." *Prayer shield*, a term made popular by Dr. C. Peter Wagner, refers to the protective prayers of watchman-intercessors who feel called to be the silent partners of God's frontline warriors. The watchful prayers of these dedicated intercessors form shields that deflect the arrows of the enemy, opening the way for victory on the spiritual battlefield.

Beth Alves learned the importance of such prayers right on the spiritual battlefield. More than once, she has infiltrated enemy lines without being noticed. Who would think this cheerful Texas grandmother is really a ninja warrior?

She began her ministry in the early 1970s with the simplest of prayers: "Lord, teach me to pray." One thing led to another, and soon she was teaching Bible and prayer seminars across the world. The author of several books, including *The Mighty Warrior, Becoming a Prayer Warrior,* and *Intercessors: Discover Your Prayer Power* (co-authored with Tommi Femrite and Karen Kaufman), her ministry, Increase International (formerly Intercessors International), is a worldwide prayer ministry that equips intercessors to undergird the work of leaders in the Church and in the business world. (Out of admiration for all she has done and our long friendship, I co-dedicated this book to Beth.)

In the introduction to his book *Prayer Shield: How to Intercede for Pastors and Christian Leaders,* Peter Wagner wrote about Beth Alves, who had been serving as one of his personal watchman-intercessors:

> Knowing that my prayer partners are on the front lines on my behalf, I sleep well. I go to bed around 10:30 P.M., spend a peaceful night, and awaken around 6:30 A.M. My intercessors, on the other hand, have told me of some of the nocturnal battles they have fought for me. I remember one conversation that I had a few years ago with Beth Alves, one of our personal intercessors. She greeted me by asking how I was, and I responded that I was very well—thanks to her. Beth got a playful look in her eyes and said, "I know what you mean! You should see the spiritual black and blue marks I have all over me because of you!" We both laughed, but each of us knew that what she had just said

was very true. One of her assignments from God was to do spiritual warfare on my behalf.[4]

Watchman-warriors who hold up prayer shields for others may take hits on the battlefield in behalf of others. But, like Beth Alves, they will go out and do the same thing again the next day without worrying about their own welfare. Watchmen are willing to stand watch in all kinds of weather, day or night, despite a few bruises and bandages. But they carry the shield of faith and are able to extinguish the fiery darts of the evil one.

PRAYER

Lord, I volunteer for guard duty; please show me my post. As one of Your watchmen, what part of the wall should I guard? What do You want me to watch over, and how? Should I watch and pray on my own or alongside others? Position me however You want, and instruct me so I can do a good job. Fortify my spirit with Your Spirit's love, wisdom and strength. Increase the scope of my vision so I can more fully understand my assignment. Convince me, especially when the night seems long and cold, that my job in Your Kingdom is just as important as any other. I pray in the name of the greatest Watchman of them all, Jesus. Amen.

DAY 14

BECOMING A GUARDIAN IN PRAYER

1. Do you feel you have a calling to hold up a prayer shield for a particular leader or cause? How might this calling manifest itself in your life?

2. How has your righteousness (or lack of it) affected your ability to be a watchman-intercessor? Think back to times when you feel you got so distracted by personal problems that you were unable to pray well for others or you forgot to pray altogether. See if you can identify the root cause, the underlying sin. Is it fear of harm and/or self-protectiveness? Anger? Evil thoughts? Envy? Greed? Repent, if you have not done so already.
3. Are you naturally combative, or not? How does your personality both help and hinder you as a watchman-warrior?
4. How have you personally encountered Satan's malice? How did you receive the grace to endure? Measure your victory over the enemy against the damage he inflicted. Explain how your faith and trust in God grew as a result.

SECTION 3

The Lifestyle of Consecration

Joshua told the people, "Consecrate yourselves, for tomorrow the LORD will do amazing things among you."

Joshua 3:5

Therefore, brethren, having boldness to enter the Holiest by the blood of Jesus, by a new and living way which He consecrated for us, through the veil, that is, His flesh, and having a High Priest over the house of God, let us draw near with a true heart in full assurance of faith, having our hearts sprinkled from an evil conscience and our bodies washed with pure water. Let us hold fast the confession of our hope without wavering, for He who promised is faithful.

Hebrews 10:19–23 NKJV

READING FOR DAY 15

Daniel: Taking a Firm Stand

Daniel's life story is told in the twelve-chapter book that bears his name. By immersing yourself in the story, you can learn many things, including the prevailing importance that God attaches to faultless and dedicated living—in other words, to consecration and excellence. For our purposes in this reading, I want to take Daniel's unfaltering dedication and apply it to his phenomenal breakthrough in prayer on behalf of his exiled people. Usually people talk about Daniel as a prophet or as a God-worshiper in a foreign land. I want to take a look at Daniel as a watchman and an intercessor whose firm moral character enabled him to take a stand for righteousness.

Even as a youth, Daniel was remarkable. When he and his three friends were taken as captives to Babylon from Jerusalem along with most of the population, they were on the brink of adulthood. Handsome and strong, all four young men had come from noble families in Judah. Soon they caught the eye of the chief of staff of King Nebuchadnezzar, who had ordered him to select the cream of the crop of exiles in order to train them for royal service in his court. The king said:

> "Select only strong, healthy, and good-looking young men. . . . Make sure they are well versed in every branch of learning, are gifted with knowledge and good judgment, and are suited to serve in the royal palace."
>
> Daniel 1:4 NLT

King Nebuchadnezzar assumed that by starting their training when the four young men were still quite young, it would prove easy to influence their minds and hearts as he wished. He did not reckon with their strong character and their unshakeable dedication to the laws of their deeply held faith.

The first evidence of their principles concerned their diet:

> The king assigned them a daily ration of food and wine from his own kitchens. They were to be trained for three years, and then they would enter the royal service.
>
> Daniel, Hananiah, Mishael, and Azariah were four of the young men chosen, all from the tribe of Judah. The chief of staff renamed them with these Babylonian names:
>
> Daniel was called Belteshazzar.
>
> Hananiah was called Shadrach.
>
> Mishael was called Meshach.
>
> Azariah was called Abednego.
>
> But Daniel was determined not to defile himself by eating the food and wine given to them by the king. He asked the chief of staff for permission not to eat these unacceptable foods.
>
> Daniel 1:5–8 NLT

God gave Daniel favor; his request was granted. In fact, he and his companions thrived on their simple diet of vegetables and water, and King Nebuchadnezzar was most impressed with them after their three years of training were completed:

> When the training period ordered by the king was completed, the chief of staff brought all the young men to King Nebuchadnezzar.

> The king talked with them, and no one impressed him as much as Daniel, Hananiah, Mishael, and Azariah. So they entered the royal service. Whenever the king consulted them in any matter requiring wisdom and balanced judgment, he found them ten times more capable than any of the magicians and enchanters in his entire kingdom.
>
> Daniel 1:18–20 NLT

Once again, we see Daniel and his companions were set apart from the ways of the world so they could be effective in the world. Little things do eventually matter.

Born to Lead by Example

Little did anyone know how gifted and valuable these outstanding young men would prove to be. Daniel, in particular, stood out. Early on, he was able to interpret a dream for the king, and Nebuchadnezzar was so dazzled and grateful that he appointed Daniel to the primary rulership position in Babylon, with his friends serving immediately under him (see Daniel 2).

As events unfolded, Daniel continued to prove himself. This young Hebrew was unshakable in his integrity. When some of his rivals tried to trip him up by getting the king to issue an edict forbidding worship of any god except a large golden idol, Daniel and his three friends persisted in dedicating certain hours of the day to their prayers to the God of Israel, as had been their long-standing pattern, and they did not try to hide what they were doing. The king's attempt to execute them by incineration in a furnace was resoundingly unsuccessful (see Daniel 3).

Then the king had another dream, and Daniel interpreted it again. This one was prophetic. Daniel attempted to advise the king to reform his wicked behavior in order to avoid dire consequences:

> "This is what the dream means, Your Majesty, and what the Most High has declared will happen to my lord the king. You will be driven from human society, and you will live in the fields with the wild animals. You will eat grass like a cow, and you will be drenched with the dew of heaven. Seven periods of time will pass while you live this way, until you learn that the Most High rules over the kingdoms of the world and gives them to anyone he chooses. But the stump and roots of the tree were left in the ground. This means that you will receive your kingdom back again when you have learned that heaven rules.
>
> "King Nebuchadnezzar, please accept my advice. Stop sinning and do what is right. Break from your wicked past and be merciful to the poor. Perhaps then you will continue to prosper."
>
> Daniel 4:24–27 NLT

From personal experience, Daniel knew that prosperity is connected to righteousness. But the king was too proud to stop sinning, and the dream came true. Even the most enduring image of all came to pass, that of the noble and mighty Nebuchadnezzar crawling around in the open on all fours, out of his mind and eating grass like a cow (see verses 28–33).

In due time, the king was restored. But eventually he died and a new king, Belshazzar, took his place. This king did not know or care about Daniel—until the fateful night when a disembodied hand wrote on the wall of the banquet hall. *Mene, mene, tekel,* and *parsin*, its message said.

Daniel was summoned once again into the king's presence because of his skill at interpreting spiritual messages. And just as he had taken a firm stand under one strong ruler, now he did it again. Daniel predicted King Belshazzar's days were numbered, and he died that very night. He was then replaced by Darius the Mede, and Daniel once again enjoyed high status in the Babylonian court (see Daniel 5).

In fact, Daniel was so highly regarded that Darius appointed him as first in charge over the entire empire (see Daniel 6:1–3). Once again, Daniel's rivals wanted to discredit him. This time, he ended up in the den of lions—and, as every Sunday school student knows, he emerged unscathed (see verses 4–23). Once again, Daniel's personal consecration and his trust in God had ensured he would live and prosper.

A Humble, Fervent Prayer

By now, Daniel had spent his entire adult life in Babylon, exiled from Jerusalem without any expectation of ever seeing his native land again. Yet he never stopped worshiping the God of Israel, and he never ceased striving to achieve the highest possible level of uprightness and godliness. His Hebrew name, Daniel, means "God is my Judge," and God judged him to be head and shoulders above his contemporaries, even those who were of royal blood.

Some Bible commentators believe that it was in the 63rd year of Babylonian captivity—which would have meant Daniel was getting up in years—that he read from the prophet Jeremiah, investigating in depth what the prophet had foretold regarding the children of Israel. Daniel knew they had been taken captive in the first place because of their sin and disobedience, but what should they expect next? He read Jeremiah's prophetic words:

> For thus says the LORD: After seventy years are completed at Babylon, I will visit you and perform My good word toward you, and cause you to return to this place. For I know the thoughts that I think toward you, says the LORD, thoughts of peace and not of evil, to give you a future and a hope.
>
> Jeremiah 29:10–11 NKJV

The passage said the exile would end at seventy years. Here in the 63rd year, that meant it might not be much longer! (Lesson in wisdom: You cannot have a short-timer's mindset when it comes to praying through the promises of God.)

After Daniel read that prophecy, did he sit back with a satisfied sigh? Did he say, "Well, praise the Lord—God said it, I believe it, and that settles it"? Hardly. Disregarding his ordinary responsibilities, not to mention any potential vilification others might unleash on him, Daniel's response was immediate, sustained and comprehensive:

> So I gave my attention to the Lord God to seek Him by prayer and supplications, with fasting, sackcloth and ashes.
>
> Daniel 9:3 NASB

Daniel knew God wanted him to do something so that this staggering prophetic promise could be fulfilled. Possessed of a holy tenacity born of his long years of faithfulness, he applied himself to this all-important matter. The sin of his people had resulted in this exile. Even though Daniel had not committed the sins that brought the exile about, he could shoulder responsibility for them. God would hear and forgive—if only someone would speak up and ask.

Daniel knew nothing would change if he did not try. He decided to start by confessing the sins of his people as if they were his own:

> I prayed to the LORD my God and confessed and said, "Alas, O Lord, the great and awesome God, who keeps His covenant and lovingkindness for those who love Him and keep His commandments, we have sinned, committed iniquity, acted wickedly and rebelled, even turning aside from Your commandments and ordinances. Moreover, we have not listened to Your servants the prophets, who spoke in Your name to our kings, our princes, our fathers and all the people of the land.
>
> "Righteousness belongs to You, O Lord, but to us open shame, as it is this day—to the men of Judah, the inhabitants

of Jerusalem and all Israel, those who are nearby and those who are far away in all the countries to which You have driven them, because of their unfaithful deeds which they have committed against You. Open shame belongs to us, O Lord, to our kings, our princes and our fathers, because we have sinned against You. To the Lord our God belong compassion and forgiveness, for we have rebelled against Him; nor have we obeyed the voice of the LORD our God, to walk in His teachings which He set before us through His servants the prophets. Indeed all Israel has transgressed Your law and turned aside, not obeying Your voice; so the curse has been poured out on us, along with the oath which is written in the law of Moses the servant of God, for we have sinned against Him. Thus He has confirmed His words which He had spoken against us and against our rulers who ruled us, to bring on us great calamity; for under the whole heaven there has not been done anything like what was done to Jerusalem. As it is written in the law of Moses, all this calamity has come on us; yet we have not sought the favor of the LORD our God by turning from our iniquity and giving attention to Your truth. Therefore the LORD has kept the calamity in store and brought it on us; for the LORD our God is righteous with respect to all His deeds which He has done, but we have not obeyed His voice.

"And now, O Lord our God, who have brought Your people out of the land of Egypt with a mighty hand and have made a name for Yourself, as it is this day—we have sinned, we have been wicked. O Lord, in accordance with all Your righteous acts, let now Your anger and Your wrath turn away from Your city Jerusalem, Your holy mountain; for because of our sins and the iniquities of our fathers, Jerusalem and Your people have become a reproach to all those around us. So now, our God, listen to the prayer of Your servant and to his supplications, and for Your sake, O Lord, let Your face shine on Your desolate sanctuary. O my God, incline Your ear and hear! Open Your eyes and see our desolations and the city which is called by Your name; for we are not presenting our supplications before You on account of any merits of our own, but on account of Your great compassion. O Lord, hear! O Lord, forgive! O Lord, listen and take action! For Your own sake, O my God, do not delay, because Your city and Your people are called by Your name."

Daniel 9:4–19 NASB

Here was this man of God, this man of an excellent spirit, confessing the people's wickedness and insubordination as if it was his own, even though he had not personally committed any sin. Daniel had never for a moment bowed his knee to a foreign god. He had been scrupulously honest and obedient, never rebellious, even when he was under intense pressure. His consecration and excellent character were unimpeachable.

Daniel's prayer was a strong one, uttered in weakness and dependence. And it penetrated straight into heaven. From there, God dispatched the archangel Gabriel to reassure Daniel and to explain what would happen next (see Daniel 9:20–23; 10:11–21). It took a long time, and it required some major spiritual warfare behind the scenes, but eventually the revelatory word to Jeremiah was fulfilled and the children of Israel were allowed to return to their homeland.

Without Daniel's lifestyle of persistent purity and integrity, though, history would have been different. A good part of his excellent character could be summed up in one word: *consistency*. Daniel never gave up. He kept his eyes on God, and he made it his aim to please Him. He kneeled in prayer three times a day, looking out the window toward Jerusalem. He pressed on even when he was being threatened with punishment and death. At the end of his life, even though he himself would be too old to make the long journey home to Jerusalem, he presented himself to God, pleading on behalf of his people that their seventy-year exile would come to an end.

Daniel was not only a leader of the highest caliber; he was also a humble watchman who looked after the welfare of his people in exile. As such, it fell to him to remind the Lord—with fasting and humility—of His predetermined plan, so that the necessary spiritual forces could be set in motion and that plan could be fulfilled.

Daniel was remarkably willing to shoulder the responsibility for sins he did not commit in hopes that God would hear his prayer on behalf of the sinners. He was able to undertake such an important prayer assignment only because of his mature, exceptional character. He could not have seen it through had he been a lesser man than he was. Daniel never wasted time defending himself against criticism. He was willing to lay down his life when required, and because he knew his life was irreproachable, he could plead successfully for the everlasting benefit of others.

Your Own Consecration

To be effective in praying for the complex situations in the world today and in the future—particularly in places like, say, the Middle East—we need men and women of consecration and excellence like Daniel. The long days and weeks of our lives may be leading up to a culminating event that only God knows about. We dare not relax or retire from active watchman duty or from the practice of holy living that makes us able to plead God's promises with consistency and integrity. Remember what the passage in Isaiah says of watchman living:

> On your walls, O Jerusalem, I have appointed watchmen; all day and all night they will never keep silent. You who remind the LORD, take no rest for yourselves; and give Him no rest until He establishes and makes Jerusalem a praise in the earth.
>
> Isaiah 62:6–7 NASB

You do not have to be a Daniel in order to make a clean sweep of the enemy through your prayers. Realizing that only someone like Jesus could be as virtuous as Daniel, remember that you carry Jesus' Spirit within you. By God's grace, you, too, can walk in holiness and excellence. You and I are part of the priesthood of all believers (see 1 Peter 2:5), and we know we are supposed to stand firm for the Kingdom in holiness and triumph.

Taking Daniel as our example, we, too, can practice our faith consistently over long periods of time, even when we happen to live in uncongenial circumstances. We, too, can stand in the gap, whether we are praying for one individual or an entire nation, with full assurance that God will answer our prayers on behalf of others.

As we round the corner into our third week of readings, remember that watchmen must depend on the three-cord strand of intercession, sacrifice and consecration in order to be effective in such a time as this.

PRAYER

Father, I know that Your mercy triumphs over Your judgment. Your heart is tender toward those You love. You are ready to save, holding Your hand out all the time, yet too often I ignore You. Caught up in my petty problems, I react in sinful ways and fail to understand why Your blessings seem so elusive. Distracted by personal matters, I falter when You need me to undertake a burden for a crisis that affects strangers. Please pick me up and set me on my feet as many times as necessary. I cannot do this alone. Create a clean heart in me, and renew a right spirit within me. Show me my sin, and help me repent of it. Lead me in Your everlasting way. Humbly Yours, Amen.

DAY 15

BECOMING A GUARDIAN IN PRAYER

1. There will only ever be one Daniel, and your assigned watching place will certainly not be the same as his. Where has God appointed you to be a watchman? How does He want you to stand watch?
2. What is the Father doing and saying right now? If you don't have a clue, ask Him to show you, and humble yourself with fasting, if necessary.
3. In your praying, how does God want you to be more persistent, consistent and insistent? What would this look like?
4. Humble confession of sin draws God's grace onto the scene. Ask the Lord to root out areas of sin in your life, including unforgiveness and criticism, so you can more effectively pray blessing over others.

READING FOR DAY 16

Watching for Israel

> Pray for the peace of Jerusalem: "May they prosper who love you. Peace be within your walls, prosperity within your palaces." For the sake of my brethren and companions, I will now say, "Peace be within you." Because of the house of the LORD our God I will seek your good.
>
> Psalm 122:6–9 NKJV

For decades, I have been involved in prayer for Israel and the Jewish people. So this book about watchman intercession would not be complete without a chapter about it. However, a single chapter can only skim over highlights of the subject. After all, millennia of history, biblical prophecies fulfilled and yet to be fulfilled, historical conflicts between people groups in the Middle East that continue to boil over to this day . . . how can a few pages cover everything?

If you already have a watchman's heart for Israel, let this chapter reinforce your commitment. If you want to know more, I refer you to the thorough discussion offered in my books *The*

Coming Israel Awakening and *Praying for Israel's Destiny* and Derek Prince's *The Key to the Middle East*.

Above, I quoted from Psalm 122 because I believe its words capture the heart of God toward the Jewish people—those whom He called the apple of His eye in Zechariah 2:8—as well as toward Jerusalem, the beleaguered capital city of the nation of Israel.

Did you know Jerusalem is the only city named in the Bible that we are supposed to pray for? It is true. It may be hard to believe, but God wants peace to prevail in that beautiful and battle-weary city. The day will come when the fighting will cease between the antagonistic descendants of Abraham's two sons, Isaac and Ishmael.

Jerusalem and the nation of Israel are like God's timepiece; we can set our watchman's clock by them, discerning the times as we observe what is happening in Israel and the Middle East. What is God doing with the Jewish people now? Why has this latest conflict erupted? What does the future hold? Who can discern the right path? How can we be vigilant as we watch and pray?

We can do our part, echoing the words of the psalmist, "I will seek your good."

Discerning the Times

As watchman-intercessors, we must dedicate ourselves to seeking God's heart and mind so that we pray according to His will. We serve as watchmen for the people of God, whoever they may be—even the ones who do not yet identify themselves as the people of God. We do not hide our heads in the sand and ignore the troubling issues of the times in which we live.

In the Old Testament, we read about the sons of Issachar, who were "men who understood the times, with knowledge of what Israel should do" (1 Chronicles 12:32 NASB). The sons of Issachar have come to represent all people who seek to discern the times in which they live and who make their decisions based on the discerning wisdom God gives them. May God's watchmen be like sons of Issachar, seeking the mind of God as His Spirit reveals to us how to pray, just as Jesus said:

> "But when He, the Spirit of truth, comes, He will guide you into all the truth; for He will not speak on His own initiative, but whatever He hears, He will speak; and He will disclose to you what is to come."
>
> John 16:13 NASB

When praying for the Jewish people, we must understand what God is saying from three perspectives:

1. His promise to save all of Israel and bring it into His fullness (see Zechariah 12:10–11; Romans 11:12, 15, 26)
2. The temporary blindness of the Jewish people concerning Jesus as the Messiah (see Matthew 13:13–15; Romans 11:7–10, 25–28)
3. The promise that this spirit of blindness will be removed when "the times of the Gentiles are fulfilled" (Luke 21:24; see also Romans 11:25–26)

God asks volunteer watchmen like you and me, believers in Jesus, the Messiah, to shoulder a burden for the Jewish people and all of the descendants of Abraham. God's plan is to bring Jews alongside Gentiles (who are non-Jews) into full, saving knowledge of the Christ. He wants to win over Jews, Arabs, Chaldeans and all residents of the Middle East to His Son. The day will indeed come—and we have a key part in hastening it—when "the earth will be filled with the knowledge of the glory of the LORD, as the waters cover the sea" (Habakkuk 2:14 NASB).

The Jewish people will be won over by the love of the Gentile Church (see Matthew 25:40; John 13:35). Because we "wild olives" have been grafted into the original tree, we have no excuse for arrogance (see Romans 11:17–22). Arrogance all too quickly brings us down. Soon our hearts become hardened, too.

This is not the example of Paul, whose heart was broken when he observed how far from God some of his fellow Jews were:

> With Christ as my witness, I speak with utter truthfulness. My conscience and the Holy Spirit confirm it. My heart is filled with bitter sorrow and unending grief for my people, my Jewish brothers and sisters. I would be willing to be forever cursed—cut off from Christ!—if that would save them. They are the people of Israel, chosen to be God's adopted children. God revealed his glory to them. He made covenants with them and gave them his law. He gave them the privilege of worshiping him and receiving his wonderful promises.
>
> Romans 9:1–4 NLT

Paul, once a persecutor of his own people, labored all his life at great personal cost to bring as many people as possible—both Jew and Gentile—fully into the Kingdom of God. He used every means of persuasion available and urged those of us who have followed him to do the same.

Now, Satan is not ignorant of this grand plan and purpose of God to bring all Israel to Himself; it has been announced by prophets and proclaimed in public places for millennia. So he stirs up anti-Semitism and causes destruction. The enemy figures if he can eliminate the people of Israel from the face of the earth, he will win. With whole nations under his dark influence, it is not hard to imagine what the eventual Antichrist will look like (see Zechariah 12:2; 14:2; Zephaniah 3:7–8; 1 John 4:3).

As watchmen, we must be careful not to take all of our cues from the daily news or from political sources. The ever-shifting situation in Israel and the Middle East mirrors the malicious advances of Satan's unseen forces. In the midst of the confusion, only watchmen with spiritual discernment can see well enough in the dark to sound the right alarm at the correct time.

The Church as Watchman

The apostle Paul, who was Jewish from birth, wrote to the Roman church, almost entirely comprised of Gentiles, to explain much of God's plan for the people of Israel. He wanted them—and us—to know that even though the Jewish people have refused to acknowledge one of their own, Jesus, as the Son of God and Messiah, there is still hope and it lies with the Gentiles. As Paul explained, evidently the Jewish Messiah embraced the Gentiles in part to make the Jews jealous (see Romans 11:11). The Gentiles, who have been "grafted" into God's family tree, need to know that God wants to graft the natural branches back into it. He wants "all Israel [to] be saved" (Romans 11:26; see also verse 24).

Consequently, the Gentile Church has a call to fulfill. The worldwide Church must intercede for God's purposes to be accomplished in Israel and wherever else Jewish people are found. The Gentile Church must support the people of Israel with compassion and energy, embracing them as brothers. The Jewish prophet Isaiah wrote: "The Lord God, who gathers the dispersed of Israel, declares, 'Yet others I will gather to them, to those already gathered'" (Isaiah 56:8 NASB).

The Church, the Body of Christ on the earth, is the watchman on the wall described in Isaiah 62:6–7. Historically, though, we have failed to fulfill this mission. Just think of the relatively recent horrors of the Holocaust of World War II. We deplore the

Spanish Inquisition, too, but the Church still has the bloodstains on her hands. Anti-Semitism still influences critical decisions and derails efforts to introduce the people of God to their Savior. While Jesus is known as the Prince of Peace, the Church has too often demonstrated the opposite spirit, trampling on unbelievers in every generation.

Where is our love? Where is our wisdom? What has happened to the grace and mercy of God? Can we rise to the challenge of turning our own Body around, even as we begin to do a better job of looking out for our Jewish brethren?

The Esther Connection

It is as if the evil spirit of Haman never left the earth when he met his rightful end on the gallows of King Artaxerxes. We may well be destined to relive the story of Esther in our generation. For that reason, I want to urge all of you Mordecai-watchmen out there to watch carefully and then to act wisely.

You will remember the story as it is told in the book of Esther. Esther's strategic victory is celebrated to this day by the Jewish people in the feast of Purim. But she would not have been able to do anything for her people without the sage advice of her guardian, Mordecai, who was her spiritual authority. He watched in the gate, discovered a plot against the Jews and told Esther about it. In other words, without Mordecai, there would be no book of Esther. Not only that, but an entire population of Jews would have been annihilated.

Mordecai intercepted the intelligence about Haman's evil scheme, and he revealed it to the right parties. Esther employed all of her courage and charm. God made sure the king read the right document in the middle of the night. All was saved.

This story's connection to current events is clear. The anti-Semitic Haman spirit still roves around, seeking to annihilate the Jews. The Church, which represents Esther, may or may not be ready to intercede. We need the Mordecai-watchmen to step up with the right words at the right time. Only Mordecai could spot the danger, and only Mordecai-watchmen can inform the Church before it is too late for the Jewish people.

Together, Mordecai and Esther are their only hope. It is fine for today's Jews to celebrate Purim as a mighty historic victory, but in actual fact, the genocidal anti-Semitic Haman spirit has returned—and it has brought reinforcements. It is time to declare an Esther fast again.[1]

Israel and the Nations

With unseen forces of evil instigating anti-Semitism and every combative event in the Middle East today, often you cannot figure out who is right. Many people claim the same land, and their arguments seem plausible. How should we pray?

One suggestion is offered in Ezekiel 36, the chapter right before the famous "dry bones" story. God says:

> "Son of man, prophesy to Israel's mountains. Give them this message: O mountains of Israel, hear the word of the Lord! This is what the Sovereign Lord says: Your enemies have taunted you, saying, 'Aha! Now the ancient heights belong to us!'"
>
> Ezekiel 36:1–2 NLT

"Israel's mountains" and the "ancient heights" mentioned here would be Judea and Samaria, which go up into Galilee—what is called the West Bank today. The "enemies" would be the radical Islam spirit (not the Arabs themselves).

In the same prophecy, God promises to help them:

> "I will vindicate the holiness of My great name which has been profaned among the nations, which you have profaned in their

> midst. Then the nations will know that I am the LORD," declares the Lord GOD, "when I prove Myself holy among you in their sight. For I will take you from the nations, gather you from all the lands and bring you into your own land. Then I will sprinkle clean water on you, and you will be clean; I will cleanse you from all your filthiness and from all your idols. Moreover, I will give you a new heart and put a new spirit within you; and I will remove the heart of stone from your flesh and give you a heart of flesh."
>
> Ezekiel 36:23–26 NASB

This is remarkable! God promises to help the very people who had contended so fiercely against Him. Do you think they will accept His offer?

The *place* of Israel is all-important to God's plan. The Messiah will return to the very soil of Israel, and before that He wants to gather the remnant of His people together: "He . . . will gather the dispersed of Judah from the four corners of the earth" (Isaiah 11:12 NASB). For centuries now, but especially since 1948, when the state of Israel was established, Jewish people have been immigrating in droves. They call it "making *aliyah*," which means "the act of going up." By coming back to the land from which their ancestors were driven out, they are fulfilling prophecy:

> "For behold, days are coming," declares the LORD, "when I will restore the fortunes of My people Israel and Judah." The LORD says, "I will also bring them back to the land that I gave to their forefathers and they shall possess it."
>
> Jeremiah 30:3 NASB

Watching Together

God is ever faithful, even when His people are faithless. He pursues His lost sheep into the wilderness, and He reaches even battle-hardened hearts with His love. He keeps His covenant.

Most of us are grafted-in, non-Jewish believers. But we can still be watchmen on the walls, even the walls of Jerusalem, watching and praying in conjunction with the gatekeepers—those who have the authority to act for good or for evil. No intercessor can tackle this assignment solo. You must watch together with like-minded others, and you must be quick to identify for the leaders on the ground what you see from the top of the wall.

We are living in a time of awakening and activation. Besides fasting and praying, some of us will find ourselves engaged in direct evangelism. Others will be tested socially or financially when we decide to identify more fully with our Jewish brethren. Throughout, we must keep as close to the Lord as we can, praying without ceasing and proclaiming the ancient prophetic words that may find their fulfillment within our lifetime.

Remember that the power of prayer does not come from the power of the individual who is praying but from the One who hears the prayers and acts. His power is immeasurable—and it is directed entirely toward good ends: "Righteousness and justice are the foundation of [His] throne. Unfailing love and truth walk before [Him] as attendants" (Psalm 89:14 NLT). Our part is to pray and obey, remembering that "the prayer of a righteous person is powerful and effective" (James 5:16).

Tom Hess: Watchman for Jerusalem and All Nations

Tom Hess is another modern-day role model for us, one I have known for almost thirty years. Tom has spent most of his life as a watchman for Israel. He has helped establish houses of prayer and prayer watches on several continents and has led prayer expeditions to far-off places like Russia and Malaysia. I first met him through our mutual friend Dick Simmons at the house of prayer in Washington, D.C., that Tom maintained for years. After spending time with him there, I visited him many times in Jerusalem, where Tom founded the Jerusalem House of Prayer for All Nations, located on the Mount of Olives, where he resides today.

Tom is an apostolic leader who has written many books about prayer for Israel, including *The Watchmen: Being Prepared and Preparing the Way for Messiah*. His thinking (and praying) has a broad scope, taking into account the many rival claims to the land of Israel and discerning the behind-the-scenes activities of the evil one. In his book *God's Abrahamic Covenants with Israel*, he writes that the enemies of Israel are

> trying to destroy the foundations and knock down the pillars of the House of Israel, and cause the Jewish people to break covenants with their God in the very places where God made covenants with His people. . . . The four places where Abraham built altars are in the very center of Israel, the very center of the land where those who do not believe in the God of Israel and His covenants say should be an Islamic Palestinian State.[2]

The words of the ancient prophets about Israel come alive and stimulate fresh prayers on the Mount of Olives from Jerusalem House of Prayer for All Nations. Take, for example, these words from Jeremiah:

> "In those coming days," says the Lord, "the people of Israel will return home together with the people of Judah. They will come weeping and seeking the Lord their God. They will ask the way to Jerusalem and will start back home again. They will bind themselves to the Lord with an eternal covenant that will never be forgotten.
>
> "My people have been lost sheep. Their shepherds have led them astray and turned them loose in the mountains. They

> have lost their way and can't remember how to get back to the sheepfold. All who found them devoured them. Their enemies said, 'We did nothing wrong in attacking them, for they sinned against the LORD, their true place of rest, and the hope of their ancestors.' . . ."
>
> This is what the LORD of Heaven's Armies says: "The people of Israel and Judah have been wronged. Their captors hold them and refuse to let them go. But the one who redeems them is strong. His name is the LORD of Heaven's Armies. He will defend them and give them rest again in Israel."
>
> Jeremiah 50:4–7, 33–34 NLT

My friend Tom Hess is a true watchman whose heart is desperately eager to see Israel come into her full inheritance. He has taken his appointed position on God's wall, where he expects to remain until God calls him home.

PRAYER

Because I love Zion, I will not keep still. Because my heart yearns for Jerusalem, I cannot remain silent. I will not stop praying for her until her righteousness shines like the dawn and her salvation blazes like a burning torch. Then the nations will see the righteousness of Jerusalem. World leaders will be blinded by her glory. And the city will be given a new name by the Lord's own mouth. I can see the Lord holding Jerusalem in His hand for all to see—a splendid crown in the hand of God.

Never again will Jerusalem be called "The Forsaken City" or "The Desolate Land." Her new name will be "The City of God's Delight" and "The Bride of God," for the Lord delights in her and will claim her as His bride. Jerusalem's children will commit themselves to her just as a young man commits himself to his bride. Then God will rejoice over her as a bridegroom rejoices over his bride.

That is why He has posted watchmen on the walls of Jerusalem who pray day and night. Those who pray to the Lord take no rest and give the Lord no rest until He completes His work and makes Jerusalem the pride of the earth.

I am praying as I go through the gates, proclaiming, "Prepare the highway for My people to return! Smooth out the road; pull out the boulders; raise a flag for all the nations to see. The Lord has sent this message to every land: 'Tell the people of Israel, "Look, your Savior is coming. See, He brings His reward with Him as He comes."'"

The Lord has promised, and He will do it. Amen.[3]

DAY 16

BECOMING A GUARDIAN IN PRAYER

1. What does it mean to have a watchman's heart for Israel? Is this terminology familiar to you? What is your starting place as you consider the challenges of undertaking concerted prayer for Israel? Does the idea excite you, intrigue you, confuse you or leave you cold?
2. Do you come from a Gentile background or a Jewish background? How does this affect your approach to praying for Israel? What difficulties do you experience (or anticipate) as you endeavor to pray for the peace of Jerusalem?

3. How can you participate in seeking the good of God's people in Israel? Encourage yourself by reviewing the final paragraph of this chapter.
4. Compose a biblical prayer for Israel based on one or more of the following passages: Psalm 2; Psalm 91; Isaiah 62; Jeremiah 3; Zechariah 2; Zechariah 3; Zechariah 8; Ephesians 6:10–20.

READING FOR DAY 17

The Watch of the Lord

> So these governors and satraps thronged before the king, and said thus to him: ". . . Make a firm decree, that whoever petitions any god or man for thirty days, except you, O king, shall be cast into the den of lions. Now, O king, establish the decree and sign the writing, so that it cannot be changed. . . ." Therefore King Darius signed the written decree.
>
> Now when Daniel knew that the writing was signed, he went home. And in his upper room, with his windows open toward Jerusalem, he knelt down on his knees three times that day, and prayed and gave thanks before his God, as was his custom since early days. . . .
>
> So they answered and said before the king, "That Daniel, who is one of the captives from Judah, does not show due regard for you, O king, or for the decree that you have signed, but makes his petition three times a day."
>
> Daniel 6:6–10, 13 NKJV

As we saw in the reading for Day 15, Daniel's Babylonian rivals wanted to get rid of him, so they laid a "fail-proof" plan that took advantage of his obvious dedication to the God of Israel. Fully aware of their plot, what did Daniel do? He went home and prayed, as he had always done—three times a day, out loud, with his windows open. Anybody could see and hear him. Predictably, his enemies hurried to tell the king about his infraction, and the king (who favored Daniel), was forced to arrest him under the terms of his own decree.

Daniel was ready. He was willing to be imprisoned with the lions and to die for his God. What followed has become one of the favorite stories in both Jewish and Christian history: Daniel's miraculous overnight deliverance from the ravenous and violent beasts in the king's den of lions. He suffered not a scratch, and the king let him return to his home (where, presumably, he picked up where he left off with his prayers), and the king threw his enemies to the lions instead. (See Daniel 6:24.)

Daniel's story gives us a glimpse of the active—and sometimes risky—practice of what can be called "the watch of the Lord": sustained, committed, repeated times of prayer. Daniel's exemplary commitment has become legendary because of the dramatic outcome, but his deliverance from the lions always gets more attention than Daniel's praying. I want to highlight his praying. That is what Daniel's foes targeted him for doing.

As you can imagine, watching and praying is not very exciting most of the time. It usually takes place behind closed doors. Characterized by sober vigilance and patient endurance, including sleeplessness and fasting, it requires a certain level of personal commitment and untiring faithfulness.

The question must be asked: *Why* should a person watch and pray? What is the point of praying so much? Could not the same results be achieved another way? In many ways, watching looks like a waste of time, and under certain circumstances (such as Daniel's), it appears to be downright dangerous.

The Why of Watching

The primary reasons for watching prayerfully come straight from Jesus' instructions to His disciples. In telling them how to respond to threatening developments like wars and rumors of wars, His key word was *watch*. Look at these imperative, even urgent, statements:

> Jesus answered: "Watch out that no one deceives you. For many will come in my name, claiming, 'I am the Messiah,' and will deceive many. You will hear of wars and rumors of wars, but see to it that you are not alarmed. . . .
>
> "Because of the increase of wickedness, the love of most will grow cold, but the one who stands firm to the end will be saved."
>
> Matthew 24:4–6, 12–13

> "Therefore keep watch, because you do not know on what day your Lord will come. But understand this: If the owner of the house had known at what time of night the thief was coming, he would have kept watch and would not have let his house be broken into. So you also must be ready, because the Son of Man will come at an hour when you do not expect him."
>
> Matthew 24:42–44

> "Watch therefore, for you know neither the day nor the hour in which the Son of Man is coming."
>
> Matthew 25:13 NKJV

> Then He said to them, "My soul is deeply grieved, to the point of death; remain here and keep watch with Me."
>
> . . . And He came to the disciples and found them sleeping, and said to Peter, "So, you men could not keep watch with Me for one hour? Keep watching and praying that you may not enter into temptation; the spirit is willing, but the flesh is weak."
>
> Matthew 26:38, 40–41 NASB

Jesus said to them: "Watch out that no one deceives you."

Mark 13:5

"When these things begin to happen, watch out!"

Mark 13:9 NLT

"Watch out!"

Mark 13:23 NLT

"Be dressed ready for service and keep your lamps burning, like servants waiting for their master to return from a wedding banquet, so that when he comes and knocks they can immediately open the door for him. It will be good for those servants whose master finds them watching when he comes. Truly I tell you, he will dress himself to serve, will have them recline at the table and will come and wait on them. It will be good for those servants whose master finds them ready, even if he comes in the middle of the night or toward daybreak."

Luke 12:35–38

He replied: "Watch out that you are not deceived. For many will come in my name, claiming, 'I am he,' and, 'The time is near.' Do not follow them. When you hear of wars and uprisings, do not be frightened. These things must happen first, but the end will not come right away."

". . . Be always on the watch, and pray."

Luke 21:8–9, 36

Notice how many times Jesus used the key word, *watch*. He could not be clearer in His message to His disciples—and, therefore, to the generations in the Church since then. We watch so that we will escape deception and obtain wisdom and guidance. We watch because He wants our company. We watch for danger and in order to give warning to others. We watch so we will be ready to meet the Lord when He comes.

Today we are still living in the troubled time between Jesus' first coming and His final coming. According to our Lord Jesus, the prescription for handling all of the end-times trouble is still the same as it was when He was teaching His first disciples: watching and praying.

Jesus tells us to watch and pray. How does He want us to conduct ourselves? Resolutely, faithfully, carefully but bravely—much as Daniel did. Daniel, who is considered a "type," or a representation, of the forthcoming Son of God, modeled for us the kind of faithful praying that comes from living and breathing the atmosphere of the Kingdom.

Watching in the New Testament

Jesus, of course, modeled the watch of the Lord. He fasted and prayed for forty days in the wilderness at the beginning of His time of active ministry (see Matthew 4:1–11; Mark 1:12–13; Luke 4:1–2). Then when He was in the midst of teaching His disciples and ministering to the throngs of people, look how often He withdrew from others in order to pray:

> When Jesus heard what had happened [about the death of John the Baptist], he withdrew by boat privately to a solitary place.
>
> Matthew 14:13

> Very early in the morning, while it was still dark, Jesus got up, left the house and went off to a solitary place, where he prayed. Simon and his companions went to look for him, and when they found him, they exclaimed: "Everyone is looking for you!"
>
> Mark 1:35–37

> It was at this time that He went off to the mountain to pray, and He spent the whole night in prayer to God. And when day

came, He called His disciples to Him and chose twelve of them, whom He also named as apostles.

Luke 6:12–13 NASB

At daybreak, Jesus went out to a solitary place. The people were looking for him and when they came to where he was, they tried to keep him from leaving them.

Luke 4:42

Jesus often withdrew to lonely places and prayed.

Luke 5:16

If the Son of God needed to take extended prayer times on a regular basis, even at the expense of sleep and comfort, what makes us think we can get along without the same?

The early Church understood the importance of extended times of prayer. They watched, sometimes in response to threats and sometimes because of simple obedience. Their first watch came right after Jesus ascended to heaven, as He told them to watch and pray until the Holy Spirit would come:

After his suffering, he presented himself to them and gave many convincing proofs that he was alive. He appeared to them over a period of forty days and spoke about the kingdom of God. On one occasion, while he was eating with them, he gave them this command: "Do not leave Jerusalem, but wait for the gift my Father promised, which you have heard me speak about. For John baptized with water, but in a few days you will be baptized with the Holy Spirit." . . .

Then the apostles returned to Jerusalem from the hill called the Mount of Olives, a Sabbath day's walk from the city. When they arrived, they went upstairs to the room where they were staying. Those present were Peter, John, James and Andrew; Philip and Thomas, Bartholomew and Matthew; James son of Alphaeus and Simon the Zealot, and Judas son of James. They

> all joined together constantly in prayer, along with the women and Mary the mother of Jesus, and with his brothers.
>
> Acts 1:3–5, 12–14

When it says, "They all joined together constantly in prayer," that means they were watching and praying. They were not chatting, sleeping, cooking or eating meals. They were not checking their email. They were, for ten days straight, standing and sitting in that simple room, praying aloud and reminding each other of the promises of Scripture and the instruction of the Lord.

In other times of special need, the members of the early Church gathered to watch and pray for long stretches of time. Remember the story about Peter's miraculous release from prison? The Church watched and prayed then, too: "Peter was therefore kept in prison, but constant prayer was offered to God for him by the church" (Acts 12:5 NKJV). After the angel set him free, Peter went directly to the house where the believers had gathered to watch and pray for his release:

> And when Peter had come to himself, he said, "Now I know for certain that the Lord has sent His angel, and has delivered me from the hand of Herod and from all the expectation of the Jewish people."
>
> So, when he had considered this, he came to the house of Mary, the mother of John whose surname was Mark, where many were gathered together praying.
>
> Acts 12:11–12 NKJV

In other words, he knew where he would find them. He knew they were watching and praying.

The Church continued to grow and spread far and wide, and the apostle Paul played a key role in its success. It was never easy. Paul uses the word *watchings* when he describes the hardships of his ministry as an apostle:

> But in all things approving ourselves as the ministers of God, in much patience, in afflictions, in necessities, in distresses, in stripes, in imprisonments, in tumults, in labours, in watchings, in fastings.
>
> 2 Corinthians 6:4–5 KJV

> Thrice was I beaten with rods, once was I stoned, thrice I suffered shipwreck, a night and a day I have been in the deep; in journeyings often, in perils of waters, in perils of robbers, in perils by mine own countrymen, in perils by the heathen, in perils in the city, in perils in the wilderness, in perils in the sea, in perils among false brethren; in weariness and painfulness, in watchings often, in hunger and thirst, in fastings often, in cold and nakedness.
>
> 2 Corinthians 11:25–27 KJV

So we see that the first disciples were following Jesus' example when they watched in prayer. But this was not a new concept.

Watching in the Old Testament

The people of Israel had been watching for generations. Daniel, of course, was one of them, and we have already noted his faithful adherence to the times of prayer he had learned when he was growing up in Jerusalem.

We see another example in the account of the patriarch Jacob, alone in the wilderness, wrestling with an angel in order to secure his destiny. He persevered all night until he prevailed, having said to the angel of the Lord, "I will not let you go unless you bless me" (Genesis 32:26).

The long vigil of the first Passover was a significant watchnight, too, as the angel of death went from house to house, slaying all of the firstborn sons in Egypt but passing over the homes of the Hebrews that had been marked with the blood of the lamb. (See Exodus 12.)

Watching, watching and more watching . . .

By reading what they wrote, we know the prophets of the Old Testament considered themselves watchmen for the Lord. Habakkuk declared, "I will stand my watch and set myself on the rampart, and watch to see what He will say to me" (Habakkuk 2:1 NKJV). God told Ezekiel directly, "Now as for you, son of man, I have appointed you a watchman for the house of Israel" (Ezekiel 33:7 NASB).

The prophet-priest Samuel started watching through the night when he was only a boy and heard the voice of the Lord calling his name in the night. For Samuel, watching became a default response to dire developments, such as the time when Saul was rejected as Israel's king and Samuel: "And it grieved Samuel, and he cried out to the LORD all night" (1 Samuel 15:11 NKJV).

In a number of the psalms, David mentions watching:

> In the morning, O LORD, You will hear my voice; in the morning I will order my prayer to You and eagerly watch.
>
> Psalm 5:3 NASB

> You are my strength, I watch for you; you, God, are my fortress.
>
> Psalm 59:9

> On my bed I remember you; I think of you through the watches of the night.
>
> Psalm 63:6

> A thousand years in your sight are like a day that has just gone by, or like a watch in the night.
>
> Psalm 90:4

> I watch, and am as a sparrow alone upon the house top.
>
> Psalm 102:7 KJV

Nehemiah is another faithful and faith-filled Old Testament leader who modeled sustained, fervent praying, even day and night:

> I said, "I beseech You, O Lord God of heaven, the great and awesome God, who preserves the covenant and lovingkindness for those who love Him and keep His commandments, let Your ear now be attentive and Your eyes open to hear the prayer of Your servant which I am praying before You now, day and night, on behalf of the sons of Israel Your servants, confessing the sins of the sons of Israel which we have sinned against You; I and my father's house have sinned."
>
> Nehemiah 1:5–6 NASB

You cannot miss the fact that godly people have been watching for centuries—and they are still watching today.

Watchers Watching Today

Are you beginning to think watching and praying are the exclusive domain of towering biblical figures? I hope not, because in their own human strength, those godly people were no more capable of praying day and night with persistent faith and passion than you or I. We can count on the same Spirit of God who helped them for support and guidance as we watch and pray.

Watchers want what God wants, and they volunteer for active service, quick to set aside their own personal comfort or agenda. Sometimes they are able to gather with like-minded others; sometimes they operate solo. They look and listen by the hour so they can apprehend the heart of God and pray according to His will. They keep alert so that they will not miss the slightest divine movement. They invite heaven to invade earth in specific ways, and they shore up others in prayer so they will not flag in zeal or strength. They guard against incursions of evil, and they learn how to fight with spiritual weapons.

Praise and worship become effective weapons in the mouths of intercessors. Another effective weapon is called the *prayer of agreement*. Jesus told His disciples that where two or three have gathered in His name, there He would be in their midst (see Matthew 18:20). So, in the prayer of agreement, the first person with whom we want to come into agreement is God Himself. As we do that, it is much easier to come into agreement with others. The potential is now enormous!

Watchers know the strength of their prayers increases with numbers. That is why they have established hundreds and thousands of houses of prayer across the world over the years. One of them has captured my heart: the one-hundred-year prayer watch of the band of Christians known as the Moravians. I profiled them in my book *Prayer Storm*, saying the following:

> In 1727, in Herrnhut, Saxony, under the leadership of Count Nicolas Ludwig von Zinzendorf, night-and-day intercession arose in a small community in what today is eastern Germany. The people in the community had come from Moravia, so they became known as the Moravians. This prayer vigil continued for over 110 years, and it fueled a missionary movement that touched the world. The men and women of Herrnhut committed themselves to hourly intercession in order to, in their words, "win for the Lamb the rewards of His suffering."[1]

Historically, it happened this way:

> In 1722, Count Nicolas Ludwig von Zinzendorf was asked by a group of Christians if they could cross the border from Moravia in order to live on his lands. He assented, and they settled in a town they called *Herrnhut*, which means "the Lord's Watch." Zinzendorf had always been interested in a life of prayer and devotion to God, and, after his tenants suffered a season of

> prolonged disagreement and difficulty, he began to lead daily Bible studies for them in 1727. A sudden time of revival occurred, which many have called "the Moravian Pentecost." The effects of this move of the Holy Spirit have been far-reaching, indeed.
>
> One of the first results of the revival was that 24 men and 24 women covenanted to devote one hour every day to concerted prayer. It was a very simple model, and soon others joined them. This was the beginning of what became a 100-year-long prayer watch. Every hour of every day, someone was praying. While others were working, someone was praying. They prayed 24 hours a day, 7 days a week, 365 days a year. The "altar fire" never went out. . . .
>
> These men and women were young. Even their patron, Count Zinzendorf, was only 27 years old at the beginning. Almost immediately, they began to launch evangelistic missions to foreign lands as far-flung as the West Indies, Greenland and Lapland, and Turkey. As the years passed, they grew old and passed the baton to others; Zinzendorf died in 1760. But the prayer continued unabated.
>
> By 1792, 65 years after the prayer watch began, that one small band of Moravian believers had sent 300 missionaries to all parts of the globe.[2]

Among the many people who were significantly affected by the Moravians was John Wesley, who went on to reach countless more for Christ. I wonder how many people are in heaven today as a result of that one remarkable prayer watch?

People who may not know about the Moravians' one-hundred-year watch have been touched by the same Holy Spirit who impelled them to gather and pray. Some of these watchmen conduct their guardian intercession in such a hidden way that nobody knows they are doing it. Others find enough others with the same passion that they can pool and multiply their prayer efforts.

It is not as exciting as a stadium event or a spectacular healing service, but watching on behalf of the King is every bit as important. Those of us who consider ourselves watchmen are privileged to participate in watching, waiting and listening in order to detect both potential threats and the still, small voice of the Holy Spirit.

Watching and praying bear much fruit for God's Kingdom. Spending extended periods of time before the Lord transforms a person. Fundamentally, watching is an expression of abiding in Him. Remember Jesus' familiar words? He said, "I am the vine, you are the branches. He who abides in Me, and I in him, bears much fruit; for without Me you can do nothing" (John 15:5 NKJV).

Mahesh Chavda: Living the Watch of the Lord

If you ever want to be part of a night of watching and praying, you can join the seasoned watchmen and women of Charlotte, North Carolina, at the Watch of the Lord. There, Mahesh and Bonnie Chavda, founders and co-pastors of All Nations Church, have been leading all-night prayer meetings on Fridays for more than twenty years. To help educate people about the practice, the Chavdas have written several books, including one titled *Watch of the Lord*, and continue to produce other resources to explain the scriptural precedent for prayer watching; the experiential realities of all-night prayer; and the notable, often miraculous, results of their prayer watching.

Their weekly night watch has multiplied into a network of watches across the world, with new ones starting up regularly. The various groups of watchers support each other, sharing wisdom and prophetic words.

Mahesh and Bonnie write about the Watch of the Lord on their website:

> The Watch of the Lord is a global prayer network begun in 1995 in response to the Lord asking us to "Watch with Me."
>
> In January of 1995 we invited about twenty people to spend the following Friday from 10:00 p.m. until 6:00 a.m. on Saturday keeping the "night watch," fasting sleep for spiritual reasons.
>
> We gathered to wait on God in worship and prayer and share in communion through Jesus' body and blood in the Lord's Supper. Every Friday since we have done the same. We have celebrated the watch with as many as a thousand watchmen present. And now there are many watches throughout the United States and abroad. We find ourselves in the midst of a renewed visitation that is manifesting the glory of the Lord!
>
> The sure promise of God through Scripture is this: "If you pray, I will answer." The delivering power of God which came to Israel was through the blood and flesh of the slain lamb! All Israel who looked for deliverance through the lamb that was slain watched all night after partaking of the Passover meal. In Luke 6:12 we find that it was Jesus' habit to spend all night in prayer to God. It was out of this lifestyle that He asked His slumbering disciples, "Could you not watch with Me even one hour?"
>
> Today we look to the same deliverer, Jesus Christ the Lamb that was slain before the foundations of the world. We answer His call to watch and pray, and we are seeing Him come to deliver.[3]

Recently, I was able to spend four hours alone with Mahesh, my dear friend of forty-plus years. As we shared back and forth about our families, our ministries, supernatural miracles we had witnessed and our relationships with the Lord, do you know the main subject Mahesh kept coming back to? The watch of the Lord. Yes, this veteran of fasting and moving in the gift of the Holy Spirit brought our endearing conversation back to the power of all-night prayer watches. He kept emphasizing the importance of maintaining it.

It is a fact: Prayer changes things. And in the lifestyle of a watchman, every prayer and sacrifice counts!

PRAYER

Holy Father God, I want my life to be characterized by willingness, even eagerness, to watch and pray with You. I do not want to prefer my sleep and comfort above spending time seeking You, day or night. Do You have an assignment for me? Do You want me to commit myself to pray all night or for long stretches of time? Do You have a place where You need a watchman?

Watching seems like a daunting thing to do, and I know I will need a lot of help from Your Holy Spirit. Please fortify me with Your Word, with the encouragement of others who have a passion for watching in prayer and with anything else I might need in order to watch successfully. Keep me from giving up. I am certainly no better than Your hand-chosen disciples, who failed to watch with You even one hour in Gethsemane. Therefore, may Your forgiveness of my weaknesses remain at the forefront of my mind even as I respond to Your invitation to watch with You. I ask this in the name of Your Son, Jesus, Amen.

DAY 17

BECOMING A GUARDIAN IN PRAYER

1. Have you ever participated in an all-night prayer watch? (This could include all-night vigils at someone's bedside

or long, drawn-out prayers of desperation uttered during a crisis.) What was it like?

2. Why did Jesus' disciples fail to watch with Him in the Garden of Gethsemane? What difference would it have made if they, or even some of them, had stayed awake and attended to the watch?
3. In the midst of your ordinary responsibilities to family and employer, how can you find time to pray like this? In order not to deprive anyone to whom you are obligated, what could you sacrifice? How might the sacrifice resemble fasting?
4. Even the holiest individuals must come into God's presence with humility, acknowledging their utter dependence on the saving sacrifice of Jesus Christ and the help of His Holy Spirit. Compose a short prayer that you can use at the beginning of an extended time of prayer to position yourself at His feet and to open up your heart to receive whatever He wants to give you.

READING FOR DAY 18

Prophetic Intercession

"But if they are prophets, and if the word of the LORD is with them, let them now make intercession to the LORD of hosts."

Jeremiah 27:18 NKJV

In the Old Testament, the priests pleaded the needs of the people before the Lord while the prophets pleaded the interests of God before the people. The two roles are combined in what we call *prophetic intercession*, where a watchman-intercessor prays back to God an inspiration regarding a human concern that comes from God's own heart.

Abraham, Anna and Daniel were all prophetic intercessors. Themselves prophets, they tapped into God's very heart when they apprehended His promises, which God expressed directly to them or showed them in the words of other prophets. Recognizing that they had a role to play in bringing those divine promises into being, they began to watch and pray. The verse quoted above from Jeremiah gives a glimpse into what I am trying to describe.

Prophetic intercession is near and dear to my heart. I love the way God nudges me to pray about something so that He can intervene. I have seen so many amazing answers to prophetic prayer! Such prayers strike the mark much more often than those I invent out of my own limited heart and mind.

Praying the Promises

Here is how I usually describe prophetic intercession. Prophetic intercession is waiting before God in order to hear or receive His burden—it could be a word, a concern, a warning, a condition, a vision or a promise—and responding back to Him with prayerful petition, sometimes with corresponding actions. Prophetic intercession paves the way for the fulfillment of prophetic promises.

Here are selected Scriptures that show how prophetic intercession works:

> Surely the Sovereign LORD does nothing without revealing his plan to his servants the prophets.
>
> Amos 3:7

> For we are co-workers in God's service.
>
> 1 Corinthians 3:9

> The LORD said, "Shall I hide from Abraham what I am about to do?"
>
> Genesis 18:17 NASB

> Gabriel, whom I had seen in the vision previously, came to me in my extreme weariness about the time of the evening offering. He gave me instruction and talked with me and said, "O Daniel, I have now come forth to give you insight with understanding."
>
> Daniel 9:21–22 NASB

> "No longer do I call you slaves, for the slave does not know what his master is doing; but I have called you friends, for all things that I have heard from My Father I have made known to you."
>
> John 15:15 NASB

God has made and continues to make promises. I believe every promise finds its fulfillment only when the Holy Spirit, the Advocate, pleads it before the heavenly throne through one of God's chosen intercessors. The promises may be historical covenant promises that God made to His people; truths that have been preached; prayer burdens; or spontaneous, Spirit-inspired utterances. What makes them prophetic is the fact that they reveal something that was hidden in the heart of God until it was expressed.

On behalf of someone else, the intercessor takes up a case of justice before a sovereign and entirely righteous God. God is looking for the man or woman who will take up the plea, and He can hardly believe it when no one volunteers to stand in the gap. Both Isaiah and Ezekiel portrayed this:

> So truth fails, and he who departs from evil makes himself a prey.
>
> Then the LORD saw it, and it displeased Him that there was no justice.
>
> He saw that there was no man, and wondered that there was no intercessor.
>
> Isaiah 59:15–16 NKJV

> "I searched for a man among them who would build up the wall and stand in the gap before Me for the land, so that I would not destroy it; but I found no one. Thus I have poured out My indignation on them."
>
> Ezekiel 22:30–31 NASB

Praying the Promptings

Prophetic intercession can also mean the urgings that come from the Holy Spirit regarding people or circumstances about which the intercessor knows little or nothing. God taps the watchman on the shoulder and imparts a compelling awareness that it is time to pray for a very particular need: "Here . . . pray for this thing right now!" He supplies just enough information to allow the intercessor to pray effectively about a matter, large or small, in a divinely anointed manner.

Often we call this "receiving a prayer burden," and it can mean much more than having a vague, easy-to-ignore sense of a need. If we cultivate our ability to hear the Holy Spirit (more on that in a moment), we can receive circumstantial details, specific wording for our prayers, a sense of timing and a gift of faith.

When Daniel took time to reread the prophetic words of Jeremiah, he was convinced they applied to the immediate future (see Daniel 9:2–3). The words he had read were these:

> This is what the Lord says: "When seventy years are completed for Babylon, I will come to you and fulfill my good promise to bring you back to this place."
>
> Jeremiah 29:10

Daniel began to pray for the fulfillment of the promise that prophet had delivered to the previous generation. His own prophetic senses alerted him to the imminent need expressed by the earlier prophetic promise.

Must we pray at length as Daniel did, with extreme fasting and weakness? Not unless that is what is called for. For the most part, we can cultivate our spiritual hearing in simple, practical ways.

First, we stand at our appointed post as watchmen, ready for anything. We get away from external distractions, as Jesus did when He withdrew before dawn to isolated locations (see

Mark 1:35). Quieting our internal noise, we watch to see what God may want to say, remembering, "Be still, and know that I am God" (Psalm 46:10 KJV). When we hear something, we do something—write it down, pray from it, sound an alarm, whatever is appropriate. That is what the prophet Habakkuk did:

> I will climb up to my watchtower and stand at my guardpost. There I will wait to see what the LORD says and how he will answer my complaint.
>
> Then the Lord said to me, "Write my answer plainly on tablets, so that a runner can carry the correct message to others. This vision is for a future time. It describes the end, and it will be fulfilled. If it seems slow in coming, wait patiently, for it will surely take place. It will not be delayed."
>
> Habakkuk 2:1–3 NLT

You may find, as I do, that it is easier to hear God's voice when you are performing automatic, mindless tasks, such as driving the car, showering, exercising, washing the dishes or cleaning the house, especially if you are quietly praising God at the same time. He is more eager to speak to you than you are to hear from Him.

Praying the Problems

At times, the Holy Spirit may give you insights that help explain why a problem exists. God wants you to pray with extra insight so that you can undo the invisible knots and bonds that are holding someone or something captive. In order for His justice to prevail, His authority must be reestablished wherever it has been usurped.

Now, *usurper* is one of Satan's titles, correct? How does he manage to do it so cunningly? If we watchmen can identify the doorways to darkness, we can employ prayer strategies that identify and arrest the intruding usurper and keep him from returning.

Certain conditions make it possible for Satan to set up a base of operations. The following conditions are like open doors for the enemy:

Idolatry in any form. God does not stand for anything that usurps His rightful place in our lives. (See Exodus 20:1–5; Deuteronomy 7:5, 25–26; 1 Corinthians 10:19–20.)

Temples to pagan religions. You may not need to look for a pagan religion from a faraway land. It can just as easily be a Masonic temple in your city. (See 2 Kings 17:11; 18:4; Psalm 78:58; Jeremiah 19:5; 32:35.)

Murder and the shedding of innocent blood. The shedding of innocent blood defiles the place where it occurred, and cleansing can occur only through prayer in the power of Jesus' shed blood. Look for this kind of defilement when you are dealing with locations that have seen historic enslavement, military massacres, euthanasia, infanticide or abortion. (See Genesis 9:6; Exodus 20:13; Leviticus 17:11; Numbers 35:33.)

Witchcraft. In certain parts of the world, even the Western world, outright satanic worship and witchcraft are flourishing and taking strong root. Remember also that "rebellion is as the sin of witchcraft, and stubbornness is as iniquity and idolatry" (1 Samuel 15:23 NKJV). (See Leviticus 19:31; 20:6.)

The banning of prayer and Bible-reading from educational institutions. Our children have been prevented from hearing the truth, and they are taught to see it as falsehood. (See Exodus 12:26–28; Deuteronomy 4:9; 6:7.)

Adultery, sodomy, perversion and all sexual sins. We must keep our sexuality in line with God's intention for it. (See

Leviticus 18; 20; Deuteronomy 23:17; Romans 1:24–28, Romans 13:13.)

Substance abuse. Much addictive behavior is only witchcraft or idolatry disguised as a fun, leisure-time activity. (See Proverbs 23:31–35; Romans 13:13; Ephesians 5:18; Revelation 17; 18, 21:8.)

Fighting, anger, hatred, cursing and unforgiveness. We must have clean hearts if we want to walk in liberty. (See Exodus 20:12; Leviticus 20:9; Joshua 6:26; Proverbs 17:3; Matthew 18:21–35; 27:23–26; John 19:15; Romans 12:14; 1 Corinthians 4:12; 5:1; 2 Corinthians 6:14–16; 1 Peter 3:9.)

Any of these sins become doorways to evil. Sin incurs curses, but the prayer of a righteous watchman can lift them (see James 5:16). When God's prophetic intercessors watch diligently, they can spot the hidden workings of the enemy and pray in such a way that God's light overwhelms the darkness.

Praying the Place

In the early 1990s, Steve Hawthorne and Graham Kendrick published a small book that had a big impact in the world of prophetic intercession, titled *Prayer-Walking: Praying On Site with Insight*. They learned how to pray "on location" based on the prophetic insights God would furnish for each situation. Soon watchman-intercessors all over the world were going right to the places they expected to see their prayers answered. They relied on a combination of geographical and historical research and the Holy Spirit's revelational guidance.

Prayer-walking pushed the "refresh" button for intercessors, although it is nothing new. Abraham did it (see Genesis 13). Joshua did it (see Numbers 13–14). Jesus did it, too (see

Luke 13:34–35; 19:41–44). In our day, groups of watchman-intercessors have initiated ambitious prayer-walking events on several continents.

When we are faced with intractable situations that do not yield easily to prayer, we should remember this option. Praying "on site with insight" can happen in your neighborhood, on the streets of your city, at your place of employment, at sites of consecrated use (either noble or ungodly consecration) and from vantage points that overlook a city or a region. You can pray at sites where tragic events have occurred, releasing God's blessings and chasing away the darkness. Remember, "Mercy triumphs over judgment" (James 2:13 NKJV)!

If you become aware that a certain place's name has evil origins and carries evil intent, you can call on God to bring a change. As one of His intercessors, you can look into His heart to find out the prophetic destiny He originally intended for the place, and in His name you can declare that His purposes will prevail.

On sites where grievous sin was committed in the past (such as a massacre), you can pray to cut off the evil that has become inherent there, and you can terminate the curses that accompanied the atrocity. In places where sin is ongoing, you can repent on behalf of those who cannot or will not turn to God, and then you can invite God's grace to flourish where it used to be excluded. Sometimes believers seal such prayers by receiving Communion on the site, as well.

In governmental sites, such as town halls, courtrooms, and capitol buildings, on-site intercessors can ask the Lord to raise up righteous leadership. They can counteract specific problems by proclaiming God's promises.

Alert watchmen will find plenty of times to pray on site wherever they may find themselves—at a red light, in a waiting room, at concerts, anywhere. Humble yourself, praise God's holy name, and ask God to open the eyes of your heart to His purposes. You will never be disappointed!

Cindy Jacobs: Praying with a Watchman's Eyes

My friend Cindy Jacobs travels the world, ministering as a prophet and a prophetic intercessor. Early on, the Lord called her with this word from the Bible: "Ask of Me, and I will give You the nations for Your inheritance, and the ends of the earth for Your possession" (Psalm 2:8 NKJV). She has endeavored to live it out ever since. She is an absolute globe-trotter and has probably ministered to more governmental leaders than any person I know.

She and her husband, Mike, co-founded a ministry called Generals International (formerly Generals of Intercession), which provides a platform from which they launch prayer journeys, practical biblical teaching and more. She is also the founder of many ongoing initiatives that place a focus on current-day prophetic ministry.

Cindy has written many books, including *Possessing the Gates of the Enemy*, from which I want to share an excerpt about how you can develop what she calls a "watchman's eye":

> Here are several things you can do to develop a watchman's eye:
>
> 1. Sign up for the army! Tell the Lord that you are willing to be a watchman.
>
> 2. Keep your heart pure so that you can properly discern areas for which God wants you to pray.
>
> 3. Develop a God-consciousness in your life. Be aware at every moment that you are on call. Being a watchman is very much like being a doctor who carries a beeper. At any given moment he or she may be called up for an emergency. No matter what you are doing, God may call you to change your plans, pray and sound the alarm to stop the enemy's attack.

> 4. Pray that God will teach you the proper time and place to sound the alarm. God reveals to intercessors the intimate needs of those for whom we intercede. This is a precious trust. The things God shares with us are not to be told to others. Many prayer groups are nothing more than spiritual gossip sessions. . . .
>
> 5. Do not be afraid to pray prayers that may seem unusual to you. You may be praying, for instance, and all of a sudden you start praying for a pastor in South America whom you do not even know. Many watchmen have averted disasters that threaten people they have never met.[1]

Prophetic intercessors have a watchman's pair of eyes. Let me relate something to you that happened years ago while I was ministering in Colorado Springs. Cindy and I had been invited to the first National School of the Prophets, hosted by the late C. Peter Wagner. At the end of the conference, Peter had gathered a range of speakers in a reception room. I happened to be standing near Cindy when Peter—who did not yet really know me—asked me, "Well, then, who are you?" Cindy pointed her prophetic finger at me, as I did the same to her. She said, "He is the father . . . ," just as I, in turn, said, "She is the mother . . . ," and then, in unison and unrehearsed, we finished, " . . . of prophetic intercession."

There is such diversity in the Body of Christ, and it manifests itself in every sphere: in pastoral ministry, in evangelism, in prophetic ministry and in the global prayer movement. Not all watchmen are prophetic intercessors like Cindy Jacobs, but I am grateful I can pray alongside dedicated watchmen like her when the going gets tough!

PRAYER

Lord, nothing is greater than Your love. With You on my side, I can face any enemy. I trust You completely with my life because You are the highest, strongest, wisest, most trustworthy—and You love me in spite of my weaknesses and foolishness. I am eternally grateful to enjoy right standing with You, completely free from condemnation or accusation. Nothing on earth or in heaven can separate me from Your love. Not even the worst hardship can diminish it. Because You sent Your own Son to earth, I can come into Your presence. Now He sits at Your right hand, where He always has Your ear, and I can come close, too. You have enlarged my heart so I can intercede before You on behalf of others as well as myself. I accept with joy the overwhelming victory You have bestowed on me, and I ask You for insights and grace so I can bring others to Your feet. Yours forever, in Jesus, Amen.

DAY 18

BECOMING A GUARDIAN IN PRAYER

1. Are you called to be a prophetic intercessor? How can you know? Have you ever had an experience in intercessory prayer that seemed to be informed by a prophetic sense? How was the prayer answered?
2. Define *prophetic intercession* in your own words. Beyond the examples given in this chapter, what other biblical figures can you think of who exemplify prophetic intercession?
3. What are some good ways to prime yourself to hear the Holy Spirit's promptings for prayer? Think of at least three ways that you know would work for you.
4. As you read this, where are you located? In your own home or someplace else? Indoors or outdoors? Sitting

still or riding on some form of transportation? In a familiar place or one that is new to you? See if you can receive from the Holy Spirit an on-site prophetic insight about your location, and then pray from the insight you receive.

READING FOR DAY 19

For Such a Time as This

"Who knows whether you have come to the kingdom for such a time as this?"

Esther 4:14 NKJV

We find deliverers all over the place in the Old and New Testaments. Moses was a deliverer. Joshua was a deliverer. Deborah was a deliverer. Gideon was a deliverer. Samuel was a deliverer. David was a deliverer. All of the prophets were deliverers—Elijah, Elisha, Ezekiel, Daniel. Queen Esther was a deliverer, too.

Jesus was the greatest Deliverer of them all, followed by each of His disciples, including Paul, Stephen and countless (not to mention nameless) others. Right up to the present day, God—the great Creator-Deliverer—commissions men and women to reflect His heart and bring liberation from bondage.

Would you include yourself in that list? What mighty exploits have you achieved lately? *Well, my life is just ordinary*, you might be thinking. *You know, I go to work every day. I feed the cat. I go to church on Sunday. One time I went on a short-term mission trip, but all we did was fix up a school.*

I get that. And yet, when you think about it, none of the heroes of the faith I listed above operated in peak deliverer mode all of the time. In fact, most of the time, they were just plodding along, performing ordinary duties like everyone else. They got up each day and did pretty much the same thing they had done the day before. This is even true of Jesus.

Everyday plodding does not get the acclaim it deserves because it is not glamorous. But this day-to-day stuff is simple faithfulness.

I think about my own life related to this. I am a pretty average Joe—not a high mover or shaker or influencer. I keep doing what I do, and I will not quit. I am a diligent, loyal and somewhat responsible man (at least, I hope so). But friends of mine are more like magnets. They draw crowds; they are whirlwinds who change the atmosphere. They seem to carry Holy Ghost explosives, and miracles break out wherever they go. I just plod along . . . *and then.* Well, and then His presence comes and everything changes. That happens, I believe, because I bathe everything I do in plodding prayer. And then He shows up.

This seems to be a biblical pattern. In each of the notable people's lives I mentioned above, something came up. Suddenly their duties expanded to include feats of bravery they could hardly have imagined in their wildest dreams. Dutiful David, the shepherd boy, became David the giant slayer. Dutiful Jesus left His carpenter's bench for good when His mother said, "They have no wine" (John 2:3 NKJV). Dutiful orphan Esther became the favorite of King Ahasuerus (Artaxerxes) "for such a time as this" (Esther 4:14).

Dull, dutiful labor gave way to heroic actions. Duty paved the way. By fulfilling ordinary obligations day after day and year after year, average people were prepared when an emergency—or several emergencies—arose.

Be Dutiful

I started out this section of the book with the life of Daniel. Daniel was dutiful, for sure. *Dutiful* might have been his middle name. He stretched the rules from time to time, like when he asked to be excused from eating rich food or when he failed to comply with the edict about prayer. But for the most part, Daniel just did his job. He was loyal and respectful, undertaking his duties with diligence and thoroughness, earning high marks from the king he served.

Most of all, he served God as King, and that is where Daniel's fullest consecration came from.

Daniel was resolute and strong when his dutiful character put him into dangerous situations more than once. Then his dutifulness was rewarded and recorded for posterity, and he was moved steadily into position as a deliverer of his people. When watchman duty turned into combat duty, he was ready.

I am no Daniel, that is for sure, and neither are you. But as faithful watchmen on the wall, we can cultivate the same devotion to duty, whatever that duty may be. By relying on God, we learn about reliability. By sitting at His feet, we replicate His character in our lives. Through our dependable watching and praying, we, too, will be ready when we are tapped for combat duty someday. "For such a time as this" can apply to any of us, if we have committed ourselves to serve well in whatever role God has designated for us.

Duty. Far from being a boring, unimaginative, unfulfilling word weighed down with a sense of grim obligation, it can be one of the highest forms of consecration around. Watchmen must persevere for hours at a stretch and be ready to return to their posts again after only a short break. Sometimes they may find their watch strained and tense. But much of the time, it is just tedious. The hours go by, and nothing really happens. Yet watchmen need to remain poised to spring into action if a threat appears. They cannot zone out.

Guard duty is not thrilling. For the most part, it is not rewarding. It can be fairly lonely, too; almost nobody stops by for a visit, and chatting or texting on the phone is considered a distraction, a no-no. A watchman just stands or sits there, maybe pacing back and forth. He never lies down on the job.

Sounds great, doesn't it? Oh, but it is. And what is more, it matters.

Purify Yourself

If the watchman fails in his duty, the consequences can be serious. That is why Ezekiel sounded such a stern warning:

> At the end of seven days the word of the Lord came to me, saying, "Son of man, I have appointed you a watchman to the house of Israel; whenever you hear a word from My mouth, warn them from Me. When I say to the wicked, 'You will surely die,' and you do not warn him or speak out to warn the wicked from his wicked way that he may live, that wicked man shall die in his iniquity, but his blood I will require at your hand. Yet if you have warned the wicked and he does not turn from his wickedness or from his wicked way, he shall die in his iniquity; but you have delivered yourself. Again, when a righteous man turns away from his righteousness and commits iniquity, and I place an obstacle before him, he will die; since you have not warned him, he shall die in his sin, and his righteous deeds which he has done shall not be remembered; but his blood I will require at your hand. However, if you have warned the righteous man that the righteous should not sin and he does

not sin, he shall surely live because he took warning; and you have delivered yourself."

Ezekiel 3:16–21 NASB

The stakes are high! As watchmen, we must keep to our stations and respond when we hear God speak. If we do not, we could be liable for the consequences. But if we take our position on the wall with insight that is coupled with intercession, then we can surround our cities with prayer and turn back the forces of darkness.

Without progressive purification in our lives, we will falter at critical moments. Before they could take up their assignments in the court, Daniel and his companions had to go through an extended time of preparation and purification (see Daniel 1:8–21). So did Esther (see Esther 2:8–16). You and I do not need to be groomed physically in the same way or trained in matters of a king's court, but Daniel's and Esther's experiences should serve as good reminders to us. Without that time of preparation, they almost certainly would have stumbled when they had to stand strong between opposing forces. In fact, neither of them would have lasted long enough in the king's palace to be used by God. Purification was not the only thing they needed, but it was important.

In his book *Interceding Against the Powers of Darkness*, Arizona pastor and author Terry Crist wrote, "If you are going to gather people for battle, you must free them from their captivity. . . . You can't possess the land *without* until you possess the land *within*."[1]

In order to be watchmen and spiritual warriors, you and I must "pay the price to separate ourselves through purification."[2] We need to be purified with the fire of the Holy Spirit and then washed with the water of the Word (the Bible and the truth within its pages). This is not optional for any Christian, but it is imperative for anyone who expects to stand firm as a watchman. (See Luke 3:16; Ephesians 5:26; Titus 2:14; 3:5.)

In the Old Testament, we read about something that is sometimes called the *law of battle* or the *law of purification*. To make everything ready for a battle, everything had to go through a preparation process. This also represents the process that each of us must go through spiritually, emotionally and mentally:

> Then Eleazar the priest said to the men of war who had gone to the battle, "This is the ordinance of the law which the LORD commanded Moses: Only the gold, the silver, the bronze, the iron, the tin, and the lead, everything that can endure fire, you shall put through the fire, and it shall be clean; and it shall be purified with the water of purification. But all that cannot endure fire you shall put through water. And you shall wash your clothes on the seventh day and be clean, and afterward you may come into the camp."
>
> Numbers 31:21–24 NKJV

This purification process is imperative, as we must allow no common ground between us and our adversary. Here is some more wisdom from Crist:

> The reason Jesus was so effective in spiritual warfare . . . why He was able to confront the devil so effectively . . . in the wilderness encounter [was because] Jesus recognized the law of purification. The reason Jesus could stand in such power and authority and deal so effectively with the wicked oppressor of the nations was because no common ground existed between Him and His adversary. When the devil struck at Jesus, there was nothing whatsoever in Him to receive the "hit." When Satan examined Him, there was nothing for him to find. Jesus and Satan had no relationship one to another, no common ground. There was nothing in Jesus' life that had agreement with the works of darkness! One reason so many ministers and intercessors have been spiritually "hit" by the fiery darts

of the enemy is because they have not responded to the law of purification.[3]

This makes perfect sense. Jesus at one time spoke at length with His disciples and then curtailed the session, saying, "I will no longer talk much with you, for the ruler of this world is coming, and he has nothing in Me" (John 14:30 NKJV). In the same way, a watchman, as one in the first lines of both defense and offense for the Bride of Christ (the Church), must allow no common ground with the evil one. Each one of us must learn to detect our weak places, the potential backdoor entrances for Satan, and to address them effectively with the help of the Holy Spirit and the resources He sends our way.

Pick Your Style

What does it look like to be a watchman on spiritual guard duty? You tell me. I have taken so many different approaches to watching that no one way stands out. I have watched during the dark of the night and at high noon. I have watched in airports and on long train rides. I have watched by myself and alongside other watchman-intercessors. Sometimes I pray or sing aloud when I watch; other times, I am silent. At times, I just close my eyes and groan or sigh (see Romans 8:26). I have committed myself to daily or weekly watch times, but I seem to do best with the spontaneous ones, when the Spirit of God wakes me from sleep or grabs my attention in some way and I am catapulted into an assignment.

I know people who pray every single day at a certain time and who have not missed a day yet. (Many of them belong to organizations dedicated to intercessory prayer, and they have signed up to pray at certain hours or on particular days, often so that somebody will be praying every hour of the day.) The International House of Prayer in Kansas City, Missouri, never closes its doors, their teams of watchmen and women having committed themselves to "harp and bowl" prayer around the clock and calendar.

Talk about dutiful! Some very ordinary-looking people are really epic watchman-intercessors on the inside. They are capable of pushing through marathon prayer sessions without breaking a sweat. Their greatest ambition in life is to go deeper in prayer. They do not mind if they are "nobodies," if only they can fulfill their calling to prayer. With the psalmist, they can say, "Better is one day in your courts than a thousand elsewhere; I would rather be a doorkeeper in the house of my God than dwell in the tents of the wicked" (Psalm 84:10).

Each watchman is one of a kind, which means that as a watchman, you do not have some ideal to live up to—except the ideals of duty and consecration to the service of God. And the longer a watchman serves the Lord in watchful prayer, the more he or she grows in quiet confidence, because of His deep love: "Such love has no fear, because perfect love expels all fear. If we are afraid, it is for fear of punishment, and this shows that we have not fully experienced his perfect love" (1 John 4:18 NLT).

Confident in God, who always comes through, watchmen increase in their discernment as the years go by. They can detect the still, small voice of the Lord more easily, and their spirits are obediently nimble, capable of shifting to a new line of prayer without skipping a beat.

Spiritual watch duty is unique in this way: The watchman is listening more for the voice of God than for the sounds of intruders. God will tip him off if trouble is coming. He will speak words of wisdom and strategy to his watchful heart. The watchman is never on his own, even when he appears to be all by himself in a place. He keeps the eyes of his heart fixed on the Lord at all times:

> To You I lift up my eyes, O You who are enthroned in the heavens! Behold, as the eyes of servants look to the hand of their master, as the eyes of a maid to the hand of her mistress, so our eyes look to the LORD our God, until He is gracious to us.
>
> Psalm 123:1–2 NASB

Esther: A Responsive Watchman

I love to read the book of Esther because the story line is so gripping. I never get tired of seeing how, through Esther's obedience and courage, the evil Haman was deposed and the Jews were preserved from annihilation. Esther's story inspires me. A nobody becomes a somebody, and that somebody changes history!

Esther was a beautiful young woman who had been orphaned as a girl and had been raised by her cousin and guardian, Mordecai. In Persian culture, the king had the right to conscript young virgins as potential members of his harem, and Esther, without revealing that she was Jewish, was compliant when summoned.

There in the king's court, she allowed herself to be groomed for her new duties. She maintained a dual consecration: to the royal household, as well as to her people of origin. She continued to listen to the advice of her cousin Mordecai, whom she trusted.

You will remember the wonderful story—how Mordecai discovered Haman's plot against the Jews and how Esther put her life on the line and, with great tact and deliberation, interceded successfully for the preservation of the Jews and the downfall of Haman.

Early on in the story, Esther declared a three-day fast:

> Then Esther told them to reply to Mordecai, "Go, assemble all the Jews who are found in Susa, and fast for me; do not eat or drink for three days, night or day. I and my maidens also will fast in the same way. And thus I will go in to the king, which is

> not according to the law; and if I perish, I perish." So Mordecai went away and did just as Esther had commanded him.
>
> Esther 4:15–17 NASB

Esther declared the fast in a desperate effort to stave off an enemy attack. To this day, people undertake three-day "Esther fasts," especially at the time of Purim, which is the Jewish feast that commemorates Esther's story of deliverance. In undertaking an Esther fast, we, too, are beseeching God, asking that the glory of the Lord protect us from the evil one. We remember the words of Isaiah: "Then your light will break forth like the dawn, and your healing will quickly appear; then your righteousness will go before you, and the glory of the LORD will be your rear guard" (Isaiah 58:8).

Esther, counseled well by Mordecai, was able to intervene through her fasting, prayer and courageous action. She had been positioned as the person taking the lead, yet her effectiveness would have been blunted or thwarted if she had failed to cooperate with Mordecai, who held the position of spiritual authority in her life.

Just as Esther found herself in a position "for such as time as this," so today may the worldwide Bride of Christ be situated to rise up in her full magnificence to withstand the assault of evil. The Church is like a spiritual Esther, praying and fasting and seeking God's favor and protection and for the overthrow of evil in our day.

Although God is never mentioned in the book of Esther, He is there. Esther's God is the same as ours, and we have been grafted in as part of God's chosen people, the Jews (see Romans 11:17). You and I may not be as good-looking as Queen Esther, and we may not be part of a powerful household, but our God oversees the events of our lives, just as He did hers. We read the same psalm that Esther's people did: "In Your book were all written the days that were ordained for me, when as yet there was not one of them" (Psalm 139:16 NASB).

Thus, we can expect that, if we only follow Him faithfully and consistently, the Lord will deliver us from disaster and then choose us to help usher in His kingdom in the days ahead. He says to each one of us:

> "But you, Israel, My servant, Jacob whom I have chosen, descendant of Abraham My friend, you whom I have taken from the ends of the earth, and called from its remotest parts and said to you, 'You are My servant, I have chosen you and not rejected you. Do not fear, for I am with you; do not anxiously look about you, for I am your God. I will strengthen you, surely I will help you, surely I will uphold you with My righteous right hand.' Behold, all those who are angered at you will be shamed and dishonored; those who contend with you will be as nothing and will perish."
>
> Isaiah 41:8–11 NASB

And, in turn, each of us replies in prayer.

PRAYER

Hear my prayer, O Lord! And let my cry for help come to You. Do not hide Your face from me in the day of my distress; incline Your ear to me; in the day when I call, answer me quickly. You will arise and have compassion on Zion, for it is time to be gracious to her, for the appointed time has come. Save us, O Lord our God, and gather us from among the nations to give thanks to Your holy name and glory in Your praise. Forever amen![4]

DAY 19

BECOMING A GUARDIAN IN PRAYER

1. In what regard would you consider yourself to be dutiful? (Have you thought about it much?) Describe some ways in which fulfilling your ordinary responsibilities has fed into your prayer life. In what ways do you see a need for improvement in both your faithfulness (your dependability and follow-through) and faith-full-ness (your level of confidence in God)?
2. How is the Bride of Christ (the Church) like Queen Esther, in terms of intercessory prayer? What is your individual part in the corporate intercession of the Bride? How could the effectiveness of your role be enhanced?
3. Can you define some specific way in which you have been positioned within your circumstances and as a watchman-intercessor "for such a time as this," for the sake of others?
4. Holding in your heart a particular need that God has laid there, intercede for it with confidence by modifying the spirit of what Jeremiah 31:15–17 says.

READING FOR DAY 20

Praying for Authorities

> I urge that entreaties and prayers, petitions and thanksgivings, be made on behalf of all men, for kings and all who are in authority, so that we may lead a tranquil and quiet life in all godliness and dignity. This is good and acceptable in the sight of God our Savior, who desires all men to be saved and to come to the knowledge of the truth.
>
> 1 Timothy 2:1–4 NASB

Daniel shows the way for us when it comes to praying for governmental authorities; he is our finest model. He did not want to leave Jerusalem, but once he was exiled and found himself in the court of the king of Babylon, he dedicated himself to bringing the rule of God into that pagan place. He did it by dint of his stellar character and by incessant prayer. He was a true watchman on the wall.

Daniel invested himself in both the success of the king under whom he had been forced to serve and the restoration of his people in Jerusalem, disregarding potential misunderstandings and serious repercussions (such as death!). When he had come to understand the prophecies about the return of God's people to their homeland, he intensified his efforts, fasting and praying and repenting on others' behalf. He did not relax his guard or rest on the assumption that God would simply act to fulfill those prophetic promises, but he prayed all the more, helping to bring them to fulfillment.

By God's grace, Daniel had the necessary wisdom to navigate tricky political shoals. Over the years, the king and other ruling authorities came and went, and many of them were less than friendly toward him. All of them were pagans whose values did not match his in the least.

Does this sound a little bit familiar? You and I have not been banished to a foreign land for life, but the leaders and political climate in our nation seems to go from bad to worse—and as God-fearing citizens, we do not know what to do.

Or do we?

Our Prayers Are Required

In the opening passage I quoted above, Paul urged Timothy to pray even for evil authorities. He told Timothy to pray *for* them, in fact, not against them, and to pray with two goals in mind: (1) "so that we may lead a tranquil and quiet life in all godliness and dignity," and (2) so that everyone (both leaders and ordinary citizens) could be "saved and to come to the knowledge of the truth."

We can find other Scriptures that support this idea. See, for example:

> Honor all people. Love the brotherhood. Fear God. Honor the king.
>
> 1 Peter 2:17 NKJV

Fear the LORD and the king, my son, and do not join with the rebellious officials, for those two will send sudden destruction upon them, and who knows what calamities they can bring?

Proverbs 24:21–22

When the righteous are in authority, the people rejoice; but when a wicked man rules, the people groan.

Proverbs 29:2 NKJV

Everyone must submit to governing authorities. For all authority comes from God, and those in positions of authority have been placed there by God. So anyone who rebels against authority is rebelling against what God has instituted, and they will be punished. For the authorities do not strike fear in people who are doing right, but in those who are doing wrong. Would you like to live without fear of the authorities? Do what is right, and they will honor you. The authorities are God's servants, sent for your good. But if you are doing wrong, of course you should be afraid, for they have the power to punish you. They are God's servants, sent for the very purpose of punishing those who do what is wrong. So you must submit to them, not only to avoid punishment, but also to keep a clear conscience.

Pay your taxes, too, for these same reasons. For government workers need to be paid. They are serving God in what they do. Give to everyone what you owe them: Pay your taxes and government fees to those who collect them, and give respect and honor to those who are in authority.

Romans 13:1–7 NLT

Besides following the laws and living lives that are above reproach, one of the ways we can honor those in authority is by praying for them. Very few citizens do this, which makes our prayers all the more important.

Our Prayers Make a Difference

I write as a citizen of the United States, and that fact establishes my reference point. But I think also of Daniel's Babylon and the situation of God's watchmen in many other cities and nations throughout history.

Around me, the mood of the nation is both angry and resigned. Nobody is happy with the direction things are going. Hopeful developments surface from time to time, only to crash into obstruction and disappointment.

This is not only on the national level, of course. From every direction, the news is negative, whether it has to do with local municipalities or relations between world leaders. We see nothing but accusations, false promises, deteriorating ethics, exasperation and weariness. Most challenging of all, the sinful human condition is on full display 24/7, thanks to instant broadcasts.

How on earth can a single watchman—or even a group of them—intercede effectively for such a mess? (As a prophetic intercessor, part of my job involves calling forth hopeful solutions to problems. As prayer guardians, we are to bless our leaders and not to give in to critical accusations.)

South African pastor Andrew Murray grappled with this question. He was pastoring and writing during times of upheaval, and he recognized that Paul was writing to Timothy during a similar time. In those days, the Roman government ruled the world with an iron fist. Christians were universally despised by both the secular and the religious rulers. The situation was every bit as urgent as it is today, and yet Paul's primary advice was not about organizing a riot or a boycott or a coup. Rather, it was simply, "Pray!"

Murray read Paul's words to Timothy and then wrote:

> What a faith in the power of prayer! A few feeble and despised Christians are to influence the mighty Roman emperors, and help

> in securing peace and quietness. Let us believe that prayer is a power that is taken up by God in His rule of the world. Let us pray for our country and its rulers; for all the rulers of the world; for rulers in cities or districts in which we are interested. When God's people unite in this, they may count upon their prayers effecting in the unseen world more than they know. Let faith hold this fast.[1]

Amazingly, our prayers make all the difference in how things turn out. According to Jack Hayford, they "determine whether God's goodness is released toward specific situations or whether the power of sin and Satan is permitted to prevail. Prayer is the determining factor."[2]

As with any other category of intercession, we can base our prayers on the words of Scripture when we pray for those in authority over us. Dick Eastman of Every Home for Christ drew my attention to the following passages that are "prayable" in this application:

> He has shown you, O man, what is good; and what does the LORD require of you but to do justly, to love mercy, and to walk humbly with your God?
>
> Micah 6:8 NKJV

> When a country is rebellious, it has many rulers, but a ruler with discernment and knowledge maintains order.
>
> Proverbs 28:2

> "Because of your raging against Me, and because your arrogance has come up to My ears, therefore I will put My hook in your nose, and My bridle in your lips, and I will turn you back by the way which you came."
>
> 2 Kings 19:28 NASB

We can pray that leaders will govern honestly, humbly and with mercy. We can pray for them to have knowledge and understanding—which is more than mere information; it includes a grasp of history and roles and cultures and God's will. Today's tyrants are as real as the Roman Nero. Pray that God will deal with them swiftly, for the sake of His people. Pray that He will hedge in such dangerous leaders with limits and boundaries.

Our Prayers Are Personal

As Americans, each of us should take it upon ourselves to pray, preferably by name, on a regular basis for the sixteen people who, in our personal sphere, have the most influence in the United States government: the president; the nine justices of the Supreme Court; our state's two senators; the congressman or woman from our district; and our state governor, state senator and state representative. (If you are not an American, simply apply these principles within your own country's government.)

We can also single out others in various levels of government, even the "authorities" and "governments" within our homes, schools, churches or workplaces. Jeremiah wrote, "This is what the Lord of Heaven's Armies, the God of Israel, says. . . . 'Work for the peace and prosperity of the city where I sent you into exile. Pray to the Lord for it, for its welfare will determine your welfare'" (Jeremiah 29:4, 7 NLT). Did you catch that? Your welfare depends upon the decisions of those who are in direct authority over you. For a season, you may decide to pray for school officials by name or for your managers and their managers at work. Do not limit yourself to "bless me" prayers. Reach out to bless *them,* even if you disagree with their policies and chafe under their decisions.

You can turn your attention to spiritual leaders, as well, praying for everyone from your local pastor and church staff members to regional leaders, national leaders and overseers of various aspects of Church life.

In addition, you can consider business leaders, who are the equivalent of the Middle Eastern elders sitting at the gates. Why should you pray for them, in particular? What special influence do they have? Here is how I described it in my book *Prayer Storm:*

> In ancient Middle Eastern cities . . . a city would have more than one gate, and they were connected by broad walls (which you could compare to the "walls of salvation"). At least three offices would be represented or contained at the gateways of a city: commercial, judicial, and prophetic. Actual real estate transactions were handled at the gateway; deeds were transferred, signatures were collected. Court cases and judicial hearings were held right in the gate, and decisions would be announced right there. In addition, prophetic words, the word of the Lord, would be delivered to the priests in the gate (see Prov. 1:21; Jer. 17:19–20; 26:10–13). So there at the gate, a person would find commerce moving, the justice system operating, and spiritual dynamics taking place.[3]

You can also concentrate your prayers on the process by which leaders are selected in a particular sphere. Some are elected, of course, and your prayers could be important to the outcome of an election. Most, however, are hired or appointed. Some graduate into their positions over time. Regardless of how they get there, you can pray that the wisest and best-equipped people be designated for each assignment. You can base your prayers on Moses' advice to tribal leaders, in which he addressed them as follows:

> "At that time I told you, . . . 'Choose some well-respected men from each tribe who are known for their wisdom and understanding, and I will appoint them as your leaders.'

> "Then you responded, 'Your plan is a good one.' So I took the wise and respected men you had selected from your tribes and appointed them to serve as judges and officials over you."
>
> Deuteronomy 1:9, 13–15 NLT

Our Prayers Are Sacrificial

When Daniel prayed for the people of Israel to be able to return to their land from exile, he took it upon himself to repent for their sins—sins he had not committed himself. He identified himself so completely with the Jewish people that he, as a forerunner to Jesus, took their sins upon himself. Laying aside his own rights and privileges and all self-justification, he prayed with heartfelt humility, confessing their sin as his own and pleading with God for mercy for His own name's sake (see Daniel 9:4–19).

This kind of identification in intercession is something any watchman-intercessor can do when the circumstances call for it (as they may well do in a tangled governmental situation). The people you are praying for are trapped in the bondage of their sin. They are not likely to repent anytime soon. But an earnest intercessor can cry out on their behalf, asking God to hear and to have mercy. This kind of praying puts the intercessor directly into the shoes of the person being prayed for.

Moses used his authority as the overall leader of the people of Israel to plead for their lives. He was willing to lay down his own life, if necessary. Praying, he put himself on the line: "But now, if You will, forgive their sin—and if not, please blot me out from Your book which You have written!" (Exodus 32:32 NASB).

Paul felt the same way:

> With Christ as my witness, I speak with utter truthfulness. My conscience and the Holy Spirit confirm it. My heart is filled with bitter sorrow and unending grief for my people, my Jewish

> brothers and sisters. I would be willing to be forever cursed—cut off from Christ!—if that would save them.
>
> Romans 9:1–3 NLT

None of these men prayed the proud prayer of the Pharisee: "God, I thank You that I am not like all other men" (see Luke 18:11). On the contrary, in contrition and humility, they identified themselves totally with the failures of their people.

Throughout the Bible, we see that God exalts rulers and people in authority if they exercise righteous authority. (See, for example, Proverbs 14:34 and Proverbs 29:14.) Righteousness being in short supply, though, the only people who can "stand in the gap" for their leaders are the people of prayer. This means that one of the first ways we should pray for an authority figure is for him or her to become righteous. We can pray for every aspect of righteousness—wisdom, justice, compassion—to manifest itself in the life of that person.

Often I pray that the person I am praying for will "have God's heart." I pray for authority figures by name when I can, and I choose verses from the Bible that can be turned into good prayers. For example, based on 2 Chronicles 7:14, I pray, *Lord, make it possible for [name of leader] to humble himself and turn to You. May he become truly righteous, for the sake of [the area of the leader's oversight]*. I have prayed, based on Proverbs 29:14, Psalm 25:21, and 2 Corinthians 1:3–4, *Father, help [a local judge] to make rulings on behalf of the poor with truth and integrity and compassion.*

By myself, I cannot pray as fruitfully for authority figures as I can if I link arms with fellow watchmen. For this reason, I have affiliated myself and my sphere of ministry with a select number of groups of watchman-intercessors who are dedicated to specific causes. With this in mind, I also founded Prayer Storm (www.prayerstorm.com) to carry to a higher level several of the main prayer concerns of my heart.

Our God is not small, and He hears the cries of the needy (see Psalm 69:33). Remember, He sits on the throne, and He is not wringing His hands in worry. No, He invites us to come sit on the throne with Him and extend His Kingdom rule on earth as it is in heaven.

Our Prayers Are Active

As you pray for people in authority, pray also for those who will be choosing them for those positions. Pray that all involved will abide by biblical principles, which will lead to discernment and wisdom and integrity, and pray that God will bless voters and all authority figures as they navigate the steps toward the selection of new leaders. Let biblical terms and principles inform your prayers, and always remember that much of our governmental system was established by godly people according to biblical principles; therefore, you can pray for a renewal of those principles.

Also, remember that your participation in the voting process adds to your prayers in a very real way when you are praying for elected officials. Casting your vote is the equivalent of "works" to match your faith, and faith without works is dead (see James 2:17). In other words, as vital as your intercession may be, it cannot stand alone.

Looking back again to Daniel's example, we see that, although he was a slave and not part of a democracy, his righteous actions combined with his prayers made all the difference in bringing about the will of God for both Babylon and Jerusalem. He walked in his distinct anointing as a representative of God's people, and so can we.

Our roles will always be varied; no one person can pray for everything. But each one of us should take the commands of Scripture seriously, asking God to help us find our particular prayer assignment for the ruling authorities who are over us—without feeling guilty about those we do not pray for.

Beth Alves shared an experience that taught her about this:

> I agreed to accompany a friend who was part of a women's group that gathered daily to pray on Capitol Hill. These tenacious intercessors battled on their spiritual knees for the various bills brought to the floor.
>
> Intercession was prompted by the announcement that a particular bill was coming up for a vote. The women would then pray for the various lawmakers, reminding the Lord how each lawmaker had voted previously and petitioning Him to align their hearts with heaven's righteousness. They cried out for the scales to be removed from bureaucratically blind eyes and rambled on and on about details of the bill until they sensed that the bill and the man had melded together in God's will. The more they prayed, the more my conscience rebuffed me; I was overwhelmed with guilt. I still remember thinking, *This country is going down the drain and it's all my fault! I don't understand a thing they're talking about—and even worse, I don't care. This is like a foreign language that I have no desire to learn. . . .*
>
> I left for home cloaked in feelings of condemnation. When I finally met with the heavenly Father alone, I asked, "Lord, what am I going to do?"
>
> His answer jolted me: "Stick within the sphere of your anointing! . . . Your job is to lift up the hands of the leaders of the nations as I place them on your heart."[4]

When the Lord wants you as a watchman to carry a burden in prayer, He will place the burden on your heart. Do you feel burdened to pray for the seasonal election process? Please pick up that assignment. Do you find your attention drawn to one particular advisor or assistant to a major leader? By all means, pray for that individual. With each of us carrying our portion of the load, together we will make good progress. In Jesus, we make a great team.

Derek Prince: History-Changing Watchman

Over the course of his eventful life, Derek Prince, who died in 2003 at the age of 88, went from being an atheist philosopher at Cambridge to a prolific Bible teacher who traveled the world. Married and widowed twice, he left behind eleven adopted children. Among his numerous audio and video teachings and more than 50 books is *Shaping History through Prayer and Fasting*, which remains a best-selling title for Intercessors for America (IFA), the government-focused prayer group he helped found in 1973.

Derek was convinced that prayers could shape history and that often their influence was best exercised on the governmental level. Here is a quote from *Shaping History through Prayer and Fasting* that sums up his viewpoint:

> In 2 Chronicles God stated the conditions that His people must fulfill for the healing of their land:
>
> If my people, which are called by my name, shall humble themselves, and pray, and seek my face, and turn from their wicked ways; then will I hear from heaven, and will forgive their sin, and will heal their land.
>
> 2 Chronicles 7:14
>
> . . . The prophecies and promises of God's Word . . . are intended to provoke us to pray with increased earnestness and understanding. God reveals to us the purposes which He is working out, not that we may be passive spectators on the sidelines of history, but that we may personally identify ourselves with His purposes, and thus become actively involved in their fulfillment. Revelation demands involvement.[5]

One of Derek's most ardent prayers for leaders in military and political situations was simple and to the point: "Lord, give us leaders such that it will be for your glory to give us victory through them."[6]

Derek felt the Lord's call to Ezekiel to be a watchman (see Ezekiel 33:7–9) applied to him personally. He knew he must warn of danger and pray for God's mercy on leaders who were disobedient to God, in particular where the nation of Israel was concerned. The year before he died, he published an article that, in effect, warned those who would follow him as a watchman to pay attention to the Word of the Lord concerning the times in which they lived.[7]

In my Christian pilgrimage, the teachings of Derek Prince have made more of an impact on my life, worldwide outreach and prayer ministry than any other spiritual leader. From him, I learned about God's heart for Israel, how to pray for people in authority, the gifts of the Holy Spirit, deliverance from demonic darkness, the power of prayer and fasting and so much more. I can state without hesitation that this man was an effective, history-changing and history-making watchman.

May the watchmen who have picked up his discarded mantle be as faithful and unfaltering in their prayers as he was!

PRAYER

Father, in accordance with Your Word, I pray for kings and those who are in authority over me and around me. I pray that You will raise up godly counsel around decision-makers and policy-makers and that godly voices will prevail over irreligious advisors. I pray for the safety and well-being of the president of the United States and the other decision-makers who are even today making pivotal choices that will determine the future of many people in my nation, state and city.

I take the news headlines in hand and pray as Your Spirit leads me. I pray that You will reverse the social and political trends that deify man instead of God. I pray that people of influence will learn to rely upon You as their Source of daily strength and that dignity and honor would be released wherever Your name is named.

I pray also for spiritual leaders, that You would guard their ways and lead them into more love, faith and joy.

I bless every leader I can name and every face that crosses my mind's eye. In Jesus' holy name, Amen.

DAY 20

BECOMING A GUARDIAN IN PRAYER

1. Have you ever felt called to pray for someone who is in a role of authority? Has this kind of intercession become a pattern in your life, or has it been occasional only? In your prayer life, how have you applied Paul's words to Timothy (see 1 Timothy 2:1–4)?
2. Where have you been positioned in authority? Think about who is in authority over you and who is under your authority. Then consider how this should affect your prayers.
3. If you feel called to intercede as a watchman for a particular individual in authority, an officeholder or a governmental process, you may want to join your prayer efforts with those of others who are like-minded. Look online to find groups of intercessors who specialize in governmental affairs, and see if you can partner with them.

4. Based on the ideas presented in this reading, try out some new ways of praying for those who are in authority, persisting in your prayers long enough to be able to see and evaluate the results. What might be some measurable results to look for?

READING FOR DAY 21

The Praying Church

> When they had entered the city, they went up to the upper room where they were staying; that is, Peter and John and James and Andrew, Philip and Thomas, Bartholomew and Matthew, James the son of Alphaeus, and Simon the Zealot, and Judas the son of James. These all with one mind were continually devoting themselves to prayer, along with the women, and Mary the mother of Jesus, and with His brothers.
>
> Acts 1:13–14 NASB

The members of the early Church prayed—and they prayed together. Praying together was their default setting. They made it their practice from the beginning. Right after Jesus ascended to heaven from the Mount of Olives, the group of disciples walked down the mountain together, and together they headed back through the gate and into the city of Jerusalem, straight to the upstairs room where they had been staying for weeks. There, Luke reports, "all with one mind," they "were continually devoting themselves to prayer."

One translation states that they were "together together." I love that phrase. They were in one place, but they were also one in heart. That is what it takes.

The prayer gathering of these new Jesus-followers lasted until the Day of Pentecost, when the Holy Spirit fell on all of them (see Acts 2). But that was only their first prayer meeting. It set a precedent for a pattern of praying like the one they had observed in the life of their Master.

After Pentecost, the Church's growth exploded. And they continued to pray every time something came up that affected their welfare or unity—which happened often. The ever-larger group of believers did not settle for holding a once-a-week, hour-long prayer meeting. They packed out their small houses, praying all day and all night if necessary, putting aside everything else.

Watchmen on Duty

They were praying, for instance, the night Peter was released from prison.

At that time, the honeymoon was over for the Jerusalem church. Persecution had started—serious persecution, even to the death. The church must have had to gather to pray every single day of the week. And these were not leaders-only prayer meetings or clusters of widows and others who had no prior obligations. Everyone piled into the house, even children and servants, and their times of prayer were open-ended. They did not stop praying until they got the answers they needed.

And as soon as one prayer got answered, another major need would come up. One day John's brother James was killed by the authorities, and then Peter was arrested:

> After arresting him, [King Herod] put [Peter] in prison, handing him over to be guarded by four squads of four soldiers

> each. Herod intended to bring him out for public trial after the Passover.
>
> So Peter was kept in prison, but the church was earnestly praying to God for him.
>
> Acts 12:4–5

While the church was praying, Peter endured long days and nights of mistreatment. The night before he was supposed to appear before Herod for sentencing, he was sleeping in the pitch blackness between two guards with his hands chained together. Suddenly a light shone in the dark cell, but everyone was dead to the world. Peter was jolted awake only when somebody kicked or punched him in the ribs. An angel? He thought he was dreaming or having a vision:

> [The angel] struck Peter on the side and woke him up. "Quick, get up!" he said, and the chains fell off Peter's wrists.
>
> Then the angel said to him, "Put on your clothes and sandals." And Peter did so. "Wrap your cloak around you and follow me," the angel told him. Peter followed him out of the prison, but he had no idea that what the angel was doing was really happening; he thought he was seeing a vision. They passed the first and second guards and came to the iron gate leading to the city. It opened for them by itself, and they went through it. When they had walked the length of one street, suddenly the angel left him.
>
> Then Peter came to himself and said, "Now I know without a doubt that the Lord has sent his angel and rescued me from Herod's clutches and from everything the Jewish people were hoping would happen."
>
> When this had dawned on him, he went to the house of Mary the mother of John, also called Mark, where many people had gathered and were praying.
>
> Acts 12:7–12

As much as I love reading about how the angel sprang Peter loose from his captivity, I love this next part more. Peter must have known he would find his fellow believers praying together if he went to that particular house. But the people who had been praying fervently for his release could not believe it when he showed up:

> Peter knocked at the outer entrance, and a servant named Rhoda came to answer the door. When she recognized Peter's voice, she was so overjoyed she ran back without opening it and exclaimed, "Peter is at the door!"
>
> "You're out of your mind," they told her. When she kept insisting that it was so, they said, "It must be his angel."
>
> But Peter kept on knocking, and when they opened the door and saw him, they were astonished. Peter motioned with his hand for them to be quiet and described how the Lord had brought him out of prison. "Tell James and the other brothers and sisters about this," he said, and then he left for another place.
>
> Acts 12:13–17

Peter lay low for a while, then resurfaced to preach and work more miracles in Jesus' name. As the church was subjected to further intimidation and their trials continued, the story was told and retold to encourage the faith of the beleaguered but joyful band of believers.

Unity in Community

I can think of plenty of obvious reasons why praying in a group of believers is more effective than praying on your own. But one fundamental reason may not come to mind because it is less obvious, and it is the fact that we are praying to a three-in-one God, a trinity of Persons—Father, Son and Holy Spirit—and one of the greatest desires of the Godhead is to bring the Church into that same unity.

Jesus prayed to the Father "that they may be one even as We are" (John 17:11 NASB). He was not merely expressing a hopeful sentiment when He said that. He wanted His disciples—all of them, including you and me—to experience every aspect of their new life in God, all the way up to the level of His unity with Father God.

One of Jesus' closest disciples, John, later pointed out that nobody can love God without also loving other people: "We love, because He first loved us. If someone says, 'I love God,' and hates his brother, he is a liar; for the one who does not love his brother whom he has seen, cannot love God whom he has not seen" (1 John 4:19–20 NASB). That could be a discouraging thought, if it were not for the fact that the Holy Spirit helps us do both. Our growth in love may proceed incrementally most of the time, but if we "keep [ourselves] in the love of God" (Jude 1:21 NASB), we will make progress.

One of the measures of our growth will be our relationships within the Church, especially where corporate prayer is concerned. Can we tolerate—even appreciate—a wide variety of personalities, levels of understanding and preferences? Do we look forward to joining with others in prayer? Are we slow to anger and quick to forgive? Is unity even on our radar? We have a test before us: How do we walk in relational community that results in relational agreement with one another and propels us into relational agreement with heaven's plan?

Where unity in community is concerned, we could not have a more loving and tireless Helper. Thank You, Holy Spirit! All things all possible with the Helper's help.

Ambassadors in Prayer

We in the Western Church have become complacent in our relatively safe environment, and our prayers reflect our individualized approach to God. Sometimes we consider corporate prayer to be a watered-down version of focused personal praying. To us, *praying together* may mean what happens after we fire off an electronic plea. "Please pray for so-and-so in the hospital!" "Prayers needed—important interview today." These urgent requests are followed by a handful of quick replies: "Praying!"

We must not think in such a limited way about prayer. It is absolutely vital to have a strong personal prayer life, and there is nothing wrong with asking for prayer on Facebook, but we need to know that our individual prayers are meant to feed into the vibrant prayer life of the whole Church.

Corporate intercession—especially corporate intercessory worship—is a microcosmic picture of the eternal worship that continually rises before the throne of God in heaven.

In other words, it is not just "me and Jesus." And that is a good thing.

When the Body of Christ prays together, worshiping and interceding in the same room at the same time, much heavenly authority and power gets released. So why on earth do we not get together more often to pray? Do we not know what we are missing?

Much of what we do when we pray together I call *ambassadorial intercession*, because together we are representing sinners before God and asking Him to forgive them. We are ambassadors for Christ, standing in the gap for individuals, generations and groups of people who will be lost unless we do this. We echo Jesus' words on the cross: "Father, forgive them, for they do not know what they do" (Luke 23:34 NKJV).

We need to help each other when we pray like this, especially when offenses have been committed corporately. Here is how I wrote about corporate intercession in my book *Prayer Storm*:

> A crisis, especially a crisis of national proportions, is too big for isolated intercessors to handle alone. At this hour of history, what

> we need most is corporate intercessory worship and gathered-together ambassadorial intercession. What does this entail? It requires humility to pray in a corporate way. Differences of style, doctrine, personality and culture make this paramount. Nobody is the star. People come together in order to blend their voices as one. Together as a body of believers, the *group* stands in the gap. The individual intercessors pool their insights and inspirations to declare back to God biblical prayers and promises, to repent on behalf of others, and to do whatever the situation requires of them.[1]

In my experience, worship music filled with an anointed, prophetic flow increases the culture of unity in the group. This provides a sustainable way for hundreds of people to experience the presence of God, out of which can come powerful forms of intercession.

Corporate intercessory worship arrests the destroyer (Satan) and releases the judgments of God while sweeping the people of God up into heavenly places, like this psalm depicts:

> Praise the LORD.
>
> Sing to the LORD a new song, his praise in the assembly of his faithful people.
>
> Let Israel rejoice in their Maker; let the people of Zion be glad in their King. Let them praise his name with dancing and make music to him with timbrel and harp. For the LORD takes delight in his people; he crowns the humble with victory. . . .
>
> May the praise of God be in their mouths and a double-edged sword in their hands, to inflict vengeance on the nations and punishment on the peoples, to bind their kings with fetters, their nobles with shackles of iron, to carry out the sentence written against them—this is the glory of all his faithful people.
>
> Praise the LORD.
>
> Psalm 149:1–4, 6–9

This kind of praying does not bounce off the ceiling. Without a doubt, such prayers rise all the way to the throne of God in heaven. In John's great revelation, the prayers of the saints took visible form in God's throne room: "The smoke of the incense, mixed with *the prayers of God's holy people*, ascended up to God from the altar where the angel had poured them out" (Revelation 8:4 NLT, emphasis added).

The Bride's Watch

Jesus referred to Himself as a bridegroom (see Matthew 9:15; 22:2; 25:1). Who is His bride? The Church. Are you on board with this idea? It makes a difference in how you see yourself in prayer—as part of a Body that is being prepared as a Bride.

All of heaven knows that He will return to fetch His Bride in response to her (corporate) prayers and heartfelt pleas (see Revelation 22:17). One day, the Bride will rule the earth with her Bridegroom (see Revelation 3:21; 5:10). In the meantime, the Bride is watching and waiting for her Beloved.

While not lapsing into sensuality or romanticism, the language that best expresses the maturing relationship between the Bride and her Beloved, Jesus, must include words such as *intimacy*, *love*, *pleasure*, *delight*, *wholehearted*, *abandonment*, *affection* and *partnership*. It includes evocative words like *cherish* and *jealous*, too.[2] You can indulge in too much rich food or waste your time pursuing a particular activity, but there is no such thing as an excess of bridal love between Jesus and the Church who loves Him. The Bride longs for the day of her wedding, with all that it means for the rest of her life. The Bride watches—and prepares herself in hope and joyful anticipation. (See Matthew 25:1–13.)

In every generation, Jesus assures His Church, "I am coming quickly." The Bride cannot help but exclaim, "Come, Lord Jesus, come!" (See Revelation 22:20.) That is the best prayer of all.

How I love bridal intercession! I love entering into spiritual warfare in the company of others in the Body of Christ, enforcing the victory of Calvary by means of the power of corporate praise and anointed decrees when that is what is called for. Yes, the Bride wears army boots! Praise the Lord!

You: A Watchman in Training

In each of the previous twenty readings in this book, I have given you a brief vignette of someone whose life illustrates the message of the chapter. I tried to divide them evenly between biblical characters, such as Abraham and Anna; modern-day members of the Church, such as Beth Alves and Dick Simmons; and admirable Christians of the past who have gone on to their heavenly reward, such as Rees Howells and E. M. Bounds.

Now it is your turn to put yourself into the book. I choose you. You qualify because you are a saint—not some holier-than-thou individual who has reached perfection, but a member of Christ's Body on earth. You are part of His Bride, the Church. Although Jesus has redeemed the Church by His blood that was shed on the cross over two thousand years ago, He is still preparing His Bride for her wedding day. Soon enough, it will come—especially if you join your voice with others in the prayer of the ages, saying, "Come, Lord Jesus!" (Revelation 22:20).

Amen, and amen. May He come on our watch!

PRAYER

Lord God, I stand in prayer before You as one who is a member of Your Body on the earth today. I pray that our love may increase and overflow for each other and for everyone else and that You will strengthen our hearts so we can come into Your presence blameless and holy, both now and when the Lord Jesus comes with all His holy ones. May our prayers multiply forever, rising like fragrant incense before Your throne. We can enter Your throne room with confidence because of Your Son. Amen.[3]

DAY 21

BECOMING A GUARDIAN IN PRAYER

1. When did you first learn about the Bridegroom and the Bride of Christ? How has your understanding of this paradigm changed over time? Today, how do you see yourself as part of the Bride of Christ?
2. What kind of praying should characterize what I have called "the Bride's watch"?
3. In this chapter, I said, "Corporate intercessory worship is a microcosmic picture of the eternal worship that continually rises before the throne of God in heaven." How would you describe what I meant by that?
4. Now it is your turn to watch. Put down this book, grab your Bible and start praying. Better still, get together with some others and start worshiping, interceding and declaring, "The enemies of God have no standing here. Satan, stop interfering with the plan of God. Not on our watch! Jesus is in the house, and He is the Lord here!"

Notes

Chapter 1: Abraham: Confident Friendship with God

1. James W. Goll, *The Prophetic Intercessor: Releasing God's Purposes to Change Lives and Influence Nations*, rev. ed. (Grand Rapids, Mich.: Chosen, 2007), 27.

Chapter 2: Remind God of His Word

1. Andrew Murray, *With Christ in the School of Prayer* (New Kensington, Pa.: Whitaker House, 1981), 161–63, 166.

2. *Strong's* #6293. *Paga* is the word used in Job 36:32, which reads, "He covers His hands with lightning, and commands it to strike" (NKJV).

3. The Men for Nations prayer guide can be found online at pray.mtopgroup .com.

4. James W. Goll, *The Lost Art of Intercession*, rev. ed. (Shippensburg, Pa.: Destiny Image, 2016), 150–51.

5. This prayer is based on Ephesians 1:16–21.

Chapter 3: An Orchestra of Prayer

1. Illustration taken from Moody Global Ministries, *Today in the Word*, June 22, 1992.

2. Andrew Murray, *The Ministry of Intercessory Prayer: A Classic Devotional Edited for Today's Reader* (Minneapolis: Bethany House, 2003), 125; reprint of *The Ministry of Intercession* (1897).

Chapter 4: Nothing Happens without Prayer

1. You may have heard this story before, because I also shared it in *The Prophetic Intercessor.* I read it in R. E. Miller's book (now out of print) *Thy God*

Reigneth (Mar del Plata, Argentina: Argentine Bible Assemblies, n.d.), and I heard him tell it on a video.

Chapter 5: In Times of Crisis

1. Rees Howells, as quoted in Matt Lockett, "Rees Howells: How Prayers Played a Role in Ending Hitler's Reign of Death," Justice House of Prayer DC, accessed November 17, 2016, http://jhopdc.com/rees-howells-part-2/.

2. Ibid. Final quote taken from Norman Grubb, *Rees Howells, Intercessor* (Fort Washington, Pa.: CLC Publications, 1952), 283.

3. Rev. Yang Tuck Yoong, "The Redemption Story, Part 2: Chronicling Our Journey," The Bible College of Wales, accessed November 17, 2016, http://www.bcwales.org/prayer-and-revival/the-redemption-story/#Part-2.

Chapter 6: Live to Intercede

1. E. M. Bounds, *The Reality of Prayer,* repr. (Racine, Wisc.: Treasures Media, 2007), 29.

2. Wesley L. Duewel, *Mighty Prevailing Prayer* (Grand Rapids, Mich.: Zondervan, 1990), 221–22.

3. Bounds, *The Reality of Prayer*, 58.

4. Goll, *The Prophetic Intercessor*, 59.

5. This prayer is taken from the 27th lesson in Andrew Murray's book *With Christ in the School of Prayer*.

Chapter 7: Don't Give Up

1. E. M. Bounds, *The Necessity of Prayer* (1929; repr., n.p.: CreateSpace, 2014), chapter 6.

2. Ibid.

3. Claude Chilton Jr., foreword to Bounds, *The Necessity of Prayer*.

Chapter 8: Anna: Praying the Promises

1. James W. Goll, *Prophetic Intercession* (Grand Rapids, Mich.: Chosen, 2007), 143–44.

Chapter 9: The Watchman Fast

1. *Strong's* #6684.

2. Epiphanius of Salamis, *The Panarion, Books II and III, De Fide*, trans. Frank Williams, rev. ed., Nag Hammadi and Manichaean Studies 79, ed. Johannes van Oort and Einar Thomassen (Leiden, Netherlands: Brill, 2013), 509.

3. Lou Engle and I co-authored the book *The Call of the Elijah Revolution* (Shippensburg, Pa.: Treasure House, 2008).

4. I had the honor of serving as the chairman of TheCall Nashville on July 7, 2007. On that hot summer day, seventy thousand radical believers came together in Music City U.S.A. to exalt the name of the Lord.

5. Saint Basil the Great, "About Fasting," as quoted in *Christian Fasting: A Theological Approach*, trans. Kent D. Berghuis (Dallas: Biblical Studies Press, 2007), 188.

Chapter 10: Removing Obstacles

1. Dick Eastman, *No Easy Road: Discover the Extraordinary Power of Personal Prayer*, rev. ed. (Grand Rapids, Mich.: Chosen, 2003), 47.

2. This prayer is modified from the Anglican Book of Common Prayer, as quoted by Better Gatherings, "General Confessions," http://bettergatherings.com/index.php?option=com_content&view=article&id=101&Itemid=93.

Chapter 11: Waiting in Quietness

1. James W. Goll, *The Lost Art of Practicing His Presence* (Shippensburg, Pa.: Destiny Image, 2005), 103; first published in 2000 as *Wasted on Jesus: Reaching for the Lover of Your Soul.*

2. Augustine, *Confessions* 1.1.

3. Kieran Kavanaugh, O.C.D., and Otilio Rodriguez, O.C.D., trans., *The Collected Works of St. Teresa of Avila*, vol. 3 (Washington, D.C.: ICS Publications, 1985), 386.

4. This prayer is an adaptation of several prayers written by Saint Teresa of Ávila.

Chapter 12: Prayers of Heaven

1. Charles H. Spurgeon, *Spurgeon's Sermons on Prayer* (Peabody, Mass.: Hendrickson, 2007), 52.

2. Mike Bickle with Deborah Hiebert, *The Seven Longings of the Human Heart* (Kansas City, Mo.: Forerunner Books, 2006), 136–37, 144, 146.

Chapter 13: Absolute Trust

1. George Müller, *A Narrative of Some of the Lord's Dealing with George Müller, Written by Himself, Jehovah Magnified. Addresses by George Müller Complete and Unabridged*, 2 vols. (Muskegon, Mich.: Dust and Ashes, 2003), 2:291, as quoted in John Piper, *A Camaraderie of Confidence: The Fruit of Unfailing Faith in the Lives of Charles Spurgeon, George Müller, and Hudson Taylor* (Wheaton: Crossway, 2016), footnote 19 on pages 65–66.

2. George Müller, *The Life of Trust: Being a Narrative of the Lord's Dealings with George Müller*, ed. Herman Lincoln Wayland (Boston: Gould and Lincoln, 1868), 208–09.

Chapter 14: Called to Battle

1. *Strong's* #3794.

2. Dean Sherman, *Spiritual Warfare for Every Christian: How to Live in Victory and Retake the Land* (Seattle: YWAM Publishing, 1989), 52–53.

3. These categories have been modified from Elizabeth Alves, Tommi Femrite, and Karen Kaufman, *Intercessors: Discover Your Prayer Power* (Grand Rapids, Mich.: Chosen, 2000). Originally published by Regal Books.

4. C. Peter Wagner, introduction to the second edition of *Prayer Shield: How to Intercede for Pastors and Christian Leaders* (Minneapolis: Chosen, 2014), 8.

Chapter 16: Watching for Israel

1. A little-known Canadian minister named Clyde Williamson was inspired to initiate Esther fasts in 1983. He published a small book titled *The Esther Fast Mandate: A Call to End-Time Intercession for the Release, Return, Restoration and Revival of Israel and the Church* (Etobicoke, Ontario: Almond Publications, 1987). Since then, others, including me, picked it up and ran with it.

2. Tom Hess, *God's Abrahamic Covenants with Israel and the Church: Biblical Road Map of Reconciliation—Restoring the Altars, Foundations and Pillars on the Mountains of Israel* (Jerusalem: Progressive Vision International, 2004), n.p.

3. This prayer is an adaptation of Isaiah 62 NLT.

Chapter 17: The Watch of the Lord

1. James W. Goll, *Prayer Storm: The Hour That Changes the World* (Shippensburg, Pa.: Destiny Image, 2008), 24–25.

2. Ibid., 22–23.

3. Chavda Ministries, "The Watch of the Lord," accessed November 17, 2016, http://www.chavdaministries.org/Groups/1000096825/Chavda_Ministries_International/CMI_HOME/Ministries/The_Watch_of/The_Watch_of.aspx.

Chapter 18: Prophetic Intercession

1. Cindy Jacobs, *Possessing the Gates of the Enemy: A Training Manual for Militant Intercession*, 3rd ed. (Grand Rapids, Mich.: Chosen, 2009), 60–62.

Chapter 19: For Such a Time as This

1. Terry Crist, *Interceding Against the Powers of Darkness* (Tulsa, Okla.: Terry Crist Ministries, 1990), n.p.

2. Ibid.

3. Ibid.

4. This prayer is adapted from Psalm 102:1, 13; 106:47 NASB.

Chapter 20: Praying for Authorities

1. Andrew Murray, *Helps to Intercession: A 31-Day Expedition in Prayer* (Fort Washington, Pa.: Christian Literature Crusade, 2007), 35.

2. Jack Hayford, *Prayer Is Invading the Impossible* (New York: Ballantine Books, 1983), 57.

3. Goll, *Prayer Storm*, 230.

4. Alves, Femrite, and Kaufman, *Intercessors*, 198–99.

5. Derek Prince, *Shaping History through Prayer and Fasting*, rev. ed. (New Kensington, Pa.: Whitaker House, 2002), 124–25.

6. Ibid., 74.

7. Derek Prince, "A Watchman for a Nation," October 2002. Published by Derek Prince Ministries, Charlotte, N.C.

Chapter 21: The Praying Church

1. Goll, *Prayer Storm*, 105.

2. Read Scriptures such as these with the bridal relationship in mind: Exodus 34:14; Psalm 27:4; 45:10–11; 149:4; Hosea 2:16; Matthew 9:15; 25:10; Mark 12:30; John 3:29; 10:14–15; 15:9; 1 Corinthians 6:17; 2 Corinthians 11:2; Ephesians 3:18–19; Hebrews 1:9; Revelation 2:4; 3:21; 19:7–9; 21:9–10; 22:17.

3. Prayer based on 1 Thessalonians 3:12–13.

General Index

Scripture Index

Old Testament

Mark

Luke

John

Acts

Romans